W9-BDA-841

Studies in Comparative Politics

STUDIES IN OPPOSITION

STUDIES IN OPPOSITION

edited by

RODNEY BARKER

Lecturer in Political Theory and Government
University College of Swansea

MACMILLAN

ST MARTIN'S PRESS

First published *1971* by
THE MACMILLAN PRESS LTD
London and Basingstoke
Associated companies in New York Toronto
Dublin Melbourne Johannesburg and Madras

Library of Congress catalog card no. 70–167757

SBN 333 12482 0

Printed in Great Britain by
RICHARD CLAY (THE CHAUCER PRESS) LTD
Bungay, Suffolk

Contents

Rodney Barker

Introduction

VIGOROUS AND VIOLENT OPPOSITION TO POLITICAL REGIMES HAS become familiar: academics, journalists, and their hybrid intellectual progeny have dinned our ears with accounts of Weathermen and Free Welsh warriors, Black Panthers and Paisleyites – even Gay Power has emerged with novel determination. This dissension which, in the West, seems noisier than anything experienced for the past thirty years, has been matched by an almost equally eager commentary: the pages of *Government and Opposition* (from which the following articles are drawn) have already been harvested for a study of *Anarchism Today*, and publication on the subject of student protest and revolt is rapidly becoming as necessary for the aspiring academic as Jane Austen once declared a poem on autumn to be for any poet worthy of his calling.

Both commentators and their subjects have reflected and voiced a demand for uncluttered channels of protest, for extra-parliamentary opposition, for effective dissent. This demand arises from and includes two different characteristics. One is simple political frustration, a feeling that the wrong policies are being pursued and the right people going unheard. The other is the belief that there is some positive benefit to be gained from having a form of continual opposition, of whatever hue, to the acts and policies of government, of whatever kind, coupled with a fear that this necessary opposition has become moribund or stifled, and its benefits emasculated or destroyed. The first characteristic is only new and surprising to those with an obsessive concern for contemporaneity; the desire to secure effective means of communication for one's beliefs and implementation for one's policies is hardly a product of the last few years. Such desires have recently been

more violently and vociferously expressed in, for instance, the
United States than has been usual since the Second World
War, but it is little over a hundred years since that nation was
in the throes of full-scale civil war. Similarly the history of
Ireland, where a British Prime Minister has recently discerned
civil war, gives the sanction of tradition to violent dissent, not
to peaceful agreement. The second characteristic, the belief
that there is virtue in opposition *per se*, seems far more
original, even if it has sometimes been lost under the sound
and fury of the first. It has already received sufficient expression to make it both useful and necessary to distinguish it
from the mere accident of an opposition arising from political
frustration. It is the belief in opposition as such which thus
forms a point of departure for this anthology.

The establishment of opposition in itself as a subject for
debate and examination among students of politics might
seem to call in the first place for a general analysis and critique
of the idea. But what would be neglected in such an enterprise would be the much more interesting question of the
origin of the new topic. The idea of organized political opposition as a normal and beneficial component of a polity is after
all a surprising one, and seems quite out of accord with the
traditional concern of political speculation: the search for
the good state based on undivided allegiance to correct principles and practices. To recommend opposition smacks of relativism in political values[1] and of a disbelief in the possibility
of establishing general agreement among men as to the details
of their government. The ship of state may not be sailing on a
boundless ocean without map or compass, but it seems it is to
follow a zigzag course, without overmuch discrimination in its
choice of ports of call. It is today generally accepted that one
of the marks of a genuine democracy is the existence of a
vigorous, legal, alternative government which subjects the
activities of the men in power to searching public scrutiny. As
the 1964 general election approached in Great Britain, public
warnings were raised against a fourth Conservative government not because its principles might be wrong or its ministers
incompetent but because it would vitiate the alternation and
variety which were deemed to be an essential part of govern-

[1] A fact observed by Hans Daalder, 'Government and Opposition in the
New States', *Government and Opposition*, vol. 1, no. 2, January 1966.

ment in a parliamentary democracy. There have always been changes of ministry, but they have been welcomed chiefly by the friends of the incoming office-holders. To value the process of alternation itself is something newer. It is not simply that it jars with the recurring desire of those who contemplate politics to map out unified and stable Utopias, though, as Professor Schapiro has pointed out, this is a far more venerable tradition than the adulation of opposition.[2] Quite apart from the utopians, students of politics have traditionally sought to justify or prepare for unity rather than division in public policy, explaining the underlying coherence of the existing order or indicating the foundations of the new order which would or should succeed it. To ask questions such as 'What is the nature of the good life?' or 'What is the proper purpose of the state?' is to imply that answers of a universal validity may be found which will serve as the irrefutable basis for government. A major purpose of political enquiry was traditionally to discern universal truths and values, and since these necessarily had a final quality, there could be only one course for the state to follow once they had been established. This search for principles of unity, without which political society would dissolve into anarchy, had been characteristic in differing ways of most political thinkers from Plato onwards. Rousseau was quick to condemn 'factions and sectional associations' as striking at the root of public agreement.[3] Burke, while believing in Parliament as the model of a nation which it virtually represented, nevertheless believed that this varied assembly should form a common personality, 'a deliberative assembly of *one* nation, with *one* interest, that of the whole.'[4] The passion for unity was shared by Hegel and his

2 Leonard Schapiro, Foreword to *Government and Opposition*, vol. 1, no. 1, October 1965.

3 '. . . des brigues, des associations partielles, aux dépens de la grande'. J.-J. Rousseau, *Du Contrat Social*, in *Œuvres Complètes*, tome VI, Paris, 1825, p. 39.

4 Speech to the electors of Bristol, on being declared elected, 3rd November 1774, in *The Works of the Right Hon. Edmund Burke*, ed. Henry Rogers, London, 1850, p. 180. Against this view, Burke is frequently quoted in favour of the opinion that 'Party is a body of men united, for promoting by their joint endeavours, the national interest, upon some particular principle in which they are all agreed.' *Thoughts on the Cause of the Present Discontents*, 1770, in *Works, op. cit.*, p. 151. But the concept of the national interest is as important here as the view that connections may properly promote it, and the quotation should be read in the light of Burke's desire to restore to the Commons its role as a unified representative of national opinion. When the

Marxist and idealist successors, and by liberals like Mill who
saw the rational conversation of a multitudinous citizenry as
the preliminary to a firmly based and correctly determined
public policy.[5] Even writers who have observed and applauded
the operation of political opposition have justified it by
reference to traditional values: 'The more it fulfils its ultimate constructive duty,' declared Sir Ernest Barker in 1942,
'the more it hastens the pace of considered and effective
action, weighted with the volume of general consent, and
moving with the momentum which only that volume can
give.'[6] If good and bad, true and false, had any meaning, it
seemed natural that all the actions of princes and parliaments could be assessed in terms of them. The curious
esteem in which opposition has come to be held clearly requires some kind of explanation.

In attempting to discover how the idea of political opposition has emerged, and why it has come to seem valuable, the
meaning of the term needs first to be clarified. The word
'opposition' has many meanings, and unfortunately some
writers have treated these as if they were different aspects of
the same phenomenon instead of different though related
phenomena expressed by the same word. The meanings include revolution and mild criticisms of housing programmes
and food subsidies, and to attempt to conflate them is to
stretch a concept so far that like a balloon in a vacuum it is
destroyed by its own expansion – there is little profit in discussing Babeuf and Bonar Law and imagining one is talking
about the same thing. In some African languages the confusion is exacerbated by the word for opposition deriving
from the word for enmity.[7] In English we have no such excuse.

Commons achieves this, 'It will not suffer that last of evils to predominate in
the country; men without popular confidence, publick opinion, natural con-
nexion, or mutual trust, invested with all the powers of government.' The
court will learn that the interests of the monarch lie in having an administration 'composed of those who recommend themselves to their sovereign through
the opinion of their country': *ibid.*, p. 153. See also F. O'Gorman, 'Party and
Burke: The Rockingham Whigs', in the present anthology, pp. 111–30.

[5] On Hegel, however, see R. N. Berki, 'Political Freedom and Hegelian
Metaphysics', *Political Studies*, vol. XVI, no. 3, October 1968.

[6] Ernest Barker, *Reflections on Government* (first published 1942), London,
1967, p. 203.

[7] Leonard Schapiro, *op. cit.*, p. 2.

In the first place, opposition may mean total resistance to the form and basis of the state, and a determination to overthrow it by whatever means. (Not that opposition in this sense is always particularly dangerous: in England before the Great War the readiest exponents of this position were the innocuous socialist sects, the SDF. and its offshoots, while the only real threat of civil war came from the Conservative Party. Nor is the desire of the campus revolutionary to transform totally the existing order always in direct proportion to his ability to do so.) Secondly, the word may denote resistance to the power of the state when the latter is viewed as an oppressive institution. Thirdly, the word 'opposition' may refer to resistance to the group, faction, or dynasty in command of the state, and to a denial of its legitimacy. Fourthly, it may be used to denote a loyal opposition which opposes the commanding group without either contesting its legitimacy or threatening or rejecting the basis of the state or the constitution. Fifthly, opposition may be used to mean the system of checks and balances whereby the constitution guards against and corrects its own excesses, or to identify a belief in a composite or divided sovereignty. These checks and balances can be of the formal kind detected in the English constitution by Montesquieu, or of the informal kind administered by a civil service to an eager but inexperienced minister. Finally, the term has been used to describe the methods whereby the citizen or group, without condemning government as inherently oppressive, modifies its action, mellows its harshnesses, and prevents its tyrannies. Dicey was concerned to establish the principles underlying this kind of opposition, just as the later proponents of the Ombudsman have worked to give them practical effect.

Certainly there are dangers in confusing the various meanings of the word 'opposition', especially as in many cases it may be necessary to apply several different meanings in describing a single political situation or event. Some critics have proposed using different terms to describe some of these activities: Professor Sartori, for instance, has suggested that we distinguish between opposition and control (p. 31).[8] The one

[8] Page numbers in parenthesis in the text indicate where an article included in this anthology may be found. In such cases the date of original publication is given at the beginning of the article.

word will probably do, however, provided one is on one's guard for slips from one sense into another. In discussing the politics of the new states of Asia and Africa, for instance, it is necessary to talk both of legal and loyal opposition to the existing commanding group, and of factional resistance to its power and a determination to overthrow it by any means. The history of many of these states is a chronicle of an uneasy balance between the two with frequent tumbles into rebellion and violence. In an apparently calmer context, the legal and loyal opposition of the Conservative Party to the Home Rule policies of the Liberal Government in Britain after 1911 seemed to many at the time to be on the point of becoming factional and violent opposition to lawful government. When the Conservative leader, Bonar Law, told a rally at Blenheim Palace that 'I can imagine no length of resistance to which Ulster can go in which I should not be prepared to support them',[9] he was no longer speaking the language of His Majesty's Loyal Opposition. Again, the language appropriate to violent resistance to a government may be used, not with the intention of provoking civil war but as a means of raising the enthusiasm of a loyal, legal, and peaceful opposition. Like the Sorelian myth of the general strike, much of the revolutionary phraseology of European social democracy has been sustenance for legality rather than incitement to illegality.[10] On the one hand, therefore, it is necessary for analytical purposes to distinguish between the many different meanings of the word 'opposition'; on the other it is necessary to recognize the close relationship which often exists in fact between the many different activities referred to.

Once the meanings of the term are clarified, it appears that not all of them are new or strange: it is possible to establish an ancestry for most of them. Resistance which struck at the root of the state was a canker which most political thinkers tried to extirpate. But for anarchists it was a necessary feature of that 'establishment of Humanity' which, argued Bakunin, necessarily meant 'the ruin of all States'.[11] Equally even for the more orthodox there were circumstances in which a ruler

[9] Quoted by Robert Blake, *The Unknown Prime Minister. The Life and Times of Andrew Bonar Law 1858–1923*, London, 1955, p. 130.

[10] Cf. Shils, pp. 54–6 of this anthology.

[11] Michael Bakunin, *Marxism, Freedom and the State*, translated and edited by K. J. Kenafick, London, 1950, p. 53.

might forfeit his title to rule, and in which he could only maintain his position by force. In these circumstances violent resistance might be justified, and Aquinas was ready to invoke Aristotle in defence of the overthrow of tyrants.[12] Similarly hostility, not to a particular state or ruler but to the expanding power of the state as such, was represented by a vigorous tradition which existed at least until the end of the first quarter of the present century, encompassing thinkers who in a variety of ways attempted to set limits to central power: Gierke, Duguit, Spencer, Morris, and the English pluralists. The belief in a balance of power runs back through judicial theory to Montesquieu, and the desire to furnish the citizen with safeguards against overweening public power has an equally secure pedigree, much of it again in the form of legal theory.

There remains only one meaning of the word 'opposition' which appears to lack an ancestry: legal and loyal opposition to the group or person in command of the state (I shall henceforward give this use of the word a capital 'O', to distinguish it from other uses). It is not surprising that until relatively recently it has had little currency, for it is in many ways an incomplete, perplexing notion. The basis of any kind of criticism of a government might be thought to be the belief that its actions were wrong; to stop short of measures to prevent this wrong because of a belief in the rules of the game would appear to destroy the moral basis of the initial criticism. Either the actions of the government are wrong and ought to be opposed at all costs, or they are not wrong and ought to be supported. Equally, while one might accept the right of a group to resist a particular action because they believed it to be wrong, an equal right to use its powers must be conceded to the government – could it be a government if, by permitting resistance, it ceased to govern? It was an inability to see any middle ground between these alternatives which led G. K. Chesterton to stigmatize the socialist state as necessarily intolerant and tyrannical. An extension of state action could only mean an extension of the sphere of life where dissension would be suppressed:

A Socialist Government is one which in its nature does not tolerate any true and real opposition. For there the Government

12 *Summa Theologica*, Qu. 42, art. 2, quoted in A. P. d'Entrèves (ed.), *Aquinas: Selected Political Writings*, Oxford, 1959, p. 161.

provides everything; and it is absurd to ask a Government to *provide* an opposition.

You cannot go to the Sultan and say reproachfully: 'You have made no arrangements for your brother dethroning you and seizing the Caliphate.' You cannot go to a mediaeval king and say: 'Kindly lend me two thousand spears and one thousand bowmen, as I wish to raise a rebellion against you.' Still less can you reproach a Government which professes to set up everything, because it has not set up anything to pull down all it has set up.[13]

For a very long time the political arrangements of Europe made it difficult to avoid the conclusion reached by Chesterton. In an absolute monarchy, the integrity of the state and the responsibility of government could be symbolized by a single person, and it was difficult in practice to challenge the one without challenging the other. In such circumstances the treatment by Henry VIII of his opponents makes perfect sense. It would be misleading perhaps, even under the Tudors, to talk of a general belief in undivided or unqualified sovereignty. The Stuarts were not the first to discover the existence of claimants to a share in the diffuse authority of the state. Yet exile, the more gentle successor to execution, continued into the 18th century in England, and in Anne's reign it was possible to complain that 'if a gentleman stands up to complain of grievances, although this house meets in order to redress them, he is represented as a person that obstructs Her Majesty's business'.[14] The notion of legal Opposition is not one which flourishes in any soil, for it presupposes certain features in the state and certain qualities in the condition of political thinking.

The existence of legal Opposition involves some separation between the person or persons symbolizing sovereignty, and those exercising government. It also involves a corresponding existence of layers of activity and controversy within the state. At the first level lie the political arrangements of the state, the constitution, which provide for the location of authority,

---

[13] G. K. Chesterton, 'The Beginning of the Quarrel', reprinted from *The Outline of Sanity*, 1926, in *Stories, Essays and Poems* (first published 1935), London, 1965, p. 198.

[14] Townsend, *Memoirs of the House of Commons*, I, 309, quoted by Archibald S. Foord, *His Majesty's Opposition 1714–1830*, Oxford, 1964, p. 6.

the exercise of that authority by various bodies, and the rights and duties in general terms of the citizens. At the second level come such arrangements and regulation of the life of the community as do not involve an alteration of the conventions operating as the first level: the raising of taxation, the conduct of foreign affairs, the provision of public services. The distinction is to some extent artificial even in the most complex states, and there will always be disagreement about the precise location of particular activities or controversies. The problem of what is second-order matter and what directly affects the constitution is a matter of some confusion and bitterness at the present time in Northern Ireland. But unless some kind of working distinction can be made, everything affects the constitution, and the state must act like Chesterton's sultan. It has been suggested by Robert Dahl that loyal and legal Opposition can be viewed as a means 'of managing the major political conflicts of a society'.[15] Certainly where political dissension is contained within a system of Opposition one may assume either that major political conflicts are being managed, or that they are not sufficiently major to disrupt the system. But equally one of the characteristics of a major political conflict might be said to be that it could not be contained within conventional rules of fair play. It is only when the group which is out of power feels its grievances to be secondary to the primary if tacit need to maintain agreed political forms, that Oppositional politics are possible. As Lord Simon put it in 1937, 'Our parliamentary system will work as long as the responsible people in different parties accept the view that it is better that the other side should win than that the constitution should be broken.'[16] Consequently it is a mark of such a situation not only that secondary-level controversies are kept secondary but also that proposals for reform will often be couched in terms which make change appear a necessary condition for the maintenance of the essence of the existing order. It is no accident that it was the supporters of parliamentary reform in England in 1832 who put such a conservative view

[15] Robert A. Dahl (ed.), *Political Oppositions in Western Democracies*, New Haven and London, 1966, p. xv.
[16] Quoted in L. S. Amery, *Thoughts on the Constitution*, London, 1947, pp. 31–2.

forward, while the opponents talked in terms of radical measures and dangerous innovations.

When the area of government activity broadens as it did
with increasing rapidity in Great Britain from the beginning
of the present century, when the state begins actively to cultivate the broad pastures of society, it is likely that there will be
an increasing area of its activities which, though disliked, will
be relatively trivial, and though severe, of limited repercus-
sion. The big, or collectivist, state provides opportunities for
bread-and-butter politics, and hence for Opposition, which
are less likely to exist in a state with limited responsibilities.
In Great Britain since the emergence of the Labour Party as
the successor to the Liberals there have been no conflicts between the parties of the grandeur or the bitterness of those
which divided Liberals and Conservatives before 1914. The
power of the House of Lords, over which the normal operation of government was almost brought to a standstill, was a
matter which touched the heart of the constitution. Passion
and enthusiasm were aroused over the battle for authority
within the state, over the struggle for legislative supremacy
between the two Houses of Parliament, and over the assertion
by the representatives of the people of their right to practical
sovereignty. Similarly the great issue of Ireland, which affected
the territorial integrity of the kingdom, succeeded in splitting
the Liberal Party, threatening the traditional neutrality of the
monarch in party disputes, and bringing the army to the verge
of mutiny and Ulster to the brink of armed rebellion. By
comparison the politics of the inter-war years were tame and
trivial. Visionaries might see in the general strike the first
blast of the trumpet which would tumble the walls of capitalism and open the way for the armies of socialist revolution. But
the trade unions were not prepared to go to the barricades in
search of the millennium, nor was the TUC prepared to challenge constitutional propriety in pursuit of hours and wages,
however determined their use of the strike weapon. The advent of the Labour Party into effective parliamentary politics
marked in fact the end of constitutional disputes and the
beginning of a period of bread-and-butter politics. With the
arrival of a party whose main purpose consisted in securing the
fairer distribution of goods and services, and which had little
or nothing to say about the constitution, loyal oppositional

politics became securer than ever. In 1937 the Leader of the Opposition was even paid a salary.[17]

Parliamentary Opposition had been a convention of English politics for over a hundred years, however, when the Leader of the Opposition was first paid. The constitutional crises of the closing years of Liberal rule came at the end of a long period when loyal Opposition was an established feature of parliamentary life. Professor Foord, having chronicled its protracted adolescence, detects its arrival at adulthood by 1830, four years after J. C. Hobhouse had introduced the expression 'His Majesty's Opposition'.[18] For despite the continued political role of the monarchy in the 19th century, one condition of a viable Opposition party was fulfilled with its giving up the attempt to rule; it reigned, and it meddled, but once sovereignty and government were seen to be settled on different persons, it became possible to attack the latter without threatening the former. It is not surprising that in the Soviet Union in 1921 Lenin had to put the lid on opposition;[19] he was too closely associated with the legitimacy and prestige of the new state to be at the same time the target, directly or indirectly, for attacks on policies and programmes. Charisma and loyal opposition are uneasy bedfellows, and in feudal monarchies, new states, and revolutionary regimes the latter is more likely to be kicked out than embraced.

The existence of a practice is one thing; its status in political thinking quite another. Though legal Opposition can be detected in European, and more particularly English politics during the 19th century, and though its presence was recognized at the level of practical politics and political comment, it was not valued or even greatly commented on as a necessary or desirable feature of free, parliamentary states. An article by Cornewall Lewis in the *Edinburgh Review* of 1855 to which Professor Foord very properly draws attention, singled out parliamentary Opposition as a cardinal feature of the free political system enjoyed by England, and commented on the salutary fact 'that public opinion can distinguish between the

[17] Those who have detected a consensus in British politics might do well to consider whether the 1950s were not perhaps its blossoming rather than its germination.

[18] Archibald S. Foord, *op. cit.*

[19] See, e.g., Leonard Schapiro, 'Putting the Lid on Leninism', *Government and Opposition*, vol. 2, no. 2, January–April 1967.

general utility of Government and the occasional errors and
misconduct of its administrators, and that the people can obey
the law, while they criticize those who carry it into effect'.[20] But
Lewis did not accord to parliamentary Opposition the character it is often given today. He saw its essence as selfish and
factional, capable of serving a useful public purpose only when
subjected to the check of public responsibility which arose
with the publicity of parliamentary debates and the limitations which the possibilities of office placed on the Opposition's
promises and proposals. Professor Hanham has drawn our
attention to Alphaeus Tidd (p. 132), who while looking
favourably on the work of Opposition, saw its merit in its
critical function. Todd, however, did not view it as the re-
pository of political alternatives, and hence for him a Tory
Opposition served to make Whig ministers better Whigs,
rather than to dilute their Whiggishness.[21] Professor Foord has
attached the belief in 'a loyal and responsible Opposition' to
his broad definition of Western liberalism, and to its characteristics of free speech and representative government.[22] But a
belief in an organized Opposition by no means follows from
a liberal view of politics, and though it may be compatible
with it, and is generally nowadays associated with it, the same
was not the case in the 19th century. The existence of an institution is no guarantee of its recognition, and Foord himself
cites Bagehot's account of the man who, in 1830, responded to
the idea that the Opposition be invited to form a ministry,
'Sir, I would as soon choose for a new coachman the man who
shied stones best at my old one.'[23] Professor Ionescu and Dr de
Madariaga in their book, *Opposition,* have pointed to the
supersession of unanimous decisions by majority decisions as
the method of procedure in many European assemblies, and
have rightly argued that the majority principle can be conducive to the toleration of minorities in a way that a constant
search for unanimity might not be.[24] But though decisions

---

[20] *Edinburgh Review,* vol. CI, January–April 1855, pp. 1–22 and 2.
[21] See also H. J. Hanham, *The Nineteenth Century Constitution, 1815–1914,*
Cambridge, 1969, pp. 110, 122–3.
[22] Archibald S. Foord, *op. cit.,* p. 3.
[23] Walter Bagehot, *The English Constitution and Other Political Essays,*
New York, 1911, p. 396, quoted in Foord, *op. cit.,* p. 7.
[24] Ghiţa Ionescu and Isabel de Madariaga, *Opposition: Past and Present of a
Political Institution,* London, 1968, pp. 45–9.

were reached by majority in the 19th century, what was valued was still unanimity, and it would be a mistake to take political practice as straightforward evidence of political beliefs. When John Stuart Mill published his reflections on *Representative Government* in 1861, he found no place for the loyal Opposition. For him, liberalism meant something different, and his importance as a liberal thinker makes his views of great interest.

Mill recognized that in any free state there would be debate and discussion springing from diverse approaches to the problems facing government; the existence of 'many conflicting opinions' was one of the features which he expected in any deliberative assembly.[25] He was equally convinced of the necessity of critical debate in order to sustain the quality of public life. The Jewish prophets, he observed, contested the power of both kings and priests, 'and kept up, in that little corner of the earth, that antagonism of influences which is the only real security for continued progress'.[26] It was this independent critical spirit which marked off the Jewish nation from the host of less successful states surrounding it. The nearest modern equivalent which Mill could find for the prophets, however, was not an Opposition but a free press. The 'antagonism of influences' was to be sustained not by any formalization of dissent but by the spirit of free enquiry embodied in a critical press. When Mill did consider the role of Parliament as a restraint on government, he attributed the role to the whole body, not to any organized faction within it. Parliament was at once a 'Committee of Grievances' and a 'Congress of Opinions', and within it, ultimate unity is always to be hoped for in the subordination of sectional opinions to the criteria of rationality, 'where those whose opinion is overruled, feel satisfied that it is heard, and set aside not by a mere act of will, but for what are thought superior reasons, and commend themselves as such to the representatives of the majority of the nation'.[27] This criterion of rationality was to be given its proper weight in the ideal form of representative government by a differential franchise which would give plural votes to

[25] John Stuart Mill, *Considerations on Representative Government*, London, 1861, in *Utilitarianism; Liberty; Representative Government*, ed. A. D. Lindsay (first published 1910), London, 1957, p. 231.
[27] *Ibid.*, pp. 239–40.
[27] *Ibid.*, pp. 239–40.

those who, by possessing university degrees or by practising a liberal profession, gave evidence of superior intellectual ability. Only a belief that a truly national policy could be arrived at by the application of enlightened citizens could justify such a proposal, and indeed Mill invoked such a policy, 'dictated by impartial regard for the interest of all',[28] as the alternative to sectional and class policies. The idea of permanently embodying alternative policies within a formally constituted parliamentary party, of giving the proposals of such an opposition not only equal weight with all others at a deliberative stage but also equal weight with the policies ultimately arrived at and carried through by the national government, implies a relativism quite out of key with Mill's view of politics. The dissent and criticism which he envisaged did not arise out of any permanent and irreconcilable division of principle, but from an initial multiplicity of opinion on any and every question, a multiplicity which shifted and changed as the issues themselves changed.

The ignoring, even implied exclusion, of loyal Opposition at a theoretical level in Mill's defence of representative government, was matched when the actual operation of representative government in England was described. Writing six years after Mill in 1867, Walter Bagehot shared many of his assumptions about the essential features of parliamentary democracy. Unlike Mill, he discussed the part played by parties – a very necessary part, he considered. But by party he meant not the massive parliamentary and popular organization, adhering to a distinctive set of principles and policies, and forming the basis of permanent and fixed divisions in the politics of both Parliament and the nation. The parties which he recognized were shifting and convenient alliances formed to sustain ministries, not rigid ideological or bureaucratic monoliths. He observed the existence of Whigs, Tories, and Radicals, but argued that 'they are much else too. They are common Englishmen, and, as Father Newman complains, "hard to be worked up to the dogmatic level".'[29] In consequence parliamentary government was not factional government, for the 'body is eager, but the atoms are cool'.[30] Despite

[28] *Ibid.*, p. 249
[29] Walter Bagehot, *The English Constitution* (1867), London, 1963, p. 159.
[30] *Ibid.*, p. 159.

the existence therefore of parties, and the significance of terms such as Whig, Tory, or Radical, the real variety of Parliament consisted of its being '658 persons, collected from all parts of England, different in nature, different in interests, different in look and language'.[31] Consequently the most important feature of Parliament was its coherence as a representative of the national mind and temper: 'Parliament ought to embody the public opinion of the English nation',[32] and because it did so the vital and necessary antagonisms and debate were not between Government and Opposition but, as for Mill, between Government and the fluid and flexible, yet homogeneous, Parliament: 'The whole life of English politics is the action and reaction between the Ministry and the Parliament.'[33]

Thus despite the clear existence throughout the 19th century in England of something which could be termed a loyal Opposition, there was a widespread tendency to ignore it when describing the essentials of actual or ideal political systems.[34] In order to have not simply opposition in the sense of free criticism, but an Opposition, party was essential. It is possible to find numerous examples of recognition by politicians of the existence, even the necessity and desirability, of parties in a constitutional monarchy. What is missing is any extension of this private if admitted recognition into public principle.[35] The tendency of thinkers like Mill, on the other hand, was to seek for a basis for political action which transcended party. He prefaced his *Considerations on Representative Government* by stating his desire, and the necessity, of formulating a doctrine over and above the doctrines of either

[31] *Ibid.*, p. 155.
[32] *Ibid.*, p. 179.
[33] *Ibid.*, p. 151.
[34] Casting their net far wider than 19th-century Britain, Naess, Christopherson, and Kvalø list 311 definitions of democracy taken from a wide range of writers on politics. All the definitions identify popular or majority rule, and neglect Opposition and variety. Arne Naess, Jens A. Christopherson, and Kjell Kvalø, *Democracy, Ideology and Objectivity: Studies in the Semantics and Cognitive Analysis of Ideological Controversy*, Oslo and Oxford, 1956.
[35] Caroline Robbins (' "Discordant Parties": A Study of the Acceptance of Party by Englishmen', *Political Science Quarterly*, vol. LXXIII, 1958, pp. 505–29) is able readily to establish that the existence of parties was recognized at the beginning of the 19th century. What she fails to do — she is not primarily concerned to do so — is to establish that parties were publicly praised or accorded a place in accounts of the virtues of English government.

Liberals or Conservatives, 'something wider than either, which, in virtue of its superior comprehensiveness, might be adopted by either Liberal or Conservative without renouncing anything which he really feels to be valuable in his own creed'.[36] Party indeed, though a fact of the nation's political life, fitted in ill with its theories of representation. The two possible entities which an MP might represent were for Mill his constituents or his own free and responsible judgement – to interpose party would have been to interpose something at once partial and factional. Similarly the view that interests were represented in Parliament envisaged a form of political organization more variegated and flexible than was suggested by organization into parties. For Mill and Bagehot, writing towards the close of 'the golden age of Parliament', it was possible to ignore or underplay the role played by parties. By the end of the century, when from being simple parliamentary groupings parties had extended roots deep down into the soil of the electorate and developed a higher degree of cohesion within Parliament, it was less easy to avoid recognizing their importance. When this importance was more commonly realized, it was frequently deplored, while those who regarded parliamentary resistance to government policy as essentially disruptive, had their views confirmed by the tactics of the Irish party under Parnell. Henry Sidgwick, writing in 1891, was a little surprised that Mill had not given any place to a dual party situation in discussing the workings of representative government. But he himself looked upon party with a jaundiced eye, and sought to loosen the grip of party loyalty. He looked forward to the day when at least some ministers would hold their office on merit alone, immune from the changing fortunes of cabinets and parties, and to 'an increase in the number of persons taking a serious interest in politics who keep out of party ties altogether'.[37]

Applying liberal principles to the two nations which from a European perspective seemed their fount and their stronghold, Mosei Ostrogorski saw none of the benefits which subsequent writers have detected in the existence of parties.[38]

[36] Mill, *op. cit.*, p. 173.

[37] Henry Sidgwick, *The Elements of Politics* (first edition 1891), London, 1897, p. 603.

[38] M. Ostrogorski, *Democracy and the Organization of Political Parties*, 2 vols, translated by Frederick Clarke, London, 1902.

Parties, and the system of majority government and systematic Opposition which went with them, had corrupted, he thought, the democratic character of politics in England and America, and formalized and distorted the variety of national political opinion. A truly democratic polity must allow due weight both to the diversity of political opinion and to differences in intellectual ability and civic merit. Party denied both these their proper emphases, and the only solution was its destruction by electoral reforms and by a return at parliamentary level to something even more flexible than enjoyed by the English Parliament in its golden age. Collective responsibility would be jettisoned, and each minister would stand or fall on his merits. Criticism would thus be of a relevant rather than a factional kind, and there would be no organized Opposition to the whole ministry. Rather there would be principled, free, and intelligent criticism of particular actions, by fluctuating alliances whose members would have in common only their dislike of a particular policy or the actions of a particular minister. Party government, and hence Opposition, was not compatible with parliamentary government.[39]

Ostrogorski was the first liberal to face the party system and to attempt to judge it by traditional liberal values. Before the publication of his work, as both he and Bryce observed, although parties and party government existed, their existence went largely unrecognized by any thorough examination of their role in the government of nations.[40] His arguments cast doubts on the now common assumption that a belief in representative government blended naturally into a belief in party government and organized Opposition as central ingredients of classical liberalism. It was not the existence of an organized Opposition that liberals valued but the freedom to oppose and criticize, a freedom which could not be properly exercised in formal organized parties. Hence Mill's ignoring of Opposition, and Bagehot's scant attention and scanter estimation, were not simply a matter of historical accident, of their happening to write before the advent of mass parties and at a time when parliamentary organization was relatively flexible. The doctrine of party government, and the advocacy of Opposition

[39] *Ibid.*, particularly vol. 2, part 6.
[40] *Ibid.*, vol. 1, pp. xxxix–xl and liv.

which depended on it, implied forms of political life which
were inimical to liberalism.

It is not therefore surprising to find, two years after the
publication of Ostrogorski's work in English, Sidney Low having to justify his treatment of parties in the political life of
England, for, as he aptly pointed out, 'The party system is
treated as something exceptional and a little discreditable.
Men may be willing to die for party, but they seldom praise
it.'[41] Low's arguments, in *The Governance of England*, represent a coming to terms with party, and a jettisoning of older
beliefs about the checks against tyranny and the guarantees
of freedom provided by English government. The idea of a
balanced constitution, with each part preventing the possible
excesses of the others, and the belief that Parliament stood
over against government as both its conscience and its police-
man, was, suggested Low, out of tune with the facts of the
situation. These roles were now performed not by Parliament
as such but by a party which provided an alternative to the
party in power, and which was active and articulate both in
the Commons and in the constituencies, and which thus provided across the whole spectrum of the nation's political life
the possibility of a choice, and hence a standing warning to the
government in power. 'The check on the Government in
office is the existence of an alternative Government out of
office, ready and able to take its place at any moment; and
such an opposition government *in posse* is impossible without
the two great well-balanced forces, always mobilized and on
the war footing.'[42] Four years previously D. G. Ritchie had
argued that a system of two parties was necessary to stable
government, and that the organized criticism of government
by Opposition was a valuable aid to wisdom and virtue in a
situation where no party 'is likely to possess a monopoly' of
these qualities.[43] Thus by the early years of the present
century, parties had become quietly, but publicly, respectable,
having occupied for the previous hundred years and more a
position in the state quite out of accord with the formal recognition given to them and estimation placed on them in political

[41] Sidney Low, *The Governance of England*, London, 1904, p. 117.
[42] *Ibid.*, p. 123.
[43] D. G. Ritchie, 'Civic Duties and Party Politics', in *Co-operative Wholesale
Societies' Annual, 1898*, reprinted in *Studies in Political and Social Ethics*,
London, 1902, p. 92.

thinking. Opposition, democratic self-assertion formalized and organized in the excluded party, became modestly recognized as a positive good in the state. Within four years of Low's book, A. L. Lowell was writing: 'The recognition of the Opposition as a legitimate body, entitled to attain to power by persuasion, is a primary condition of the success of the party system and therefore of popular government on a large scale.'[44]

The promotion of Opposition to the position it now holds both in the popular mind and in the minds of students of politics has been a slow process. The favourable comments of Low and Lowell at the beginning of the century represented no more than a modest beginning. Twenty years later Harold Laski in *A Grammar of Politics* could give an account of parliamentary government which perpetuated the view rejected by Low, of Legislature and Executive as distinct bodies and as the real units of action within the constitution.[45] Party and Opposition, notions which divide the Legislature and imply a very different view of political life, found virtually no place in his description. In 1936 Ivor Jennings described principled Opposition as a necessary feature of democratic government.[46] But three years later Ramsay Muir was declaring that 'in a democratic system there are two factors: the Government and the machinery for exercising criticism and control of it on behalf of the people—Parliament'.[47] When the forms and essence of democratic government were being undermined and assaulted in Europe in the 1930s, the first line of defence was not necessarily a reassertion of party or Opposition but of parliamentarianism, free speech, and liberalism on the one hand, or on the other of a socialism which even in the Anglican hands of Stafford Cripps or the pedagogic fist of Harold Laski could at times seem not over-enthusiastic or optimistic about the possibilities of a loyal capitalist Opposition.[48] This second position was, though, vigorously attacked

[44] A. Lawrence Lowell, *The Government of England*, New York, 1924, p. 452.
[45] Harold J. Laski, *A Grammar of Politics*, London, 1925, pp. 328–68.
[46] Sir Ivor Jennings, *Cabinet Government* (first edition 1936), Cambridge, 1959, pp. 15–16.
[47] Ramsay Muir, *Future for Democracy*, The Liberal Book Club, London, 1939, p. 109.
[48] See Sir Stafford Cripps, 'Can Socialism Come by Constitutional Methods?', in Christopher Addison, etc., *Problems of a Socialist Government*, London, 1933, and Harold J. Laski, *Democracy in Crisis*, London, 1933, pp. 77–92.

by Bassett in a work which also credited the two-party system
with a fundamental role in parliamentary democracy.[49] Not
until after the Second World War, however, were there any
signs of great attention being paid to the idea of Opposition.
L. S. Amery in 1947 quoted Bagehot's contention that the
whole life of English politics was 'the action and reaction
between the Ministry and the Parliament', but he brought
the observation up to date: 'One might almost say today "between the Ministry and the Opposition", for it is the latter
upon which has devolved most of the original critical function of Parliament.'[50] 'On Opposition,' he contended, 'rests
the main responsibility for what was once the critical function of Parliament as a whole.'[51] Benn and Peters described
constitutional Opposition as 'a notion essential to democracy'
in 1959,[52] and in the mid-1960s a small trickle of books and
articles, and the foundation of a journal devoted to the study
of government *and* opposition', indicated the final establishment of the idea. Even then Professor Schapiro, in introducing the new journal, felt it necessary to point out that
'opposition' did not necessarily imply hostility or dissension.[53]

His warning was understandable, and a recognition of how
curious the idea of Opposition can still seem. The shift, de-
tectable in Low, in favour of party and Opposition was a
radical one. The classical liberal view of a representative
parliament which rendered government at all times answer-
able to the nation was replaced by a view which implied
plebiscitary government, whereby the customer benefits by the
competition to secure his vote, and by the scrutiny to which
the activities of the lucky party are subjected by the unlucky
one. Moreover, to value entrenched and formalized political
alternatives in a state, and to prefer this to the search for
certainty and unanimity, might seem to imply a degree of

[49] R. Bassett, *The Essentials of Parliamentary Democracy*, London, 1935.
[50] L. S. Amery, *op. cit.*, pp. 10–11.
[51] *Ibid.*, p. 31.
[52] S. I. Benn and R. S. Peters, *Social Principles and the Democratic State*,
London, 1959, pp. 346–7. In 1962, in a version of a paper first delivered in
1958, D. E. Apter was proposing to show how the disregard of Opposition in
the new nations 'is short-sighted, even though understandable'. D. E. Apter,
'Some Reflections on the Role of a Political Opposition in New Nations',
Comparative Studies in Society and History, vol. IV, no 2, January 1962.
[53] Leonard Schapiro, Foreword to *Government and Opposition*, vol. 1,
no. 1, October 1965, pp. 2–3.

relativism in political thinking. The enthusiasm of students of politics for Opposition, their preference for functions rather than principles, reflects a respect for tolerance and variety and a suspicion of grand causes and ultimate ideals. On the other hand, much of the quality of absoluteness, which was regarded uneasily when it resided in principles, has simply been transferred from them into forms of government. This remarkable change in the attitude to party and Opposition cannot be explained simply in terms of a recognition of the political facts of life. Party and Opposition had existed for a century before Low gave them credit for sustaining democracy, and even then it was almost another half-century before the academic student of politics took Opposition to his lawful bosom and made an honest woman of her. The conditions in which Opposition may arise are not identical with the conditions in which it may be accorded a high value. Even if one explains the absence of positive and favourable comment on any scale before the beginning of the present century by a time-lag between political practice and political reflection, some explanation needs to be offered as to why this lag was taken up when it was. It is necessary to seek the direct conditions of intellectual developments not simply in the real world of political history but also in the world of political thought and opinion. It may be no coincidence that Opposition came to be widely written about shortly after the announcement of the end of ideology and the death of political philosophy. But not only was Weldon tolling the bell for political philosophy earlier than this: just as the beginnings of Opposition's prestige go back to the beginning of the century, so too do those of the intellectual environment in which the notion seems finally to be flourishing.

Changes were taking place in the first quarter of the present century which, while not marking the death or even the sickness of political philosophy, prepared a ground more favourable for the reception of a stress on Opposition than had existed in the previous hundred years. Sir Ernest Barker has suggested that by the outbreak of the Great War the state as an idea was under attack from two sides: from the internationalists who wished to render it responsible to the wider community of nations, and from pluralists who wished to diffuse or dismantle its authority and powers within its own

territory.[54] But it is equally significant that these movements
marked a respite in the debate over the form and nature
of the state, and over its relationship with its citizens. Pluralism and internationalism ignored the state or tried to push
it on one side; they did not attempt to reform it, but rather
to supplement or surpass it. This was significant at a time
when, in England, the state was moving firmly into the role
of positive responsibility not simply for law and order,
internal and external security, and the prevention of social,
medical, and economic nuisance, but also for the living standards and general well-being of the population, and the control, even sometimes the direction, of its economic affairs. After
the Liberal administrations of 1906–15, and the unprecedented
powers of nationalization and control taken by the coalitions
of 1915–18, not only did Spencerian or Morrisian protests
against state interference seem little more than charming
fantasies but any future speculation was faced with the *fait
accompli* of an entrenched paternalism and collectivism which
it could no longer reasonably expect to dismantle. Political
philosophy did not die as a result. But it became prised away
from other areas of political study, while itself appearing at
times to be more interested in second-order than in constitutional politics. Much of the pluralist thinking of the first
quarter of the century exemplified this second characteristic,
as solutions were sought to problems which might formerly have been considered to be economic or religious rather
than traditionally political. Guilds, voluntary associations,
churches, and economic phalanxes rested their claims to self-
government on their being in some sense prior to the state.
In asserting their autonomy it was necessary to include them
in a political framework, even though that framework was one
which denied or reduced the political competence of the state.
This form of pluralism was a partial recognition of the new
growth, through the agency of the state, of public responsibility, interference, and supervision. Secular pluralism
sought not to remove public responsibility but to divert it
through different agencies. In this respect it was unlike conservative theory which stressed the essential privacy of much
voluntary activity. The concern of political theory with the

[54] Ernest Barker, *Political Thought in England from Herbert Spencer to the
Present Day*, London, 1915.

stratagems of pluralism facilitated the release of many students of politics from a desire for or a guilty necessity of seeking to identify or assert some common criteria for public action. For though much pluralist thinking assumed an ultimate unity or agreement by the balancing, for instance, of the interests and programmes of the various guilds or syndicates, the assumption was nevertheless made that at one level there could be a quite legitimate sectional policy which was not necessarily derived from any principle of common welfare, nor immediately compatible with the demands and desires of other groups or individuals.[55] More important, pluralism opened the way for politics at two levels to receive the sanction and explanation of a political theory: at the second level there were the politics of the guilds, at the first level the constitutional agreement which formed the basis of life in a federative or pluralist society. The first level had to rest on common agreement; it was in the nature of the second level that it would always be the setting for variety and even discord. In the first place, therefore, political theory prepared the way for a concentration on second-order political activity; in the second place, the foundations of the state, whether regarded as discredited or unassailable, dropped out of the vision of a good many students of politics as a subject of enquiry or criticism; in the third place, as questions of the role and nature of the state came to seem distant, there was a concentration on problems which appeared to be of a purely technical nature, and which did not raise any broad issues of political theory. It was not so much that political philosophy was dead, or ideology at an end; rather that politics came to be written about as if they were, or as if they were preserved and static, frozen in the Siberian glacier of distant academe, their anatomy and growth arrested, and hence both taken as read, and treated as no longer the subject-matter for enquiry. It was an attitude not least common in the burgeoning university discipline of political studies. The difficulties that had been

[55] 'Ends or goods are specific, reason with its universals is instrumental. Intelligence consists not in weaving all goods into a rational whole, but in integrating certain competing impulses with reference to certain situations.' Herbert W. Schneider, 'Political Implications of Recent Philosophical Movements', in Charles Edward Merriam and Harry Elmer Barnes (eds), *A History of Political Theories: Recent Times. Essays on Contemporary Developments in Political Theory*, New York, 1924, p. 340.

placed, by the concern with the politically good, in the way of accepting and even valuing permanent divisions of opinion and principle at some level of political activity were hence removed or obscured.

In so far as political studies in the present century may be divided into two very broad streams, 'government' and 'political science' (history and philosophy having gone their separate ways), both streams stand equally distanced from traditional speculations. The value-framed, theoretical examination of politics has not ceased; but it has taken one step away from the discussions which led to arguments about forms of politics in terms of the ultimate goals of human or political activity.[56] In such matters, empiricism has meant a conservative positivism. Democracy has become such a widely accepted good that examination is made, not so much of its grounds and character, as of the conditions in which it will be sustained or achieved, or of the devices which are most appropriate to its operation. Pragmatism has placed the test of political speculation in the crucible of practice, and efficiency, whether of institutions or systems, has achieved a new predominance. Sir James Bryce, introducing his massive survey of *Modern Democracies* in 1921, explained that his intention was 'to provide a solid basis for argument and judgement by examining a certain number of popular governments in their actual working'.[57] In the United States ambitions waxed higher. Three years after the publication of Bryce's book, Merriam was contributing to a study of modern political theory the vision of 'advances towards technical knowledge of the political process',[58] while another contributor to the same volume delivered a magisterial rebuke to less enlightened predecessors, and stepped proudly into the new empirical world: the United States had become the laboratory of democracy, where 'outgrown concepts of another age are being discarded' and 'speculation is giving way to sound induction'.[59] Some of these early enthusiasms have become mellowed with time; but the flight from traditional speculations in examinations of political activity has formed the background within which the

[56] For a vigorous assertion of the vigour of this new form of political theory, see Brian Barry, *Sociologists, Economists and Democracy*, London, 1970.
[57] Sir James Bryce, *Modern Democracies*, London, 1921, vol. 1, p. vii.
[58] Merriam and Barnes, *op. cit.*, p. 45.
[59] Malcolm M. Willey, in Merriam and Barnes, *op. cit.*, pp. 48 and 78.

academic study of politics has been undertaken, and out of which the notion of Opposition has emerged, both as a valued form of politics and hence as a proper subject for descriptive or analytical study.

The first major work based on the notion of Opposition was Robert Dahl's *Political Oppositions in Western Democracies*, which arose out of two conferences at the Villa Serbelloni in Italy. It was published in 1966. The assumption of the worth of democracy, coupled with the intention of studying the phenomenon itself rather than any abstract notions of forms of state, make Dahl sound at times uncannily like his in many other ways dissimilar predecessor, Bryce. Together with his fellow-scholars, their optimism ripened in the Mediterranean sun, Dahl set out to 'attempt to understand modern democratic politics by examining oppositions',[60] with the further intention of discovering, 'To one who believes in the essential worth of a democratic polity, how much opposition is desirable, and what kinds? What is the best balance between consensus and dissent?'[61] Dahl introduced the topic of the book, Opposition, as one of 'the three great milestones in the development of democratic institutions',[62] not realizing that while as a descriptive statement what he says is true, as a description of democracy it is still rather unusual. Dahl's contribution to the prestige of Opposition is impaired by his attempting at times to enmesh all forms of opposition to all and any acts of government as part of the same thing, an approach which would lead us to consider Mrs Mary Whitehouse in the same class as Emiliano Zapata. The position is not much retrieved by a categorization of the ways in which oppositions can differ which in essence says simply that they may differ in every conceivable way, in goal, methods, contexts, and character;[63] in fact they may differ so much that the only thing they have in common is their possession of a common label, the inflated word 'opposition'. By far the greatest significance of the work, however, is its academic canonization of Opposition, a saint which has long been performing local miracles and receiving unofficial worship, but which has at last received the

---

[60] Robert A. Dahl, (ed.), *op. cit.*, p. xviii.
[61] *Ibid.*, p. 387.
[62] *Ibid.*, p. xi.
[63] *Ibid.*, p. xvi and Chap. 11.

official pronouncement of merit to which it has long been entitled. For though on the one hand Dahl writes as a student of politics seeking to encompass and comprehend the phenomenon of Opposition, he also writes as an eager and open advocate of democracy, and of what he believes to be its necessary ingredients. 'Today', as he puts it, 'one is inclined to regard the existence of an opposition party as very nearly the most distinctive characteristic of democracy itself; and we take the absence of an opposition party as evidence, if not always conclusive proof, for the absence of democracy.'[64] A similar position is adopted by Professor Ionescu and Dr de Madariaga in their *Opposition*, published two years later in 1968: 'the presence or absence of institutionalized political opposition', they write, 'can become the criterion for the classification of any political society in one of two categories: liberal or dictatorial, democratic or authoritarian, pluralistic-constitutional or monolithic'.[65] Professor Ionescu has embodied this assumption in the journal, *Government and Opposition*, founded in 1965 under his editorship. In addition to the usual run of articles, the journal has carried occasional surveys of the progress of oppositions, with the intention of keeping a check list on the state of democracy in the contemporary world.[66] Thus Opposition shows signs of entering its kingdom, both as a valued element in democratic politics and, stemming from this status, as a subject for academic dissection and examination. Virtue has hence become lodged not in the ends to which democracy was previously considered merely instrumental but in the very institutionalization of dissent which constitutes a characteristic of contemporary forms of democratic government. This situation does not simply exemplify the results of a suspicion of grand designs or ultimate ends, a feeling that there are no brave causes to fight for or that such brave causes as there are, are voiced by villains and followed by fools. A belief in Opposition is at present after all an essentially optimistic position, even if the fortunes of any particular policy are insured by the system of built-in alternation and variety. It is also the fruit, however, of the manner in which

[64] *Ibid.*, p. xvi.
[65] Ghiţa Ionescu and Isabel de Madariaga, *op. cit.*, p. 9.
[66] *Government and Opposition*, vol. 3, nos. 3 and 4, Summer and Autumn 1968; vol. 4, no. 3, Summer 1969.

politics has been studied since the beginning of this century, and of a development which more recent conditions have merely accentuated. In this sense the distance between contemporary students of Opposition and Sidney Low or Lord Bryce is much less than that between Bryce and Low, and Ostrogorski. Bryce might have thought much of contemporary political studies odd; Ostrogorski would have found it alarming.

The following articles are the first of a series of anthologies to be drawn from the pages of *Government and Opposition*. Later volumes will deal with forms of political activity which have not been considered here – the so called 'extra-parliamentary opposition', for instance. It is not the purpose of this collection to chart the growth of the idea of Opposition. This would be valuable, but would perhaps be difficult outside an account of a history of political studies at least since the beginning of the present century, a history of which we are at present sorely in need. Nor is it intended to provide a comprehensive survey of all regimes with legal Oppositions. It is, rather, an anthology of articles which in a variety of ways illustrate the new interest in Opposition and its application in scholarly enquiry. But it is also, I hope, an anthology in the best sense of the word: a collection of articles which, though associated by some common theme or themes, are chosen in the first place for their individual merit rather than for their utility to some Procrustean editorial scheme. In this sense, what follows illustrates the eclecticism of political studies, rather than any editorial grand design.

The following sixteen essays are reprinted as they originally appeared.[67] Some of them discuss political situations which have since altered, but the essays remain as valuable studies of specific situations and events, and no attempt has been made to turn them, by 'up-dating', into works of contemporary reference. Professor Sartori, in 'Opposition and Control: Problems and Prospects' (p. 31), examines the notion of Opposition as a specific form of political activity, and discusses

[67] There are two exceptions to this. In Professor Lehmbruch's article (p. 168), certain ambiguities in his use of the English word 'control' have been removed by substituting, in consultation with the author, the word 'check' on pp. 185 and 186. Secondly, I have taken the opportunity to correct some typographical and editorial errors which occurred when the articles were first published.

B

some of the circumstances in which the activity, thus defined,
may be expected to operate. Professor Crick (p. 38) engages in
a characteristically spirited examination of Dahl's *Political
Oppositions in Western Democracies*, a book which remains
the most important contribution so far to the discussion of
Opposition. Just how well established the discussion and its
implications have become is illustrated by Professor Shils's
discussion of the new states of Asia and Africa (p. 45). Opposition, if not taken quite as the norm, is taken as the standpoint,
and it is its suppression rather than its existence, and the arguments for its termination rather than those for its cultivation,
which Professor Shils is concerned to examine and criticize.

It is the privilege of the editor of an anthology to enjoy a
freedom of selection not given to the compiler of a reader.
Professor Martines' study of the Italian city states (p. 79) is
hardly a contribution to the study of Opposition as usually
conceived; it does, however, have a peculiar appeal, not only
for its inherent interest but also as an example of the effects
which the notion of Opposition has had on the study of politics,
and of the uses to which it can be put in such apparently unlikely soil as medieval Mantua, Genoa, or Florence. Professor
Oakeshott's discussion of Magna Carta (p. 104) on the other
hand indicates delightfully, when we tremble at ascribing
oppositional politics to the early 18th century, that a form of
them can be detected in the early 13th century if we have the
imagination and boldness to look for it. Frank O'Gorman's
study of party in 18th-century England, and of its justification
by Burke (p. 111), illustrates why the 18th century has proved
so intimidating; there are both difficulties and rewards in the
study of a period when, though the words 'party' and 'opposition' were freely used, they had very different connotations
from those with which we have today become familiar. The
development of these two words, and of the activities to which
they refer, is discussed by Professor Hanham in his account of
Opposition techniques in England between the Second Reform Bill and the Great War (p. 131), thus combining with
Frank O'Gorman to introduce the course of Opposition in its
most familiar and still perhaps its most admired form.

But the Westminster model's esteem can be misleading if
it is taken for typicality. Richard Hofstadter describes the
American experience – both like and unlike that of England –

of an existence of parties before what we now think of as a party system, and of an absence of any necessary connection between oppositional practice and oppositional theory (p. 146). Professor Tosi, in his study of the ambiguous position occupied in Italy by such parties as the Communists (p. 153), provides an example of Opposition by parties whose formal theoretical equipment is out of key with the role they perform, and who may find themselves uneasily stressing both proletarian virtues and bourgeois civic ones. A different kind of ambiguity is described by Professor Lehmbruch in the case of the Grand Coalition in West Germany (p. 168), where the need for government seemed at least temporarily incompatible with the need for the criticism and alternative policies which Opposition can provide. A third example of the variety which exists within Western Europe is given by K. R. Libbey's account of referenda and initiatives in Switzerland (p. 194), devices which seem to go at least some of the way to offering the possible circumvention of party desired by Sidgwick and Ostrogorski.

The interests of scholars, however, are no more confined within Europe than were the interests of their military predecessors. J. E. Spence, in his study of South Africa (p. 216), reveals the peculiar obstacles placed in the way of Opposition when the great issue of politics is one which constantly involves the very basis and constitution of the political order, where in fact the distinction between first- and second-order issues cannot be made in the manner in which it can be made, for instance, in Britain. Professor Austin chronicles a different situation in Ghana (p. 248), where no party in power has given complete deference to tolerance and variety in political life.

The difficulties of sustaining Opposition in a state where parties outside the government initially regard Opposition as an outmoded convention, while relishing its legitimate fruits, is one of several features which emerge from Professor Wilson's account of Ceylon between 1947 and 1968 (p. 267). Professor Morris-Jones's discussion of the Indian Congress Party (p. 284) raises the question of how far some at least of the functions normally ascribed to Opposition – the proposition of alternative policies, the voicing of criticism – may be found within a party which, by dominating national politics, apparently renders such functions difficult.[68] Finally Dr Zellentin's essay leads to the question of how far the notion of Opposition, associated with the internal politics of nations, may be applied to a supra-national organization, the European Parliament (p. 302). Much more could be said of the issues raised in this and all the other essays in this volume. But it is the duty of an editor at this point to stand aside, and let his contributors speak for themselves.

[68] The main ideas of this article have been developed to take account of the course of events of 1967 and 1969, in the author's *Government and Politics of India* (3rd edition), London, 1971.

Giovanni Sartori

Opposition and Control: Problems and Prospects[*]

MY PURPOSE HERE IS ONLY TO PUT FORWARD A NUMBER OF tentative suggestions in order to provide some common basis and a starting ground for discussion. We are called on to examine the principle and the working of political opposition as one of the specific means of control. That is to say that in our context the notion of opposition is specific, the notion of control general. Accordingly, the issue may be formulated as follows: in the light of the problem of controlling government, that is, of checking absolute power, to what extent and in what ways is the existence of an opposition vital, useful or possible in both 'developed' and 'developing countries'?

Obviously, if one deals with developing countries the very idea of 'developing' needs to be dissected. Some countries are purely and simply under-developed; other countries find themselves at different stages of development. Since we are not primarily concerned with economic development, a useful way of clarifying what we mean by political development and / or modernization is to consider the 'level of institutionalization' of the countries concerned, with reference, e.g., to the degree of functional differentiation, structural specificity and institutional consolidation of their political arrangements. Whether this suggestion is accepted or not, it seems necessary to refer to specific levels or stages of development, bearing in mind that some of our comparisons are not only cross-cultural but also asynchronous.

Let it also be clear that we should not in any way limit our understanding of what an opposition accomplishes, or may accomplish. That is to say that it should not be taken for granted that the roles of opposition are only related, basically, to the purpose of controlling and restraining the exercise of

[*] Vol. 1, no. 2, January 1966.

power. While it appears that, at least in the West, the idea of opposition was, and perhaps remains, closely linked with the principle of respect for and protection of minorities (with all that this entails), it is at least conceivable that an opposition may perform a number of roles on quite different grounds.

For instance, an opposition may represent interests, and may represent them in a way that is hardly conducive to checking absolute power *vis-à-vis* minorities and dissenting opinions. An opposition may also take part in the political communication function, that is, its primary role may be confined to providing a channel of information which actually lacks, in the final analysis, effectiveness and efficacy; or it may only be a safety valve, a merely verbal outlet, in the sense that opposition is tolerated only to placate opposition. These random observations surely show the need of a more analytical classification of the conceivable roles and functions of oppositions. With these provisos in mind, our central, preliminary cluster of questions could be stated as follows:

At which stage of development, or of institutionalization, are the mechanisms of opposition likely to operate smoothly and successfully? Where oppositions exist, which roles do they actually perform? And where opposition is banned, are there alternative mechanisms or possibilities of control? Finally, and in principle, is the presence of an overt opposition a necessary requirement for any political system seeking modernization? The latter question has been answered in the affirmative, among others, by David E. Apter.[1] It appears clear, however, that the issue can hardly be discussed in general, that is, without specifying the notion of opposition. What kind of opposition? Opposition under what form and within what limits?

The following is a rough attempt to pin down the connotation of the idea of opposition as it is cherished in democratic Western politics. It is suggested that a distinction may usefully be drawn between 'constitutional opposition' and 'opposition' without qualification, that is, between a narrow and fairly precise meaning on the one hand, and a vague and broader meaning which has yet to be explored and construed, on the

[1] Cf. 'Some Reflections on the Role of a Political Opposition in New Nations' in *Comparative Studies in Society and History*, vol. IV, no. 2, January 1962, pp. 154–68.

other hand. Possibly we should at present concern ourselves more with the latter topic than with the concept of constitutional opposition. But this is all the more reason for singling out from the outset the frame of reference, the 'reference concept', that we are likely to use, rightly or wrongly, as our yardstick.

OPPOSITION AND CONSTITUTIONAL OPPOSITION

Any means of 'opposing' is not what we usually call 'opposition'. In fact, opposition is almost always a shorthand term for 'constitutional opposition'. And the qualification 'constitutional' that was applied to the practice of opposition in the 19th century was fitting, for the kind of opposition that one finds in the Western democracies is the outcome of a long and delicate process of 'constitutionalization of politics', to use the telling expression of Benjamin Constant. For one thing, and to begin with, constitutional opposition presupposes 'quiet politics', not turbulent politics. Better said, constitutional opposition belongs to a peaceful view of politics, not to a warlike approach in which the opposer is an enemy, an *hostis*. In short, constitutional opposition presupposes the domestication of politics. Whether explicitly stated or not, this seems to be the implicit assumption of our usual way of discussing the behaviour of oppositions and the merits of the majority–opposition arrangement. We say: an opposition must oppose, but not obstruct; it must be constructive, not disruptive. Indeed, in many accounts opposition is understood as a form of collaboration. We also say that opposition is different from factionalism, that a 'real opposition' has in view the general interest, not merely personal antagonisms. Finally, most authors stress that opposition presupposes consent on fundamentals, that is, consent at the community and regime level. What the opposition opposes is a government, not the political system as such. Thus 'separatism' is something different from opposition proper. And no matter whether we have a different name for it or not, we are likely to distinguish between constitutional opposition and anti-system opposition, that is, the kind of opposition that would replace the system (thereby implying the prohibition of future opposition), not merely the governors.

If one pushes the argument further it may even appear that

the principles and practices of opposition not only presuppose the constitutionalization of politics but also that they are closely related to a 'fair play' approach to politics. Indeed, there is a very real sense in which the 'game image' of politics applies to the performance of an opposition. Too much opposition, that is, an opposition pushed to extremes, may tear the political system apart. And the same is true for disloyal, or *mala fide* opposition, at least if some limits are not respected.

Why are these limits respected? If one looks for instance at British constitutional practice, one of the answers surely is that what goes on in the House of Commons is a game played by correct players to whom cheating appears more disgraceful than losing. This is not to say that the working of the mechanism of opposition necessarily requires good loosers and correct players. (One is reminded of Ortega's 'origen deportivo del estado'.) It does suggest, however, that particular operational codes – as Nathan Leites would say – are involved if the role of opposition is to be played in a constructive and successful manner.

However that may be, the notion of constitutional opposition needs to be pinpointed also with reference to the principle of alternation in power and, moreover, to the type of party system within which it occurs.

Real alternative government only occurs in two-party systems. In systems with more than two parties we usually find something different, depending on how many parties there are and on how wide (and how extreme) is the spectrum of political opinion. In the moderately pluralistic party systems – roughly, when the relevant parties are three, four or at most five – the more frequent pattern is 'coalition governments', that is, a situation in which all the parties are likely to share, at some time, a fraction of governmental power. Finally, in the highly fragmented and pluralistic party systems – e.g. in France, Italy, the Weimar Republic, Spain before the civil war – we find a third pattern, namely, a situation in which the system only allows for a peripheral 'semi-turnover': the centre party, or group of parties, never alternate, whereas the extreme parties (e.g. communist or fascist parties) never govern (until the system breaks down).

The bearing of the foregoing on our topic is that the patterns and style of opposition vary significantly from one type

of party system to another.[2] The relevant distinction here
seems to be between responsible opposition and irresponsible
opposition. An opposition which knows that it may be called to
'respond', i.e. which is oriented towards governing and has a
reasonable chance to govern, or to have access to governmental
responsibility, is likely to behave responsibly, in a restrained
and realistic fashion. On the other hand a 'permanent opposition' which is far removed from governmental turnover and
thereby knows that it will *not* be called on to 'respond', is
likely to take the path of 'irresponsible opposition', that is, the
path of promising wildly and outbidding.

What seems to follow is that to the extent that the concept
of constitutional opposition coincides with the concept of
responsible opposition (and they do coincide to a large
extent), the successful operation of the mechanics of opposition
depends not on one but on two conditions: the constitutionalization of politics and, additionally, the kind of inducements
that are provided by the particular party system. As a general
rule, internalized self-restraints are likely to be more effective
when all the parties are allowed access to power, and in particular the more the system provides for some substantial
alternation in power. However, the more parties there are, the
less this latter condition is likely to be satisfied. Therefore it
can be suggested that responsible opposition and party pro-
liferation are inversely correlated.

Whatever the merits of this latter hypothesis, Duverger
points out correctly that it is only in two-party systems that one
finds an 'institutionalized opposition'.[3] In multi-party systems
one is confronted with non-institutionalized, overlapping, and
shifting oppositions (in the plural) that do not really perform
the role of presenting clear-cut alternative policies to the
electorate. And from this point of view one may even wonder
whether we are not simply confronted, in this case, with one
of the many facets of the general principle of opposing power
to power.

As can easily be seen, a rapid survey of Western experience
already shows to what extent it is itself diversified, and points
to the fact that the classic model of opposition is hard to put

[2] Cf. the forthcoming volume by R. A. Dahl and others on *Oppositions in
Western Democracies*, Yale University Press, 1966.
[3] Cf. *Les partis politiques*, Paris, 1954, particularly pp. 454–5.

into practice even under relatively optimal conditions. For it should be remembered that until now we have been speaking only of the highly institutionalized political systems in which there is a concern for the protection of minorities, and, in general, for the protection of individual freedom, in which factional warfare has been replaced by legalized competition, and in which the operational code only allows *some* means, not *any* means of opposition.

There are, then, at least three basic types or patterns of opposition: (i) a responsible constitutional opposition; (ii) a constitutional but non-responsible opposition (ranging from semi-responsibility to full-fledged irresponsibility); (iii) an opposition which is neither responsible nor even constitutional, and which eventually could also be dealt with under the term 'contestation' understood as a broader and less specific term than 'opposition'.

Clearly enough, our praise of an opposition-based system is basically derived from the first type. It is also clear that the third type, or possibility, is only a residual category, in the sense that neither our theory nor our factual knowledge has yet really come to grips with the third case. Yet can we deny that this is a realistic way of stating the case with reference to many new nations that are starting from scratch? The question is raised for the purpose of leaving it unanswered. Indeed my task here is introductory, i.e. it is only to elicit reactions. Let it be clear, therefore, that these observations are only meant to suggest one possible avenue of approach, in the hope that others will explore the problem of opposition in their own way, provided that the issue is dealt with as analytically as possible.

CONTROL

Thus far on 'opposition'. As for 'control', let it be repeated that while the concept of opposition should be analytically defined, the idea of control should be left wide open. Among other reasons, our view of the problem of the control over government depends very much on how we stand with regard to the problem of opposition. The pessimists, so to speak, are likely to develop an interest in exploring alternative avenues and devices of control, whatever these may be. The optimists, on the other hand, may prefer to dwell on the controlling function which is provided by the very existence of an opposition. While we are interested in having the broadest possible treatment of the idea and of the techniques of control, this suggestion does not imply, however, that 'control' should remain an unspecified and loose term. Indeed, the question 'what do we mean by control?' is one that we should not avoid.

Bernard Crick

On Conflict and Opposition*

Robert A. Dahl (ed.), *Political Oppositions in Western Democracies*, Yale University Press, 1966.

PROFESSOR DAHL BEGINS THIS BRILLIANT AND EXASPERATING book by hitting the sixty-four-dollar question right on the nail. Of the 113 members of the United Nations in 1964, only about thirty had political systems during the previous decade in which legal party opposition had existed: 'Are the thirty systems that now exist merely the exotic flowers of a unique and passing historical climate? Or are they vigorous products of a long evolution, a political species now rugged enough to thrive in other, perhaps harsher, climes?' For certainly, Dahl says, legal party opposition is, in fact, 'a recent unplanned invention that has been confined for the most part to a handful of countries in Western Europe and the English-speaking world'.

When I say 'brilliant *and* exasperating' (taking the brilliance for granted for a moment, for Dahl is indeed a star of immediate light as well as of abstract height), it is because of a basic – perhaps inevitable – ambiguity in the subject-matter. For to say that parties in some thirty systems may operate legally as oppositions is not to say that even most of these parties see their purpose, or even one of their main purposes, as offering opposition. To say there is opposition is, in one sense, simply to point to a vital condition of – well, the nameless demi-god: what Friedrich insists on calling 'constitutionalism' (irrespective of whether there is a constitution or not); what Dahl and Sartori, like nearly everyone else, insist on calling 'democratic' (irrespective of how small the democratic element in these mixed governments may be, or of the fact that all governments of industrial or industrializing powers have to defer to or persuade their masses in a way unknown to an agrarian autocracy); what some call 'plural societies' (which is often just a tautology, another name – though one so abstruse and undesirable as to be free from ideologically inspired rape); and what Aristotle, Machiavelli, Bodin and (to my knowledge) two modern authors simply call 'polity' – communities which legitimate, not persecute, the activity of politics. So where republican government (isn't that the least ambiguous term – to be restored?) exists, there is opposition.

However, there are also regimes in which certain legal rights are attached to an institution specifically called 'the opposition'. Britain is, of course, the clearest case – but also, Dahl is quite right, an almost uselessly extreme example. A jolly good model perhaps, but a misleading basis from which to generalize about political behaviour elsewhere. Now the first sense of opposition seems to exhaust all politics, while the second seems far too narrow. The book is exasperating because it asks two quite different questions: (i) what are the general characteristics of limits on political activity which make social conflict compatible with a reasonable expectation of stability in a state or regime and (ii) what specific legal or conventional rights have certain groups to offer organized, regular, and public opposition to their governments?

Plainly the first question is the grand question of freedom and order. I make no criticism of anyone attempting it: quite the contrary – and Dahl one day may do it (and do it better, with respect, alone). But it is so much bigger than the second question that it might be better distinguished by speaking of 'conflict' and 'contestation' (as has already been suggested in this journal) rather than of 'opposition' in the more limited, but more precise and graspable, sense. For the second question is small enough – just – to warrant a plain factual account of how far opposition is institutionalized in public law and convention in certain countries, and some speculation, based on historical evidence, which would seek to explain both peculiarities and similarities.

This ambiguity emerges in the structure of the book. Most of the essays on separate countries deal, in fact, with the whole political system: they do not narrow their sights to see why elements of institutional opposition, in the second sense, exist. Such opposition gets dealt with in passing amid the more general question of conflict, contestation, degrees of diversity amid order. Now some of these essays happen to be extremely good: to be invidious, Hans Daalder on the Netherlands, the late Otto Kirchheimer (to whom the volume is dedicated) on Western Germany, and Val R. Lorwin on Belgium, are among the best, if not the best, summary accounts I have ever read of the character of politics in these countries. But this was not meant to be, quite plainly, yet another Baedeker of comparative government. Dahl is much too original for that.

He himself contributes a chapter on 'The American Oppositions'. One might expect an attempt by a political scientist to generalize upon the basis of the great and very distinguished store of American historical writings, both on the national and the state level, of the last generation. But in fact he gives us an interesting essay, somewhere between Louis Hartz and Seymour Lipset, on our old friend 'consensus'. He answers the question: if consensus is so great, why is there political conflict at all? The answer to that seems obvious – unless one is an Hegelian or a Marxist. On this quite unexpected subject-matter, however, he does make one important and largely novel point – on what he properly and modestly calls 'speculative' and 'doubtful terrain' (but here is a behaviourist willing to go for the problem, even when the statistical methods available peg out): that a high degree of consensus among the many, actually stimulates extremism among a few. The political dissenter, he argues, knowing that he cannot come to dominate either of the major parties, becomes feckless about practicalities and alienated from ordinary politics. Hartz and Hofstadter have tried to show that all the fantastic roster of American minority movements were really, at heart, believers in the same (almost claustrophobic) liberalism and democratic Americanism as the rest. Dahl argues that they were distinct types, though their distinction is a product of their ambivalence between hopelessness and desperation when faced by a consensus so wide and so firm.

Dahl's essay on America does not, however, attempt even to identify the long oppositions there have been in Congress: the anti-slavery men, then the South after Kansas and California entered the Union; the radical republican opposition to Lincoln in his second term and then to Johnson; the Mugwump republicans who opposed Grant... many such examples. Perhaps I beg the question by calling them 'oppositions'; perhaps they did not last long enough, nor work in concert over a

wide enough range of issues. Is that it? But it should have
been argued. And argued down to earth amid congressional
politics rather than in the, at times, too rarefied world of
Hartz's and Daniel Bell's obsession with obsessive consensus. I
have been as guilty as any of using these general explanations,
but at times – if the subject-matter is 'opposition' – one longs
to say: 'Sure, Americans have got an awful lot in common.
But what kind of lasting quarrels have they kept up within
this unhappy harmony?'

The really surprising essay on a particular country is, let
me pass on and off it quickly, Professor Allen Potter's on Great
Britain. This is simply a thirty-page account, drawn from very
familiar sources, of the working of the British party system;
it could appear and similar accounts have appeared in a dozen
textbooks. Surely it is absolutely vital to explain *how* it was
that opposition in Britain became a recognized institution of
the constitution, certainly by the end of the 18th century. A
fair amount has been written on this: Namier, Pares, Brooke,
Christie – to name only one side. English 18th-century history,
with its fascinating parallels to contemporary congressional
politics, is a not undeveloped field. Potter makes no use of this
literature at all. He concentrates almost entirely on the
modern period – which is to explain nothing, it is itself the
thing in need of explanation. He writes as if quite basic facts
of British politics and society might be as unfamiliar to his
readers as British history is to him. To blame the editor and
not the author, almost any historian might have done better:
what price inter-disciplinary cross-fertilization, eh?

The real book consists of Dahl's own three concluding chapters. Here at last is someone emerging from the excessive
methodological preoccupations of the 'American school' of
'political behavior', attempting to *use* the methods and the
methods adduced, striving towards an integration of history
and what we can discover about present behaviour and motivations by the methods of the social sciences (and can indeed,
one should add, infer about the past from this contemporary
evidence). Here is a proper eclecticism: methods begin to be
chosen to fit the problem rather than, the curse for so long, the
problems limited to what will appear objective and quantifi-
able within the method. 'A candid portrayal,' writes Dahl in

his Preface, 'of the relation between the essays in this volume and the analytical scheme which eventually emerged would have to show the final scheme less as a format for the essays than as their product. I have therefore placed the whole comparative analysis in the final chapters.' How much wiser than the famous Almond and Coleman volume on *The Politics of the Developing Areas*, in which (dare one say) the excellence of the descriptive part had little relationship to the pretentious 'conceptual framework'.

The main conclusion is negative, but nonetheless important: Dahl gives 'a confident no' to the hypothesis that there is any standard pattern of opposition in Western democracies. He identifies five primary conditions that 'help to explain' (oh admirably modest 'help'!) patterns of opposition: constitutional structure and electoral system: widely shared cultural premises; specific sub-cultures; the record of grievances against the government, and social and economic differences. These conditions may each 'within some limits that cannot be specified... vary independently of the others'. So – I am not quite sure if this is my gloss on Dahl or Dahl's on Dahl – 'system' becomes a necessary *concept* that we must apply to any society in order to understand it at all. But in so far as 'system' is an attribute of any society (as when social scientists say, 'there is a systematic relationship between political and social factors'), we cannot ever assign precise values to the relationships involved in the hypothetical system. We are limited both by our knowledge and by the flux of events. This seems to me a far more sensible and helpful new middle ground than either the conservative or the pure empiricist who says, 'But there is no system'; or the socialist or the social scientist who says, 'There must be a system, the variables are ... (then follows his pet or preferred scheme) – the precise values of which we can fill in later, mere research.'

Dahl's conditions or variables seem to me an admirable compromise between the overly specific and the too comprehensive, hence rather empty, 'affect' and 'effect' or 'in-put' and 'out-put' kind of *a priori* conceptualizing (word-spinning). He is inclined to put far more value on institutional and political factors than has often of late been the case:

Constitutional frameworks and electoral systems, it might be objected, have nothing to do with the characteristics of opposition; we must look instead to social, economic, cultural or psychological factors. This kind of objection reflects a 'reductionism' that seeks to reduce political factors to something more 'basic', as biophysicists seek to explain biology by invoking 'more basic' laws of physics. Yet just as biophysicists have encountered severe difficulties in reducing biology to physics, to ignore the effects of constitutional and electoral institutions leaves one in serious difficulties.

Thus to Dahl, if all is still behaviour, yet institutions represent a very special and relatively rigid pattern of behaviour.

I cannot summarize in any short space his very rich and interesting mixture of analysis and generalization – which if it reaches no new positive conclusions is none the less valuable both in the fact that it destroys fallacies, or – more often – cuts them down to size, and in the clear example it sets of distinguishing between concepts and theories: the language one talks and what one says in it. Far too often have concepts been put forward as if they were theories.

But three matters deserve singling out – two good and one bad. He gives the concept of 'polarization' some very sharp criticism, both on logical grounds as a concept and on empirical grounds as a generalization about political behaviour. In some ways he is too charitable; to my mind most of those who talk so profoundly about the 'polarization of forces' are lazy word-spinners, third-generation bastardized Marxists (even if anti-Marxists), or else simply those who follow the political pressures of the old hot and cold war – now subject to so many variations of temperature and measuring scales. He argues that declining differences in economic and social conditions may not lead to the decline of ideology but to its ascendance: as such differences become less clear-cut, empirical politics will have fewer guide-lines – theories about how societies work may become as important to governments as once were doctrines about how they ought to work. Unfortunately, however, right at the end the fragile unity of the book, almost restored, is shattered again: 'These questions seem to demand nothing less than a complicated assessment of democracy itself.' This I will not follow (though it is good stuff indeed), for it flies off far away from any specific sense of legal opposition, of opposition as an institution and not just as a synonym for patterns of conflict, contestation, and the rest. Dahl, if it is not presumptuous to say so, seems to have revived on a methodological level the useful distinction between 'institution' and (the hopelessly undifferentiated tautologous morass of) 'behaviour'. But he does not actually apply it. A fundamental condition for the existence of 'polity' is the existence of conflict; a fundamental condition for the stability of such regimes is the legitimation of conflict (usually, but *not* always, in the form of party competition); and a useful and common device for this legitimation (common but by no means universal) is the institutionalizing within the parliament or assembly of public opposition to the government of the day. This last point is dependent on the two former, but is worth singling out to discuss on its own. One cannot discuss everything at once – as Dahl probably feels that he has to. But he comes as near to success as possible, when the orders are misread and his brigade, instead of mopping up an important local position, charges straight for the guns down the long and corpse-strewn valley.

Edward Shils

Opposition in the New States of Asia and Africa*

THE SITUATION OF OPPOSITION PARTIES IN THE NEW STATES

The new states of Asia and Africa present a variegated picture with respect to the status and mode of action of their opposition parties. In only about a third of the new states are opposition parties regarded as constitutionally legitimate. Israel, Lebanon, Morocco, India, Ceylon, Sierra Leone, Senegal, Nigeria, Malaysia, Philippines, Sudan, and a few others allow opposition to exist in a public and institutional form. In Israel a system of a frequently varying coalition government and open opposition parties prevails, with full freedom of public discussion. In Nigeria, the multi-party system with a coalition government and open opposition parties still functions, although it nearly collapsed earlier this year because a major, but minority, party in the previous coalition boycotted the federal election – as part of its leader's unsuccessful scheme to make a *coup d'état*. In India, which has had the most stable and completely civilian government, opposition is free; parties in opposition to the ruling party are numerous and ineffectual, and for the most part work within the constitution. Ceylon permits two major parties and a considerable number of lesser parties. Both these South Asian regimes permit full freedom of discussion, although the previously incumbent Ceylonese party had sought to control the press. Pakistan and Sudan, having witnessed the dissolution of parties by military regimes, have now returned to something like party systems. Malaysia, too, maintains one, although it has very recently had to amputate one part of the country to avoid suppression of the locally-based Peoples' Action Party of Singapore. Sierra Leone also maintains a party system which has proceeded without

* Vol. 1, no. 2, January 1966.

crisis since independence. The Arab Middle Eastern states, the Maghreb states except Morocco, nearly all of the French-speaking African states, Ghana, Tanzania, Uganda, Kenya, Malawi, and Burma, do not have public opposition parties.

None of these new states is immune from oppositional activity. In about half of them, the incumbent governments in the past eight years have had to admit the factual existence of opposition by means of conspiracy, assassination or a successful *coup d'état*. Most of the acts of répression of an illegal opposition allegedly intending to employ violent means have been committed within states already denying both the constitutional legitimacy of opposition and indeed even the existence of any oppositional interests except 'reactionary' ones. Opposition has occurred in these states after it has already been legally abolished and its existence implicitly denied.

Among the one-party states, Guinée acknowledged recently that its youth might be tempted to become oppositional. It had already condemned the leaders of its teachers' union for illegal opposition – which it designated as subversion. The most stable of the one-party regimes, Tunisia, has seen one of its major architects in exile and assassinated under obscure circumstances. It has itself contended that it was the object of conspiracy. In Algeria, there has been a *coup d'état* by the military in a harshly repressive one-party state which had already experienced during its brief existence a regional-military rebellion, and the trials of conspirators against the previously ruling government. In the new one-party regime in Tanzania, no opposition is admitted to exist, but the leader of the opposition, Mr Tumbo, is banished from public life. The newly joined members of the government from Zanzibar have encouraged or permitted the resistance of their followers to the desires of the government in Dar-es-Salaam. In Ghana, the government has on several occasions made accusations of subversive intentions, alleged plots to assassinate the President and noted other manifestations of opposition to the rulers of the country. In Togo, President Olympio was assassinated by a group of army officers and non-commissioned officers and politicians recalled from exile to join in the conspiracy. Similar manifestations have occurred in many of the other one-party regimes.

Still, what is notable about the new states is not that opposition exists. That is to be expected. Nor is it surprising that they have not been as successful as the totalitarian states,[1] which some of them admire as embodiments of modernity, in suppressing the emergence from time to time of oppositional interests and sentiments. Their élites have had unwittingly to acknowledge this publicly, on the occasion of their displacement by the forcible action of a previously closed opposition.[2] What is more interesting at this point in our discussion is that in so many states in which the rulers strive for modernity, for progressive and differentiated societies, they should be so intolerant of opposition, and particularly of open opposition in the form of constitutional parties, contending and criticizing in public.

THE ATTITUDE OF DOMINANT PARTIES TOWARDS OPPOSITION

We must, therefore, seek to answer the question: Under what conditions does the ruling party tolerate the opposition? Or in an alternative formulation: Under what conditions does the ruling party either abolish the legal existence of opposition parties or force them to amalgamate with the ruling party?

As a first approximation, we may say that toleration of opposition exists where one or several of the following factors are present: (i) the ruling party alone or in coalition is obviously safe by a very substantial majority and is confident of its continued safety; (ii) the ruling party has a strong attachment to constitutional government; (iii) the conduct of the opposition is relatively unaggressive; (iv) the opposition is large and difficult to suppress without the probability of strong resistance by arms or by significant public opinion; and (v) the rulers do not regard themselves as the sole bearers of the charisma of nationality.

The ruling party suppresses opposition parties or forces them to coalesce with itself when it feels insecure about the stability of its majority and where the opposition, although

[1] Not that any totalitarian states have been able for long to avoid manifestations of opposition.

[2] Where subversive powers are strong – the army is almost always the only strong subversive power – it is easy for them to overthrow the incumbent party. The institutions of public order in most of the new states are very feeble and cannot successfully cope with strong subversive elements.

weak, is regarded as a danger to the security of the incumbent élite. The assessment of danger to the security of the state is a subjective phenomenon. It is often unconnected with any realistically assessed high probability of a successful effort of the opposition party to displace the ruling party.

Efforts to suppress the public existence of an opposition party have hitherto been successful except where the opposition has a particular territorial or regional base[3] or where it has substantial foreign support (e.g. the difficulties of the central governments in Congo-Leopoldville, Sudan, Iraq, India, and Indonesia in suppressing the territorially based opposition in Katanga and Orient Provinces, in the Southern Sudan, in Kurdistan, Nagaland, and Sumatra, and the Celebes). The condemned opposition parties have not as parties been able to resist effectively – their leaders have been gaoled or driven out of the country and their party machines have crumbled. They have not been able to call strikes or rally counter-pressure when the governing party has wished to take strong action against them.

Despite the almost always evident incapacity of open opposition parties to resist their own destruction – which would lead to the conclusion that they could not by the same token subvert or overcome the incumbent government (even if they wished) – ruling parties in the new states none the less incline very often to the suppression of those who oppose them. Indeed if the allegedly subversive opposition parties were strong enough to resist their dissolution, the ruling parties would perhaps be less ready to suppress them.[4]

It seems clear that it is not because the governments have been in real danger from the opposition parties that they have suppressed them. When it suppresses or amalgamates an opposition party the government does not often allege that it is doing so because the opposition actually endangered its position. What it reacts against is an imputed subversive intention – a subversive state of mind – rather than a factual

[3] The survival of the multi-party system in Nigeria is very much a function of the distinctive territorial bases of the various parties.
[4] Conversely, if the opposition parties were as dangerous as their ruling antagonists assert, they probably could succeed in their subversion because the ruling parties and their governments are also very fragile. Their powers of resistance are not very great, judging by the number of successful *coups* undertaken by oppositional elements.

probability of subversion. Prohibition or suppression is a punishment for a wrong state of mind rather than a forestalling of a probable pernicious action.

The argument usually given for the suppression of opposition is that there is no need for an opposition because the ruling party and the people are one. It is also said that because of a shortage of personnel for the exacting tasks of development, it is wasteful for educated persons to be encouraged to spend their time in criticizing when they should be working for the progress of their countries. Another argument is that the criticisms of opposition parties would distract the populace from its concentration on the tasks set by the development programmes. Finally, it is said that the abolition of opposition parties enhances the stability of government and thereby provides the firm framework needed for social and economic development.

There is not much empirical basis for these arguments. In no country in the world are party and people one, neither in the underdeveloped countries nor in the advanced ones. It is no more than a doctrinaire belief of political élites that they embody completely all the interests of the people whom they rule and that they care for them all equally and completely. But the fact that it is only a belief does not make it less real or less effective. In many cases it probably is a sincerely held belief.

It is certainly true that the new states must economize in the use of scarce educated talent. Very few of the new states have reached the point where they have an unemployable surplus of university graduates and technically trained 'cadres'. (India is the most outstanding exception.) But the suppression of opposition does not result in the employment of the talents of the opposition. They are very often, as in Ghana, incarcerated or exiled. Even if left at liberty they are seldom given important posts in the government – although in Kenya at least some of the leaders of the Kenya Democratic Union were thus employed when it was amalgamated with the Kenya African National Union. Still, the belief that talents must be conserved and used for the fulfilment of an overridingly important goal is a reality, too.

There are no grounds for believing that the inefficacy of so many measures for the improvement of agricultural technique

and output, and for the promotion of industrial production in
the countries which have permitted open opposition, are attributable to the demoralizing effect of the public criticism of
government measures by open opposition parties or a free
press. The economic misfortunes of Guinée certainly cannot
be assigned to such a cause, because there is no public opposition in Guinée. People do not work harder or more efficiently
when they are not allowed to know of criticisms of government policies. States without open opposition do not have
higher rates of economic growth than do states which tolerate
opposition. Where, as in the case of the Ivory Coast, the economic growth rate of a one-party state is relatively high, it is
largely a consequence of foreign aid.

As regards the argument from stability, this, too, has no
empirical foundation. The one-party governments – governments which have suppressed their oppositions – are not less
unstable than the types of regime they do not wish to re-
semble. Attempts at *coups d'état* have happened more
frequently in one-party regimes than in regimes with open
opposition parties (e.g. Mali, Ivory Coast, Togoland,
Dahomey, Syria, Iraq).

Since the arguments which are used to justify the suppression of opposition by governing parties seem to be empirically
baseless, why are they employed? They are employed in part
to give a justification, in terms of a principle involving the
common good, to actions which serve the particular advantage
of the ruling party. They are invoked because the ruling party
is attached to the symbols and roles of power and does not
want to be displaced. They are also invoked and applied because they are actually believed.

Why are they believed? The beliefs in question appear to
derive from an unarticulated political metaphysic,[5] from a
conception of the nation as a metaphysical essence which
finds its purest manifestation in those who believe in and give
expression to it by the fact of their incumbency in the positions of authoritative responsibility for the custody and pro-

---

[5] Professor Arthur Lewis in his forthcoming work, *Politics in West Africa*,
writes: 'A struggle for independence is highly emotional ... The men who
thrust themselves forward ... feel that they are Heaven-sent, and that anyone
who stands in their way is a traitor to Heaven's cause.'

pagation of that unitary national essence.[6] The metaphysic of the 'national essence' grew into a mind-filling reality in the course of the agitation and negotiations for independence. Those who agitated for the independence of the still scarcely existent nation became possessed by this essence, which they sought to emancipate from the accidents which encumbered it, such as the rule of the ethnically alien, the influence of traditional indigenous authorities, and others who manifested in their political action or in their tribal and communal attachments their non-participation in that essence.

According to this 'metaphysic of the nation,' one cannot simultaneously be of the nation and yet antagonistic towards its highest and fullest embodiment. Where society is very different from the state, the occupants of the ruling positions in the state regard themselves as the exclusive custodians of what is essential in the society. The empirically existing society, with its tribal divisions, its traditional leaders, its educated class with divergent loyalties and aspirations, is a bad accident of history, of mistakes by dead and living persons who did not or do not see that their existence is fundamentally anomalous. That is the way in which the rulers conceive of themselves and their competitors.

How could such a conception have arisen? It has two major external intellectual sources: Rousseau and the doctrine of the dictatorship of the proletariat, to both of which many French-speaking African politicians, were susceptible in the latter part of the 1940s and more so in the 1950s. Of the four English-speaking African states which have suppressed or amalgamated with their publicly organized opposition, at least one has been markedly influenced by the Leninist idea of the dictatorship of the proletariat, and the others have been somewhat influenced by it. But the doctrinal influences do not explain why the opposition has been suppressed in so many countries which have not been influenced at all by Rousseau and very little by Marxism–Leninism. The dominant political élites have their prejudices and some of them come from and are reinforced by political theories. But by and large,

[6] This metaphysic, although of a quite different historical origin, bears a close structural similarity to the historical metaphysics of Marxism–Leninism, which places the Communist Party in an analogous position in the communist countries.

political theory seems a factor of minor significance – almost an epiphenomenon – entering into a pattern of thought which is generated from experience, from passion and the necessities of collective pride, individual dignity and vanity, and from the colonial situation.

There is an inherent dynamic in the colonial situation of proud persons with a need for dignity and a resentment against those who deny it to them. There is a need for self-identification, which enhances dignity. The nature of this self-identification is influenced by the scope of the rejected but still obtaining colonial authority, and the ineffable experience of a distinguishing colour. It gains intensity from the self-identification which arises first from an active leading role in the independence movement and then from the fact of incumbency in the central positions of authority in the new states. The very thinness of its spread in the rest of society makes for a more acute consciousness of one's own circle of *confrères* as the exclusive bearers of the quality of nationality.

We must not, however, overlook the simple facts of attachment to power and the prestige and perquisites associated with power, of irritation at simply being made the focus of criticism, and of touchiness in response to criticism for shortcomings of which one is more or less aware. There is also the further unpleasantness of being criticized by persons who were once one's colleagues, indeed almost brothers. This wounded and aggressive response to criticism, actual and anticipated, draws additional force from the antagonism felt towards critics from ethnic groups other than that of the leaders of the dominant party, an antagonism and rivalry which are prior to the relationship of ruler and critical opponent.[7]

The sense of exclusive custodianship of the national essence

[7] Ethnic antagonisms within the broader circles of the élites and counter-élites of the new states are aggravated by the strain of the ethnic attachments within the self of those who seek to transcend them in a higher national identity.

It must, however, be pointed out that in spite of the anxieties of the élites of the ruling parties about the dangers of disintegration because of divergent ethnic attachments, the suppression of open opposition parties in order to avoid such disintegration has not been justified in the result. The problem of national unity is an urgent one, but the suppression of parties has not prevented the South Sudanese from revolting. On the other hand, no state already established and functioning has broken up because of secessionist tendencies among its ethnic minorities.

which results in the identification of state, party, and society is not equally pronounced everywhere. There are countries where it has become attenuated by experience and the passing of time and where it has to face a deeper tradition of constitutional government. In these countries, although ruling politicians become irritated with their critics, they do not proceed repressively against them because they acknowledge their fundamental right to existence. India is the chief example of a new state where a longer process of growth of the sense of nationality and a longer experience of political activity, as constitutional as was possible under a colonial regime,[8] gradually established a powerfully compelling tradition of respect for the institutions and procedures through which collective decisions are made. Ceylon shows similar features. Pakistan, despite its failures and the military interregnum and despite the rather short history of the sentiment of Pakistani nationality and the grave ecological obstacles to its formation, likewise seems to have benefited to some extent from this prolonged exposure to the culture of constitutionalism.

Sierra Leone and Israel are also the bearers of a well-established constitutional culture, and of a longer history of the sense of nationality that is to be found in most of Africa. In Israel, it has been imported with the political culture of the dominant parties. In Sierra Leone, it is part of a relatively well-established general culture and also owes much to the exceptional personal qualities of the brothers Margai. In these more tolerant regimes, the image of the nation and the sense of national identity have become sufficiently flexible to co-exist with perceived differences which are not held to diminish the reality of the nation. Nationality there does not require uniformity.

Elsewhere in the third world, where opposition parties are permitted to exist as long as they maintain a discreet and modest attitude – as in Morocco and in Senegal – or where they are so strong that to attempt to suppress them would precipitate a crisis more serious than the rulers care to face – as in Nigeria and Lebanon – and in Malaysia until a short time

[8] Colonial regimes were not congenial to the growth of a discipline of constitutional or civil politics. In most of the new states a number of parties came into existence only a short time before the granting of independence, when nationalistic enthusiasm was extremely intense.

ago – political prudence on the part of sober and artful political leaders seems to be a major factor. Of course, in all these cases there is a mixture of motives.

THE MODE OF ACTION OF OPPOSITION PARTIES

The necessity of contending with an incumbent élite which is so fundamentally distrustful of opposition – and above all of public opposition – renders the situation of opposition parties difficult. 'Dining with the opposition' – in the phrase attributed to Sir William Harcourt – is a necessary condition for bringing the opposition into the consensual relationship with rulers which is the foundation of constitutional opposition parties. Where the incumbent élite, which, in most cases, has the upper hand, believes that those who oppose them in particular matters are their enemies in all that counts in life, a corresponding attitude is bred in the opposition. If enmity is cultivated, enmity is harvested.

The traditional pomp and elaborate procedural machinery of parliamentary institutions which in advanced countries restrains the impulses of opposition parties has not brought about the same consequences in the new states. The formalities have not corresponded to or evoked deeply rooted attitudes. Parliamentary experience has had too short a life and too recent a birth. India, where experience of parliamentary debate is older, is an exception. The speaker's position there is more generally esteemed and the strong machinery of party discipline by the ruling party leadership has established an air of decorum which wild opposition cannot unsettle, and which imposes a tone of sobriety on the opposition parties. But in India, too, 'walk-outs' are not infrequent, even among oppositional parliamentarians who think they are committed to the parliamentary system.

In most of the other new states, when opposition parties were allowed to exist, they opposed with relatively little regard for parliamentary procedure and even less regard for parliamentary etiquette. African political language is very rough – those who use it may not mean it as aggressively as it must sound to those who listen to it. It is filled with threats and accusations which may or may not be seriously intended but which heighten the tension of parliamentary life. The government speaks in such terms and opposition parties reply in kind. As a result, the opposition party appears to be more inimical to the incumbent government and to public order than in fact it is.

Nor does the structure of the party system as it operates in the new states do much to bring the opposition into the partially consensual relationship necessary for the effectiveness of an open opposition party. In none of the new states of Asia and Africa has the opposition party enjoyed the beneficial influence of a two-party system, which disciplines opposition by holding before it the possibility of assuming office and then bearing the responsibility for doing a better job than those it has been criticizing. In some of them when independence was achieved, one major party, considerably outweighing all the other parties, at first either maintained or extended its preponderance. India, Burma, Pakistan, Ghana, Tanganyika, and Tunisia were instances of this. It is both discouraging to opposition and injurious to its action when one heavily dominant party appears to be immovable. People do not like to back a certain loser and the opposition parties are therefore bound to be small and to become discouraged and desperate under these conditions. Discouragement about their prospects of growth not only keeps them small, it also makes them smaller by stirring up the jealousies and disputes which are endemic in failing organizations. Despair drives the opposition into wild accusations, 'walk-outs', boycotts of parliamentary sessions, obstructive actions, nonsensical charges, triviality, etc. Such behaviour dooms the opposition party to ineffectiveness. The aggressiveness of oppositional rhetoric, which is promoted by these conditions, also lays them open to charges of subversive intent, with which the dominant party is in any case ready enough.

Some of the new states came into existence with a number of approximately equal competing parties – as in Indonesia, Israel, and Nigeria – and a coalition was necessary for the establishment of government. No more than government by congress-like parties do coalition governments, unless they are conducted with tact and loyalty, generate the parliamentary culture to 'civilize' the conduct of opposition parties, both outside and within the coalition government. On the contrary, the weaker parties in a coalition, having to compromise their principles so much before the demands of the major party, fear that their followers will suspect their probity. They must, therefore, give some evidence to their following and to those whose support they might seek in the future that their principles have not been wholly compromised. Thus they oppose within the government and outside as well. Much of their opposition is symbolic, because when they are moderately responsible or fairly attached to a share in office, they do not wish to break up the coalition. Hence they are oppositional in rhetoric, as if to hide their attachment to office. This has the effect of stimulating the opposition outside the government, since the outsiders must, to maintain their oppositional self-respect, oppose even more vehemently.

These features of minor parties within coalition governments appear also in cases in which the dominant congress-like party of the moment of independence – as in Burma or Pakistan – begins to falter and disintegrate as a result of the wear and tear of office and of the demoralizing effects of long-unchallenged supremacy. Factions within the party become more pronounced; they become almost embryonic parties. In public speeches and at party conventions, opposition to the internally dominant group becomes embittered and aggressive. It becomes difficult to patch up these conflicts to give a convincing picture of a unified party to the public. Although this situation is sometimes welcomed by political analysts who think that it foretells the formation of a fruitful dominant party – opposition party pattern, it does not ordinarily work that way. It increases acrimony simultaneously with appeals to party unity. The ruling party becomes more inefficient and indecisive but it continues in power because the opposition parties are so feeble.

The prospect of disintegration encourages the opposition parties outside the government, but it does not 'civilize' them. It only excites them. The small and ineffective oppositional parties of the time are not made stronger or more reasonable by the imminence of the breakup of the congress-like ruling party. They know that they will not be called upon to govern. The best they can hope to attain is portfolios in a coalition in which, while enjoying the fruits of office, they too can maintain their integrity by oppositional rhetoric. Thus the prospect of disintegration of a once unchallenged monolithic party increases the agitation of a clamorously negative opposition party. Disintegration has an unsettling effect, as occurred with the disintegration of the Muslim League in Pakistan and seems to be going on in India now.

An insecurely placed dominant party sometimes takes to itself as partners in a coalition one or more lesser opposition parties to enable it to keep its ascendancy over its major rival. Sharing in government does not domesticate such oppositional parties. The persisting strength of their oppositional dispositions coupled with their awareness that they have a good bargaining position rigidifies their outlook. They must not discredit themselves before their followers, and they have an opportunity to strike a blow for their ideals; the result is a combination of the conduct of minor coalition partners and of minor opposition parties in the presence of a progressively weakening dominant or congress-like party. A 'culture of coalition' which is so much needed in the new states is prevented from developing under these conditions.

THE STRENGTH OF OPPOSITION PARTIES

For all their fiery rhetoric, open opposition parties in the new states are seldom dangerous to the ruling parties either in open electoral campaigns or in parliamentary voting or in conspiratorial activities. They are usually too weak to be dangerous. Conspiratorial and subversive activity is most commonly reported from the one-party states which do not permit opposition parties. In Senegal, it was not the existing or once public opposition parties which conspired to assassinate the president or to seize power. In Ghana, the last alleged plot to assassinate the president came from within his own monolithic party. It was not an open opposition party which assassinated Prime Minister Solomon Bandaranaike or President Sylvanus Olympio. It was not a public (or even a clandestine) opposition political party which instigated the mutinies in the three East African states. The rebellion in Sumatra in 1958 was not the work of an open opposition party, although party politicians were associated with it. It was only in Zanzibar that an open opposition political party undertook to overthrow the incumbent government by conspiratorial, revolutionary means.

Nor, for that matter, have military *coups d' état* been carried
out in collaboration with open opposition parties – neither in
Pakistan, nor in the Sudan, nor in Burma have the open
opposition parties worked with the military in their prepara-
tions to take power to themselves. Rather, in two of the three
cases, it was civilian politicians of the ruling party who drew
the military into politics. In Nigeria it was one of the partners
in the ruling coalition, the NCNC, which tried to involve the
army in a seizure of power in January 1965. Thus, although
ruling parties sometimes allege that the opposition parties
must be proceeded against because otherwise they would be
strong enough and malevolent enough to damage the political
order, this is not the case.

The causes of their weakness are various. One of them is
poverty. There are few rich indigenous businessmen[9] willing
to support opposition parties. The class as a whole is not
numerous, and even when they are rich enough, they are also
usually prudent enough not to endanger their fortunes by
intensifying the antagonism of the ruling party – already
sufficiently hostile to private capitalist enterprise not to need
the additional incentive for confiscation which involvement in
opposition would provide. Moreover, with such far-reaching
government control of the economy, private businessmen have
a positive reason for supporting the ruling party – otherwise,
how could they get the licences, the foreign exchange, etc.,
which they need to carry on their business under circumstances which are intended to create difficulties for them?

How can a political party live in a new state? How can it
keep its members from becoming disgruntled and giving their
support to its opponents? It must live in part from the government treasury. Its cadres must have employment, and employment is mainly government employment. A certain amount of
use of government money diverted for the immediate use of
the party is sometimes necessary for the ruling party to keep itself coherent through the maintenance of the loyalty of its followers. Opposition parties have no access to public money.
And lacking private funds they cannot support party function-

---

[9] In those countries which have not yet driven out foreign businessmen, the
latter are extremely cautious in avoiding any activities which might jeopardize
their relations with the ruling party. They do not contribute to the treasuries
of opposition parties.

aries, or pay for electoral campaigns on a country-wide scale, such as would be necessary to turn them into real competitors of the ruling party. Since they cannot build up a country-wide machine to call meetings, arouse voters, and gain votes because they cannot pay local party agents the pittance they need for their maintenance, open opposition parties tend to concentrate their activities in urban areas. The dominant parties usually have the mass machines which cover the country and reach into rural areas because they have the money.

The impecuniousness of the opposition affects its stability and strength in another way. Paid government office is not available to the members of an opposition party – only support for the governing parties can offer that. This is why members of opposition parties in parliamentary bodies sometimes cross over. Being in opposition is like middle-class morality. As Mr Doolittle said, it is all very well for those who can afford it. Those who cannot afford it are tempted to make their peace with the ruling party in order to enjoy some of the benefits which association with the ruling party provides. Thus, though open opposition parties are sometimes coerced into amalgamation with the dominant party, the parties and their individual members are also sometimes tempted into amalgamation. The alternatives which face a feeble opposition party are extinction and exclusion and possible persecution on the one side, and a share in income and eminence on the other – with perhaps a little influence as well.

Poverty is not the only reason for the weakness of opposition parties. The oppositional position attracts intellectuals, who are quick to see imperfections because they also have high – sometimes unrealistically high – standards. They also, being urban in residence and attachment, tend to confine their political activities to the urban population. This keeps their parties at a disadvantage *vis-à-vis* the more populistic majority party which, with its larger number of less well-educated middle and lower-rank functionaries, is able to maintain closer connections with the villagers and peasants. Furthermore, intellectuals, especially those in opposition parties, are not very skilful as organizers and administrators. This, too, contributes to the weakness of their parties.

The urban or otherwise local concentration of the support of opposition parties in contrast with the dominant party is to

C

some extent a matter of poverty. It is also a product of the processes of political competition. Pre-independence politics were largely agitational politics, but as the franchise was extended and as agitation became more persistent and widespread before independence, they also required organizational skill. The factions or parties with organizational skill acquired the leading positions in the new governments. The factions or parties of the pre-independence period which could not muster the organizational skill, because their leading personalities tended to conceive of politics only as oppositional agitation and intellectual argument against the ruling power, were left behind as an almost exclusively agitational rump. The truest heirs of the oppositional tradition of pre-independence politics are the opposition parties of the independent new states. Organization and the tradition which prizes organizational skills were not in their heritage.

The 'party of independence' has other advantages over the opposition party in electoral contests. Ignorance,[10] apathy, a traditional submissiveness to established rulers, as well as loyalty and fear of loss or coercion have given strength to the incumbent parties. Opposition parties, even if they were on a level financially or organizationally with the incumbents, would be at a disadvantage.

There is one further reason for the weakness of opposition parties in most of the new states. That is the rather comprehensive, even if unacknowledged, consensus in most of the societies between the governing party and the opposition parties and groups with respect to modernization through socialistic policies and governmental action. They are also uniformly anti-colonialist. Even though incumbent governments might not be as dynamically socialistic as some of the most vehement opposition[11] wishes them to be, nor as aggressively anti-colonialist, the ruling party usually does not allow itself to

[10] Governments have been changed by general elections only in Ceylon which had the highest literacy rate of all new states at the time of independence. The Congress Party has been defeated in a state election in Kerala which has the highest literacy rate in India.

[11] Although many of the ruling parties in Asia and Africa compromise with their expressed principles and allow considerable room for private business enterprise, they do not acknowledge that at the level of principle. In principle, they nearly all say that they are socialist. So do almost all oppositional parties. There are very few parties which explicitly designate themselves as parties of free enterprise.

be outdone by the opposition on these themes. Thus even though there are discrepancies between the views of an opposition party and the action of a compromising ruling party, which permits private enterprise and makes arrangements, which some of the opposition think improper, with the Western powers, their language will be much the same. All parties claim to be non-aligned between East and West, and though the governing party inclines towards the Soviet Union or China on the one side or France, Britain, and the United States on the other, its rhetoric does not give the opposition party much room to establish its own unique identity. The opposition is deprived of much of its argument, and it suffers further from its inability to formulate its criticism in detailed factual analyses and recommendations. As a result the unsophisticated electorate – which is usually not very much interested in matters of principle in any case – finds it difficult to distinguish between the outlook of the opposition and that of the governing party.

THE EFFECTIVENESS OF OPPOSITION PARTIES

Where groups in opposition to the government have been allowed to exist publicly, how well have they done their work? One of the major tasks of an opposition party is to provide for succession. Among the new states, India and Ceylon have held several general elections with contending parties. In India, the dominant Congress Party has always been successful on a national scale and in practically all the states. Because it has not, however, always had a clear majority in the latter, it has had to form governments with the support of independents and representatives of local parties. When the communists formed a government in Kerala, it could not maintain public order and it was deposed by the central government. Thus India has never yet put opposition parties to the test of forming a successor government. It is only in Ceylon that the opposition party has on a number of occasions succeeded in winning over the incumbent party.[12] It is difficult to assess the accomplishments of each of the successive governments in Cey-

[12] The numerous reconstitutions of government in Pakistan before 1958 were the outcome of arrangements among politicians and not of a succession realized through a nation-wide election.

lon or to decide whether the prospect of forming a government after a general election has made opposition parties more responsible and more competent than they otherwise might have been when they did accede to power.

The Nigerian general election of 1965 was a fiasco, perhaps because of the hopelessness of unseating the dominant party electorally. In Lebanon, the very prospect of a general election has several times precipitated a succession crisis and once a civil war, because the incumbent president did not wish to renounce office although constitutionally required to do so. In all the other new states, succession, where it has taken place, has been the result of a *coup d'état* by the military, of assassination (once in Ceylon by monks and civilians, without affecting the dominance of the ruling party), or of a *putsch* (Congo-Brazzaville and many other countries).

In most new states the dominant party has remained dominant. The opposition has nearly always been a poor competitor for the succession. This failure to perform one major function of an opposition is not attributable to itself alone. Incumbent élites in many of the new states have taken the measures available to them as controllers of the apparatus of the state to prevent their replacement. But even where they permit a constitutional attempt at replacement the opposition has seldom been successful.

The ineffectiveness of opposition parties as contenders for the succession is in turn the factor which determines the ineffectiveness of the opposition as a critic and corrector of the policies of those governments which have allowed them to exist. Where the illiteracy and political impermeability of the populace render ineffective the efforts of a poorly organized opposition party, the governing party has nothing to fear from it. There is no need for it to modify its policies to avert or to satisfy criticism. It need have no fear that the criticisms of the opposition party will instruct the electorate about its shortcomings and turn them against it. The ruling party is usually aware that the opposition party cannot reach the mass of the population and that the activists in their own party are bound to them by ties of pecuniary advantage and belief.

What would an opposition party have to do in order to influence the leaders of the governing party? It would have to be able to address itself persuasively to the bearers of political opinion, to which the governing party is sensitive.[13] In many of the new states, however, the most effective political opinion is likely to be the opinion of activists within the ruling party, the leaders of youth organizations, and locally and territorially based notables. The activists are bound to the ruling party by belief and by the prospect of a continuing flow of material benefits. Youth organizations tend to be auxiliary organizations of the dominant party, which alone has the resources to pay for them. The leaders of youth organizations are often paid officials of the dominant party. Locally or territorially based notables, unless they are already the pillars of a primarily ethnic or communal opposition party, are difficult to reach because to do so requires more financial resources and manpower than most of the opposition parties dispose of. Moreover, concerned as they are with local interests and attached as they are to their own local community, local notables are not likely to take the risk of arousing the wrath of the ruling party, which has almost everywhere shown its ability to discipline recalcitrant traditional élites.[14] The latter generally find it convenient and profitable to present a show of conformity with the wishes of the ruling party.

Are there any other more independent and weighty bearers of public opinion whose opinion and whose organized power the government fears? Professional persons – university and secondary school teachers, students, engineers, accountants, journalists, writers, scientists, businessmen, leaders of voluntary associations, and trades union leaders are the possible publics for the opposition party's criticisms of government. But what is the likelihood that an opposition party can win these groups to its support and thereby make the governing party more responsive to its criticisms to the extent at least of modifying certain criticized policies, even if it does not accept the positive demands of the opposition party for particular policies?

[13] One of the most substantial achievements of an opposition party in bringing a government to change its policy was the decision of the Nigerian government to revise the defence pact which it had made with the United Kingdom. This victory for a critical opposition party was greatly facilitated by the vigour of the free Nigerian press.

[14] It is perhaps thanks to the relatively firm constitutional outlook which prevails in India that traditional territorial notables there have been permitted to support an opposition party. Witness the role of the *quondam* princely families in the Swatantra Party in Bihar and Rajasthan.

It is extremely difficult for trades unions to become independent in new states. The ruling parties correctly see that the only potentially strong civilian organizations which can challenge their power are the trades unions, however poor and small they may be compared with the trades unions of highly industrialized countries. Political prudence and doctrine both dictate a policy of strong governmental control over the leadership of the trades unions. In most cases, the trades unions were created for political purposes by the 'party of independence'; many of the leaders of the unions are still closely linked to the élite of the dominant party. Furthermore, the latter usually take some pains to control the new generation of trades union leaders. Trades union leaders who wish to be effective on behalf of their rank and file and who therefore wish to be a little free of the control of the dominant party will therefore be circumspect about the open defiance of the dominant party élite implicit in association with an opposition party.

India and Ceylon present instances where trades union leaders are allowed this luxury, but again, this is made possible because the constitutional tradition of the dominant party permits it. It does not happen in states where the dominant party is hypersensitive to danger and unrestrained by constitutional tradition.[15] It certainly does not happen in one party or quasi-one-party regimes.

Businessmen will not give financial support to opposition parties, nor will they otherwise show sympathy with them. Where the major large-scale *entrepreneurs* are nationals of the former ruling power or members of an ethnic minority, they will not be inclined to do anything to arouse the displeasure of the ruling party. Being businessmen and ethnically alien are sufficient causes in their own right to make them suspect to the ruling party. Only where there are indigenous businessmen (or businesswomen) who have a stake in the country and feel free to think of their own advantage – and when there are enough of them to give the additional weight of the consciousness of numbers to their self-esteem – will they form a

[15] The success of the Nigerian strike action and the failure of the Ghanaian unions in a similar action merit further consideration. The former was the most unique achievement of a trades union movement in an Afro-Asian state; the conditions for its success are obscure to me.

potential support for opposition parties. On the whole, however, they prefer to work through the dominant party for reasons given earlier.

Finally, the professional classes, the engineers, the teachers, the scientists, and the journalists and literary men. In most countries except India, Pakistan, and Nigeria, they are few in number and unorganized. They are, moreover, disproportionately in the employ of government and they are therefore relatively unresponsive, in practice, to an opposition party, however sympathetic they may be in sentiment. Their scanty numbers make for weak self-confidence. They have little or no autonomous professional culture; their institutional structure is too weak and to dependent on the government for their self-consciousness as intellectuals to establish them as an 'estate of the realm'.

University teachers form perhaps the only section of the professional classes which possesses some of the qualifications for constituting a 'critical opposition', though not an opposition party. Some of them have expert knowledge in the spheres in which governmental policies operate. Their university institutions enjoy in many instances legal autonomy. They themselves are members of a sustaining international intellectual community. They are, in principle, experienced in detached and disciplined judgement. All these characteristics should contribute to the exercise of matter-of-fact and independent opinion. Many of them, moreover, continue the oppositional traditions of their forerunners in the independence movement. None the less these do not add up to effective support for open opposition parties.

In India, Pakistan, and Indonesia, where they are indigenous and numerous, they are neither esteemed by others nor are they sufficiently self-esteeming.[16] Very few of them are well informed about current affairs, nor do they have a tradition of expressing themselves forcefully and in a well-documented way in print. They do not have organs through which they can express themselves, either. In Ceylon they are too few in number, and the same restraints obtain there too. In the Middle East the situation is not too different from South Asia. They are discontented with their governments but they are afraid

---

[16] Economists in India and Pakistan are beginning to acquire the status which is a necessary condition for influence.

to express themselves openly. In Black Africa, on the senior level they are still largely expatriates and therefore *hors de concours*. At the junior level, where indigenous persons are more common, they are too young and too inexperienced to respond to and to contribute to the life of an opposition party. Thus, oppositional sentiments of the university intellectuals do not redound to the advantage of an opposition party. University students in the new states are often oppositional in sentiment and very active too but they lack organization and discipline. Moderate oppositional parties find little response among them. Governments are wary of them but do not take them seriously.

Thus the points of support in public opinion for opposition criticism, outside the legislative body and outside the political parties, are really quantitatively too slight, too low in prestige, and too unfocused to enable oppositional parties to make their criticisms carry weight with the governing party.

CLOSED OPPOSITION: OPPOSITION OUTSIDE OPPOSITION PARTIES AND THE INSTITUTIONS OF PUBLIC LIBERTY

The decision of a ruling party to paralyse or to extinguish its rival parties simply removes opposition, except in severe crisis, from where it can be seen. Oppositional activities and assertions receive little or no publicity except *post facto*: after they have been defeated and condemned or after they have been victorious. (In the latter case, the previously secret opposition gives evidence of its previous existence by its displacement of the hitherto incumbent regime.)

The existence of oppositional activities in regimes which have committed themselves to their abolition can, of course, not always be hidden or suppressed. In the Sudan, the final abdication of the regime of General Abboud was precipitated by the public activities of students in the last days of the regime and the final appearance in public of the secret opposition of the civilian politicians. The repeated upheavals in Iraq and Syria have occurred in regimes which had declared that there was no need for a diversity of parties because the ruling party spoke for all the people except for remnants of the *ancien régime* which had to be crushed. The conspiracies against the government in the Ivory Coast, in Dahomey, and in Togoland were carried out by legally non-existent groups. All these indicate that there is opposition in the mono-lithic new states but the opposition which is thus manifested is concerned to perform only one function of opposition – namely to succeed the incumbent élite. The absence of in-stitutionalized and open opposition parties only makes it more probable that the problem of succession will be attended by subversive action.

Closed oppositions, like open oppositions, wish to accede to power but they are also concerned with policy. Indeed, in certain respects, their concern with policy is sometimes more genuine than that of open opposition parties, because they are not contending for electoral support.

The new states are full of problems of policy which generate conflicting interests and give rise to opposition. There is much mute opposition. No adequate explanation of the failure of economic policies is possible which does not refer to the re-fusal to collaborate of a hostile peasantry.[17] Failure can of course be attributed to poor planning, to the setting of un-realistic targets, which assume capital to be available when it is not. But some of the poor planning consists in predictions and efforts to control peasant behaviour which turn out to be incorrect. To describe the failure simply as a cognitive shortcoming on the part of the planners is to overlook the obstinate non-compliance of the peasantry. Apathy, unin-formedness, and sheer indifference are not the same as opposi-tion but there are also many peasant actions which cannot be accounted for solely by unawareness or inefficient communica-tion. The fact that they do not 'receive the messages' of the planners, politicians, and civil servants is not a result of a mechanical gap. The peasants do not listen. They 'play doggo' because they distrust those in authority and do not wish them well. If the governing party will not do what they wish, they for their part will not do what that party wants them to do.

The peasantry then constitutes the foremost, most massive, most powerful opposition in all new states – in those without opposition parties as well as in those with opposition parties.

[17] Disobedience to the enactments of governmental authority arising from indifference, and deliberate breaking of the law are at the margin of opposition.

Parties have little to do with it. The peasants might vote for
the ruling party because it has some semblance of a rural
organization and because they hope to win some particular
favours from its politicians in return for their votes. But they
will do little to comply with the exhortations and targets of
the ruling élite. They are not interested in programmes but
in particular services which the politicians can perform for
them. They give their votes in return for these favours, but
they do not give their collaboration to the government's
schemes for rural modernization. Their non-compliance is an
opposition of withdrawal and non-co-operation. It does not
argue for a policy, since it has no one with whom to argue or
who will argue on its behalf.

The trade unionists are a little better off: they have an
organization and they have leaders who must please them and
who move in the circles of the mighty. Their opposition is
most likely, therefore, to be a closed, positive, policy-oriented
opposition, frequently a radical intra-party opposition, which
often overlaps with the opposition of the educated youth.

Incumbency of positions of authority has a 'conservative'
effect. It is difficult to get much done in a new state. The ob-
durate immobility of the peasantry, the shortages of highly
trained manpower, the shortages of capital, the cumbersome-
ness of the rapidly expanded machinery of government, the
greater conservatism (or realism) of civil servants as compared
with politicians, all make it difficult for politicians aspiring
to rapid modernization to accomplish as much as the myth of
modernity seems to call for. Incumbency also makes, at least
in a minimal measure, for a sense of responsibility. It teaches
the lesson that not everything is possible simultaneously, that
the public peace must be kept because disorder might result
in expulsion from power. As a result, however 'progressive' a
government may be in doctrine it cannot please those whose
aspirations are unqualified by the intractable reality of trying
to govern a poor and unconsensual society. Those who are left
dissatisfied constitute a radical closed opposition, composed as
Professor Arthur Lewis has recently said of Africa, of unem-
ployed primary school graduates looking for unavailable clerical jobs, primary school teachers, small traders who cannot
compete with the Lebanese, men who resent chiefly authority,
unsuccessful claimants to chieftaincy.

This radical closed opposition is tolerated because it cannot be suppressed without great difficulty, and, more important, because it enjoys the protection of certain members of the innermost élite who regard it as a valuable adjunct for their own potential opposition to those who are in the most central positions or who might challenge or threaten them. It is a useful instrument for the convocation of demonstrations, for producing a display of violence when that is thought necessary to intimidate recalcitrants. The radical wing has its own organs of expression. It sometimes is allowed a distinctive organization; this is most likely when it is largely congruous with the youth wing of the party. It sometimes has its own publications, subsidized by the ruling party. This relationship of patron–beneficiary testifies to the fact that the radical wing is often very much an instrument of the closed opposition of a senior politician in the inner circle, to be used for putting pressure on rivals or intimidating potential or residual opposition outside the party. This patron–beneficiary relationship also appears to indicate that the radical wing is not an autonomous oppositional force. It has no power of its own. If it had no friends at the centre of authority, it would be courting suppression. (This does not mean that it will always be so; it might conceivably break away from its usually more conservative patrons and controllers and become an autonomous group in its own right.) Sometimes, concessions often more symbolic than substantial, are made to it.

There are other possible loci and bearers of closed opposition in the new states. Traditional leaders – chiefs, sultans, monks, the ulema, civil servants, journalists, intellectual leaders. Traditional leaders have been swept aside with remarkable ease in most countries. Not that they have lost the affections or deference of their people. Despite their subservience to the colonial powers, their people did not desert them. Their 'collaboration' injured them mainly with the intellectuals, who would have been against them in any case. The small scale of their sovereignties, the shambling administrative machinery through which they exercised their authority, their military insignificance, have all contributed to their defeat at the hands of the modern political élites. They are an opposition group, but a powerless and silent one. They are not acceptable enough to the ruling party to become an

internal closed opposition; they are not permitted to organize
politically, or if they are organized, their organizations are too
flimsy and too narrow for them to be effective. They have little
that they can withhold except their approval. Where they
have no monastic organization to sustain them, as do the
monks in Ceylon and South East Asia and the quasi-ecclesiasti-
cal organizations of the ulema, they have nothing to sustain
their resistive power. Furthermore, in most cases, in consequence of land reform or because of the traditional system of
land tenure, they have no financial resources to enable them to
exercise the powers which patronage provides. Even in
Lebanon, the power of the great families of *za'im* over their
traditional clients is declining. The upshot of all this is that
the traditional landlord and chiefly élites can withhold their
support and therewith the legitimacy which their prestige still
carries with it, but they can exercise little positive influence on
the policies of the modern political élites organized in the
ruling party.

As far as intellectuals are concerned, the weaknesses to
which we referred in discussing the obtacles to their provision of resonance for opposition parties operate here, too.
The educated classes outside government are too small, too
lacking in solidarity, too lacking in prestige and self-confidence
to impose their views on the incumbent political élites. Individual intellectuals do have some influence – but largely as
economists and as economic advisers in government service.
No intellectual organ in any new state, except perhaps the
Economic Weekly in India, has any influence on what officials
in governments think – and there, too, it is through its influence on civil servants and economic advisers in ministries
and in the Planning Commission that it has some positive
oppositional influence. The intellectual press, both professional and publicistic, is weak economically, too ill-informed,
and too lacking in prestige to establish the ascendancy required to impress the politicians of the ruling party.

Thus we see that in one-party and quasi-one-party states,
positive policy-oriented closed opposition is the prerogative of
politicians and civil servants, and marginally and intermit-
tently of military men and trades union leaders. In the two
former instances, opposition is real and sometimes effective,
but it is closed. When trades union leaders express opposition-

al attitudes, it is most usually done behind closed doors. It is only when they very occasionally break out of the public façade of unanimity by instigating strikes that their opposition comes before a wider audience. When in Congo-Brazzaville and in Guinée and Ghana, public trades union opposition broke the permitted boundaries, the result was subversion in one case and suppression in the others. The opposition of the military also has only those two alternatives. The military being better organized and stronger than the trades unions is more often able to achieve the former and avoid the latter alternative. Except for civil servants, whose opposition is institutionalized as closed opposition, the other carriers of un-institutionalized, closed opposition are impelled towards secrecy as well.

In India, with its freedom of economic and social inquiry and journalistic reporting and editorial analysis, the cleavages between opposition and ruling party can be seen fairly clearly. In Israel, the energy of the parties to the coalition makes the lack of unanimity quite obvious to the public eye. It is approximately the same in Nigeria and Sierra Leone. Not only the acts of opposition are visible, but the promulgation of the grounds of opposition and the preparation for its exercise are also open.

In contrast with these countries, in one-party states, the un-institutionalized situation of closed opposition makes also for secrecy in its promulgation of policy and its preparation of action. It becomes more conspiratorial in character and therefore more susceptible to accusations of subversive intention. It is bound to lead a more tenuous, more delicately poised existence simply because it is closed. The public is excluded from awareness of closed opposition and contributes and gains nothing from its operation. It is the passive recipient of such improvements as might be brought about by closed opposition. The wider society is not even a spectator of closed opposition; the delicate filaments which link leaders and constituents in situations of open opposition are almost entirely lacking in systems of closed opposition.

It is contended that the interests and desires of the populace are adequately cared for under these conditions, particularly inasmuch as there are elections in which a choice between alternative candidates is permitted and parliamentary bodies whose approval is required for the actions of government which are to take legislative form. It is necessary to consider the extent to which closed opposition allows for the representation of sectional interests and desires.

THE FUNCTIONS OF OPPOSITION AND THEIR PERFORMANCE IN NEW STATES WITH REGIMES OF CLOSED OPPOSITION

All states of any degree of complexity require for their orderly survival: (1) the disciplining of conflict through the institutionalized representation of conflicting 'interests' and their containment within the bounds of public order; (2) the expression and therewith communication to the government of interests and desires which might be neglected or otherwise disregarded; (3) the provision for an orderly succession; (4) the improvement of the performance of the government by criticism of mistakes, omissions, and injustices of past performance, thereby enabling the government to avoid such actions as would lay them open to especially damaging criticism and to disorderly subversion. States which allege that they are in some sense democratic or the élite of which is populistic are further committed in principle to (5) the instruction and enlightenment of the public, the improvement of its discipline in expressing its demands, the improvement of its qualifications for approving or disapproving of the actions of its rulers and for deciding whether to give or to withhold their support.

These are tasks which are more or less well performed in advanced countries with well-developed party systems. For reasons already given, they do not appear to be well performed in the new states, although some of them are performed better than others. The level of performance also varies from state to state within the world of multi-party systems. Are they performed better in one-party states in Asia and Africa; are open opposition parties superfluous because the tasks are adequately faced and resolved in a one-party state?

In a society in which the sense of 'interestedness' (or interest-affectedness) is not acute because of ignorance, apathy or lack of organization, the conflicts, in so far as large sections of the society (i.e. the 'masses') are concerned, need not become very severe. None the less, there will certainly be some who believe in their interests and will wish them to be realized, or at least represented and expressed. If their interests are not those being promoted by the ruling party, the absence of a publicly organized opposition will reduce the likelihood that those persons or sectors of the society will be able to make their desires known to the ruling party through organs which they regard as in some sense extensions of themselves

One-party states claim that there are no real interests other than the interest of the whole society which is represented by and cared for by 'the party'. Sectional interests are from this standpoint illegitimate and disintegrative. This metaphysical belief is not often taken very seriously in practice. Repressive measures on the one hand, and claims, on the other, that the 'party's' internal system of upward communication enables it to understand and respond to the 'masses' better than any other system show that the doctrine of unity is not regarded as entirely adequate. But even if the argument is made that 'the party' can in fact perceive the desires of the mass of the population through its mass organization, with the corollary that the mass organization permits desires to be transmitted upwards into the party hierarchy to the point of decision, what is the assurance that they will be taken into account by the leadership? It is to the 'interest' of a public opposition party or a public oppositional non-party organ to speak on behalf of these otherwise neglected interests. It is not necessarily to the interest of a *parti unique* to do so.

In fact, what seems to happen in regimes without open opposition is that even if some desires are correctly perceived and transmitted upward to the point of decision, they are often disregarded if no one there believes in their validity or thinks that to disregard them will endanger the security of the regime – and the latter might as easily result in repression as in gratification.

Conflicting interests – but not necessarily neglected interests – and ideals might become incorporated into the structure of a one-party regime as factions. Much of the activity of a faction once it gets consolidated is the preparation for its assumption of the dominant position in the party. Since, however, it is not admitted by others or by itself (publicly) to have that intention, it is bound to be regarded as conspiratorial. Factions can certainly perform some of the functions of opposition, but because they are not acknowledged as legitimate by those who are members of other factions, they are in danger of being regarded as treasonable, and are therefore liable to suppression. But even if they are not, they aggravate conflict and they arouse great tensions about succession. Furthermore, even where a factional system is well established, by virtue of its closed character it neither instructs the populace nor does it receive its sentiments.

The underlying conception of a one-party regime is that it represents a comprehensive consensus which embraces everyone in the society, or all except a few enemies of society, motivated by class, tribal, or simply self-interest. The proponents of one-party regimes assert that within the party there is full, frank and fearless criticism and discussion of alternatives. It is questionable whether this is so, even where the leader of the party would seem to wish it to be so. For one thing, it is difficult for critics to obtain the information necessary for criticism. Then, too, it is often unsafe for critics to criticize because they are in danger of being called fomenters of factionalism.

The emergence of new factions is more of a shock to the dominant group of a single-party than is an open opposition party to a ruling party within a two- or multi-party system in which, however repugnant, the divergences are at least predicted and accepted. Because factions are not institutionalized and therefore verge on the treasonable, they intensify conflicts over the succession and increase the acerbity of the response which the ruling group in a dominant party makes to its closed opposition. This, in turn, makes it more difficult for a faction as a form of closed opposition to act as an effective critic of the policies of the dominant group within the party. The relations of dominant group and faction tend more towards the *Freund/ Feind* relationship than to the consensual one. None the less, despite these liabilities, it is quite certain that factions will exist in a single party, even though strong-minded, powerful and artful leaders like Mr Bourguiba or President Nasser can keep them in check and prevent them from influencing their policies.

In so far as factions confine themselves strictly to the representation of interests and to attempts to influence the performance and policy of the dominant group in the party, either from an 'interested' or a 'disinterested' standpoint, they stand more chance of being tolerated by the dominant group. They probably also stand more chance of being tolerated if they are intermittent in their operations, being formed from shifting membership and with changing boundaries, as occasions arise. Yet there is a tendency for factions to become stabilized and for the same group of persons to take corresponding positions on a variety of issues. This can scarcely be avoided, because the major positions on any particular issue have logically, morally, or traditionally corresponding positions on other, not directly related, issues. Furthermore, the actions of a group of men on a particular issue in which they took similar stands at any one moment, alienates others who nurture their grudge long after its initial occasion. This, too, leads to stabilization of faction, and although it might make the faction more effective for a time, it also heightens antagonism towards it and renders more likely its suppression or an effort at its paralysis. Persistence in criticism from a faction of stable composition, on behalf of particular interests or ideal conceptions as to how the society should be ordered, heightens the danger for the critics of expulsion from the party, or demotion.

The fundamental fact of the closed character of opposition means that the focusing and concerting of interests and desires outside the ruling party are inhibited. From the point of view of the security of the ruling party's retention of its position, this is an advantage. From the point of view of social justice and the adjudication and compromise of conflicting interests, it is not an advantage.

The closed character of opposition excludes the populace, and the educated classes which are not in the élite of the ruling party or of the organizations which the ruling party permits, from any intelligent participation in and contribution to the formulation of the general lines of policy which will affect them. If closed opposition could be combined with public liberties, especially in academic social sciences, journalistic and editorial activities, the deficiencies of closed criticism would perhaps be compensated for. Unfortunately, this combination seldom occurs. Nor is it likely to do so.

The improvement of governmental action through *informed* criticism and the enlightenment of public opinion by such criticism within and outside governmental institutions are particularly difficult to achieve in new states, regardless of

whether they are one-party or multi-party regimes. The difficulty is in the first instance a result of a deficiency in the
supply of reliable information. Practically all new states suffer
from an inadequate press. This is not solely a function of
limits on the freedom of reporting and publication – although
the absence of that freedom is a severe handicap – but rather
of the resources of the press and the quality of journalistic
personnel. These are in turn partly determined by the poverty
and illiteracy of the mass of the population, which deprives
journalists of financial support and an exacting public. The
independent gathering of information by experienced reporters occurs relatively rarely in the new states, partly because there are too few experienced reporters and because
there is insufficient appreciation of the value of that type of
journalistic activity. There is neither a tradition which can
sustain it nor do the leaders of one-party states desire it. The
privately-owned press in the new states, handicapped by the
poverty of its potential audience, which deprives it of revenue
from advertising – there are also relatively few firms rich
enough or expansive enough to advertise – is further handicapped by the denunciatory and hortatory traditions of a
journalism formed in the days of the struggle for independence.

As a result, politicians do not have much factual basis for
their criticism of governmental actions and interests. This
applies equally to public and to closed opposition. The situation is aggravated in regimes of closed oposition – one-party
states – by the legal and political restraints on the freedom of
journalists to discover, disclose and comment. Nor is this shortcoming made up for by other organs of opinion, such as a
periodical press, less concerned with the account of day-to-day
events, and a professional social and economic research press,
more concerned with detailed documentation and long-term
evaluation. Here, too, it is not solely a matter of the repression
of intellectual freedom. Even in countries like Uganda, Kenya,
Sierra Leone, or Pakistan, or wherever intellectual freedom is
relatively unrestricted, this informative and evaluative function – which is indispensable to effective opposition – is not
being performed because not enough information is generated
by the personnel of the periodical press or the research in-
stitutes. They are too few in number to create a dense mass of

information in the light of which government actions can be described, interpreted, and assessed.

Where there is no independent gathering and criticism of facts, the government's own reporting function is unconstrained by the danger of authoritative contradiction. The ruling party can claim successes which no one can contradict, either because he does not know what the real facts are, or because he would get into trouble if he were to make known such facts as he does know.

Now it is quite conceivable that even though public criticism and opposition are not tolerated, the government might establish within its own narrow confines an independent investigative, reporting and information service which would enable at least the leading members of the governing party to know what the government is achieving and where it has fallen short. In a sense, there is such a service. The government intelligence service, the party apparatus at the 'grass roots' level[18] and the experience of politicians as they travel about and enquire, as well as the inspectorates of the various ministries, provide such a reporting service. The government does not act, therefore, in utter darkness.

But can critics, even within the closed circle of the ruling party, get at this information? Within the leadership of the party, they probably can, particularly if they are members of the dominant faction or have close connections with it. Such information is not available to the public outside the party; and given the difficulty of extracting it from those who possess it, it is not so likely to be available to the minority factions. Moreover, without the spur of possible criticism from outside, there is no incentive on the part of those who are responsible for the implementation of policies to report facts which will disclose the deficiencies of their performance.

In consequence, mistaken policies are often persisted in rather than corrected. Of course, even if information were available, it might not correct policies which are wrong, be-

---

[18] All the mass *partis uniques* claim to have this institution and put it forward as a justification for not permitting expression of opinion through opposition parties. Tanzania, Mali, and Guinée seem to make an effort to make the system work, but in other countries local agents regard it as their job simply to get out the votes and to take note of critical attitudes for security purposes, but they do not pay much attention to the upward flow of opinion from the lower strata of society.

cause doctrinaire prejudices, wrong economic theories, and vanity might blind the leadership of the ruling party to the more correct representations of their civil servants and advisers, and their intra-party critics. But correct factual information, especially publicly available information, at least makes rulers more circumspect about policies which fly in the face of accredited facts. In the course of time, it might even bring about a change in policy.

This informative-evaluative-corrective function is one of the most important functions of any opposition. It is a function which not all public and institutionalized opposition parties perform. It cannot be performed when the body of facts simply does not exist, and when the possibility of the assembly, presentation, and interpretation of those facts is prevented. It cannot be performed where there is no freedom of enquiry, publication, or public discussion.

Lauro Martines

Political Conflict in the Italian City States*

POLITICAL OPPOSITION IN ITALIAN CITY STATES WAS NOT FOR men who valued themselves more than they valued politics. The stakes were too high. Exile or loss of life and property were too often the penalties. The difficult legal circumstances which attended organized political opposition went back to the early commune, to the fervour of the civil struggles that began late in the 12th century. These were to affect the character of the opposition down to the 16th century. If the contenders in political strife sometimes expressed a readiness to compromise, they revealed, just as often, an inability to do so. And in critical times the desire for the physical elimination of political opponents easily emerged.

Major rivalries of the 11th and 12th centuries inadvertently favoured the rise of local government. The communes – rendered bolder in many cases by their quickening economies – profited from the conflicts between papacy and empire, between the emperor and the German princes, and between the episcopal and comital powers in Italy. As imperial authority waned, local groups all over north and central Italy pressed forward to take over the administration of their own affairs.

When a local group of men, usually eminent or powerful nobles and *cives*, formed a sworn association, putting *in comune* their feudal jurisdictions and prerogatives, they consolidated their control over a sizeable and expanding portion of the public power in a given territory.[1] The commune in the

[1] G. Volpe, 'Questioni fondamentali sull'origine e svolgimento dei comuni italiani (secoli x-xiv)', in his *Medio Evo Italiano*, new edn., Florence, 1960; A. Solmi, *Il comune nella storia del diritto*, Milan, 1922; L. Chiappelli, 'La formazione storica del comune cittadino in Italia', *Archivo storico italiano* (*ASI*), 86, 88 (1928, 1930); N. Ottokar, 'Il problema della formazione comunale', in *Questioni di storia medioevale*, ed. E. Rota, Como-Milan, 1946.

* Vol. 3, no. 1, Winter 1968.

full sense of the word had come into being. By the end of the 11th century many of the most famous communes were already in existence: Milan, Genoa, Pisa, Pavia and Mantua. Verona, Lucca, Florence, and Siena swiftly followed. Although the commune was by no means an urban phenomenon alone, the city led the way and it is the city we shall be watching.

STATE AND COMMUNE

As the empire, in the 12th and 13th centuries, was drained of its *de facto* power in Italy, cities under communal government (*a comune*) gained in authority, jurisdiction, and territorial expanse. But state and commune were different. The state as a sovereign entity was the state as manifested in the empire, however weak or divided. The commune, a sworn association endowed with part of the totality of public power in a given territory, was an autonomous local entity which acknowledged *de jure* the sovereign authority of the empire. It was self-governing, but only within the legal and political limits circumscribed by the empire's higher authority. During its early history the commune did not make laws (the empire alone could do that): it laid down norms for its own regulation and conduct. But in the course of the 12th century it began gradually to take on the characteristics of a small state. In many matters, foreign and domestic, it carried on for all the world as if it were a state. Although state and commune were different, an enormous change had begun to take place. The more authority and jurisdiction the commune acquired (painfully and in piecemeal fashion), the nearer it came to transforming itself into a sovereign power. A new state was coming into being: the territorial city state. It was never to have the absolute sovereignty of the modern state,[2] but its distinctive identity was already apparent by the middle of the 14th century, when Bartolus provided its legal rationale in his desscription of the *civitas per se sufficiens et sibi princeps* – the city state which owned no superior *de facto*.[3]

[2] G. Astuti, *Lezioni di storia del diritto italiano: la formazione dello stato moderno in Italia*, I, Turin, 1957.

[3] C. N. S. Woolf, *Bartolus of Sassoferrato*, Cambridge, 1913; F. Ercole, *Da Bartolo all'Althusio: saggi sulla storia del pensiero pubblicistico del rinascimento italiano*, Florence, 1932; and W. Ullman, 'De Bartoli sententia:

Close and intimate, the site of great economic vitality, featured by narrow streets and well-defined neighbourhoods (*contrade, rioni, sestieri, porte*, etc.), the walled city under communal rule afforded an intense mode of life. The leading Milanese historian has observed that the whole communal age was an age of crisis.[4]

In its struggle to become a state, to take over or reconstitute the vanishing local power of the empire, the commune had to take action which soon exposed all its weaknesses. Who was to run the commune, which of the city's social groups? This question led to the greatest troubles and laid bare the commune's gravest deficiencies. The signs of a serious *malaise* first appeared in the later 12th century, with the commune's fitful passage from consular to 'podestaral' government. Men exchanged collegiate rule for a system of modified collegiate government with a stronger executive – the *podestà*, who was very often a foreigner of noble blood.[5] From the hills of Umbria to the valley of the Po and beyond, from Perugia to Bergamo, nearly all the great communes, suffering intense inner conflict and rivalries, modified their collegiate regimes. Though seldom realized, it was the hope of some citizens that the *podestà* would stand above class and faction to administer the affairs of the commune impartially. The problem of achieving impartial government came foremost. To see the disturbances associated with the rise of the *podestà* as one with the commune's struggle to become a state is the product of an historical assessment. Taken in detail, the struggle was no more than the commune's search for a political *modus vivendi*. It was the struggle for power of social groups and blocs of leading families, each striving to devise a political arrangement by which one group or a cluster of groups, mixed or more nearly homogeneous, would rule authoritatively over the commune.

Concilium repraesentat mentem populi', in the sixth centenary papers, *Bartolo da Sassoferrato*, 2 vols, ed. D. Segoloni, Milan, 1962, II, pp. 707-33.

[4] F. Cognasso, 'Le origini della signoria lombarda', *Archivio storico lombardo (ASL)*, Ser. VIII, 6, 1956, p. 12.

[5] E. Salzer, *Ueber die Anfänge der Signorie in Oberitalien*, Berlin, 1900, pp. 20-1, 66 ff.; G. Hanauer, 'Das Berufspodestat im 13 Jahrhunderts', *Mittheilungen des Instituts für Oesterreichische Geschichtsforschung*, XXIII, 1902, pp. 377 ff. V. Franchini, *Saggio di ricerche sull'istituto del podestà*, Bologna, 1912; E. Sestan, 'Ricerche intorno ai primi podestà toscani', *ASI, LXXXII*, 2, 1924, pp. 177-254.

The very weakness of the state and the struggle of influential groups within the commune to enjoy and dispose of the highest of all worldly prizes – the 'things' of the state: this is what in part made civil conflict so intense that it could not be settled by a state which had fallen apart or by one struggling to be born. The violent nature of political strife was itself the expression of an historic effort, if one may say so, to put the state together again.

Often feeble in the face of its vigorous constituent groups, invested with a great deal of public authority yet only half a state, the commune of the late 12th and early 13th centuries provided a civil setting in which any organized opposition was at once so threatening as to seem conspiratorial. This early experience was to leave its imprint on the entire history of the opposition in Italian city states.

THE CORPORATE SPIRIT

Speaking of the political troubles in 14th-century Siena, one historian has noted that although the commune had its origin in a union of groups, it 'never succeeded in fusing them into a whole, composed of elements equal among themselves and equally subordinated to the government. Out of the conflict of social classes, military companies, guilds, interests of all kinds, that longed-for product, the modern state did not emerge.'[6] This observation applies as much to communes in general as to Siena. By the end of the 12th century most communes were composed of vigorous associations or had these to contend with. The range included neighbourhood military companies, societies of noblemen or commoners, merchant guilds, as well as guilds of small shopkeepers and artisans.[7] As the city absorbed a continuous influx of men from the country and expanded at a startling rate, new social and occupational groups gained admission to the commune or pressed to enter it. Since

[6] F. Schevill, *Siena, The History of a Medieval Commune*, new edn., New York, 1964, pp. 215–16.

[7] On the corporate movement, see F. Valsecchi, *Comune e corporazione nel medio evo italiano*, Milan, 1948; G. de Vergottini, *Arti e popolo nella prima metà del sec. xiii*, Milan, 1943; F. Niccolai, 'I consorzi nobiliari ed il comune nell'alta e media Italia', *Rivista di storia del diritto italiano (RSDI)*, XXIII, 1940, pp. 116–47, 292–342.

the state seemed unable either to enhance or fully to protect his opportunities and civil rights, the individual was ready to be drawn into a well-organized corps. What neither state nor commune could do, the corporation could. This helps to explain the universality and boldness of the corporate spirit in the 12th and 13th centuries. When the corporation stood outside the commune, it fought for recognition and entry; once inside, it functioned as a pressure group. Often, therefore, the first commitment of citizens was not to the commune but to a lesser community. Loyalty went first to an order of society (*popolo* or *nobiltà*), to a party or faction, to a guild or guild structure, or to a family bloc. These lesser communities, powerful in their own right, gave the individual his identity within the larger community; they defended him; they had given him, or would give him, a political place; they understood him best, and they would improve his position by providing him with a greater accumulation of advantages.

But the power of these communities could be acquired only at the expense of the greater community – the commune. The time came, before about 1240, when political exiles at the head or in the ranks of a foreign army began to march on their native city, moved by the powerful desire to overthrow the lesser community which then stood at the head of the commune and claimed to speak for it. Bergamo, Verona, Padua, Milan, Cremona, Bologna, Siena, Genoa, and other cities were all attacked by their own exiles. Even Venice, the sturdiest of all city states, was to become the military target of some of its citizens early in the 14th century.[8]

Opposition to the government of the commune, when it came from a tightly-knit group, such as the corporation, was less a deliberate assault on public authority than the natural assertion of a lesser community which knew its own value and which could help to prevent one of the other orders or groups from substituting itself for the government of the commune. Although the commune might be threatened by its lesser parts or units, it also relied on them to help to ward off the attempt of any one of them at wholesale usurpation.

---

[8] S. Romanin, *Storia documentata di Venezia*, III, Venice, 1855, pp. 25–31; G. A. Avogadro, 'La congiura Tiepolo-Querini', *Archivio veneto*, II, 1871, pp. 214–18.

SOCIAL AND POLITICAL STRIFE

The commune ruled over large numbers of men who belonged
to it only in the sense that they were its subjects. It was proudly
and firmly exclusive about its full-fledged memberships. Yet in
the course of the 12th and 13th centuries, more and more men
and groups made their way into it, and obtained a voice in
public affairs. Since admission to the commune was variously
predicated on property, birth, and tax qualifications, the citizens who were full members of the commune were among the
more affluent. The social world excluded (and ruled over) by
the commune involved the majority of men, the average and
the humble, although this was to be less true in the second
half of the 13th century. It is also in the second half of the
century that the threat of powerful and lawless individuals,
called *magnates*, became such that the security of the commune necessitated their political ostracism.[9] The opposition of
magnates to communal authority was as likely to take the form
of disorganized, individual acts of disobedience as of organized
subversion.

There have been attempts to de-emphasize the incidence
and importance of class conflict in the 13th-century commune.[10] The question cannot be taken up here. It is enough
to state that without further study of economic life, and if no
account is taken of the old class emphasis (which is found in
the chroniclers themselves), the great political changes of the
13th century cannot be satisfactorily explained. To take the
fierce rivalry between *popolo* and *nobiltà*, as it emerged in
most communes, and to analyse it in terms of private feud,
personal ambition, legal formulae, or the gossip of the age falls
short of providing a convincing explanation of the political
rise and triumph of the *popolo* in commune after commune.[11]

[9] G. Fasoli 'Ricerche sulla legislazione antimagnatizia nei comuni dell'alta
e media Italia', *RSDI*, XII, 1939, pp. 86–133, 240–73.

[10] E.g., N. Ottokar, *Il comune di Firenze alla fine del Duecento*, 2nd edn.,
Turin, 1962; V. Vitale, *Il comune del podestà a Genova*, Milan-Naples, 1951;
E. Fiumi, 'Fioritura e decadenza dell 'economia fiorentina', *ASI*, CXV–CXVII,
1957–9; E. Cristiani, *Nobiltà e popolo nel comune di Pisa*, Naples, 1962; also
the formulation of questions in E. Sestan, 'Le origini delle signorie cittadine',
Bullettino dell'istituto storico italiano per il medio evo, LXXIII, 1961.

[11] *Popolo*: the commoners of substance viewed as a political order in conflict with the nobility. Guilds and military companies were the *popolo's* chief
means of expression, agitation and combat. Noblemen who joined the *popolo*

Between about 1220 and the end of the century, Piacenza, Cremona, Milan, Verona, Bologna, Florence, Siena, Lucca, Genoa, Pisa, Perugia, and more than a score of other communes witnessed the rise of the *popolo* to political hegemony. In most cases this victory was preceded by about a half-century of violent civil strife, often resulting in the mass exile of all the most active members of the defeated party, the confiscation of their property, and the razing of their family houses. But it would be a mistake to try to cast the social struggles of the 13th century into the mould of the conflict between Guelf and Ghibelline. Here foreign policy was often a determining factor. In some communes the *popolo* went Ghibelline (in Cremona, Siena, Genoa), in others it went Guelf (Milan, Bologna, Florence). Now and then the alignments changed.

The nobility retained full control of communal government up to the late 14th century. Merchants and even artisans, having occasionally gained entry into the commune, sometimes appeared in the governing councils, but not in sufficient numbers to offset the presence and influence of the men born into ancient urban families, into the families of rich ex-vassals, or into houses still possessed of feudal rights within the city walls and beyond. In some cities, the coastal ones in particular, noblemen unceremoniously took up large-scale commercial and maritime enterprise.[12] As long as they controlled the chief executive offices, the nobles ran the commune. Legislative proposals were introduced to the major council by the consulate, which alone was empowered to convoke that body. The *concio* or general assembly of the commune met yearly, or less often, or only in emergencies. Assembled under the leadership of the consuls and their advisers, the *concio* usually acceded to their will.

By the late 12th century, a booming urban economy had brought forth so many prosperous and aspiring new men that in most central and north Italian cities their determination to enter the commune as full-fledged citizens, to have a distinct voice in its political destinies, began to be felt. A formidable opposition was growing up *outside* the commune. This opposi-

---

changed neither the ultimate social character of alignments nor the issues which divided the two sides.

[12] Though some students hold that the great feudal nobility seldom went into trade. Fiumi, *op. cit.*

tion was soon organized, sometimes in secret. In Milan, for example, it was named the *Credenza di Sant'Ambrogio*. In 1198 this organization suddenly stepped into the open and sought to deal with the commune almost as an equal.[13] Making the nobles (*capitanei* and *valvassori*) its chief object of criticism, the *Credenza* insisted on a share in the management of Milanese public affairs. From this time on, and down to 1277, it was to be a powerful force in the *enlarged* commune. The Visconti themselves did not dare to suppress it until the early 14th century.

Faced with the mounting discontent and pressure of some of the economy's main beneficiaries, the consular nobility – never truly a homogeneous class – began to suffer defection and division. The opposition building up outside the commune exercised a fatal influence on the old communal oligarchy. And from about the last third of the 12th century this oligarchy began to break out in rivalries which at times – as in Siena, Milan, and Genoa – issued in conflict between the urbanized feudal nobility and the old municipal aristocracy. Partly provoked and sustained by the rising political challenge of new groups, the conflict caused first one noble faction and then another to seek the support of the emerging *popolo*. Intra-class jealousies and class conflict were separate but in the result acted together, and the one, class conflict, served to step up the virulence of the other.[14] As early as the 1140s, budding civil dissension in Genoa was already partly connected with the government's resolve to bar any citizen from public office who became the vassal of a feudatory.[15] At Siena in the 1250s and 1260s the *popolo* obtained the support of well-known feudal families in its fight against the old municipal aristocracy.[16] In the second half of the 13th century the Milanese petty nobility, organized into a *consorteria* or association known as the *Motta*, sometimes gave its political support to the *Credenza di Sant'Ambrogio* and sometimes to the great nobility.

[13] I. Ghiron, 'La Credenza di Sant'Ambrogio, o la lotta dei nobili e del popolo in Milano, 1198–1292', *ASL*, III–IV, 1876–7.
[14] Revealed by the nobility's habit of turning violently against noble houses which enjoyed the favour of the populace.
[15] F. Donaver, *La storia della repubblica di Genova*, Genoa, 1913, I, p. 48.
[16] F. Tempesti, 'Provenzan Salvani', *Bullettino senese di storia patria (BSSP)*, 43, I, 1963, p. 11; and implications in E. Sestan, 'Siena avanti Montaperti', *BSSP*, LXVII, 1961, pp. 56–61,71–2.

The commune's passage from consular to 'podestaral' government came with the large-scale, organized rise of new social groups. That the two were part of a single process is revealed by the fact that while the guilds and *societates populi* tended to prefer government organized around a *podestà*, the older, entrenched families preferred consular government, unless they were sure of controlling the *podestà*.[17] Only later, from about the middle decades of the 13th century, when the *podestà* had been reduced to subservience by a still tenacious oligarchy, was the *popolo* to set up a 'captain of the people' in opposition to the *podestà* and the 'major' commune.

At times obscured by the play of private vendetta and driving personal ambition, the issues connected with the conflict between *popolo* and *nobiltà* were not any the less real for that. In some communes, until about the middle of the 13th century, *popolo* and *nobiltà* carried unequal tax burdens and the advantage was with the nobleman, who often enjoyed time-honoured privileges and special immunities. In Milan commoners were long barred from some of the most lucrative appointments and benefices in the Milanese church; this gave rise to deep resentment. In other communes certain of the lesser guilds continued to pay feudal dues to leading municipal families down to the end of the 13th century. In Genoa and elsewhere some noble families enjoyed long-standing rights to part of the public income from different customs and tolls.[18] But the most basic of all divisive issues concerned the question of the groups to be represented in the communal assemblies and in the decision-making councils. When that question was settled, as it finally was in favour of a relatively close oligarchy,[19] then all other questions, even the crucial issue of public finance, *seemed* to be drawn into the purview of possible solution.

In some cities – e.g. Perugia, Florence, Bologna, Genoa, Bergamo – the strife between parties went on even after the major social struggles were resolved in favour of particular groups or classes. The continuation of this strife was possible

[17] G. Volpe, 'Il podestà nei comuni italiani del '200', article of 1904 in *op. cit.*
[18] Vitale, *op. cit.*, pp. 55–8.
[19] Shown by what happened to local governing councils in communes which definitively passed under signorial or even distant republican rule. Cf. A. Ventura, *Nobiltà e popolo nella società veneta del' 400 e' 500*, Bari, 1964.

because the state, such as it was, disposed of an incomplete
authority and because the contenders were the great families
long accustomed to being in the forefront of public life. Hence
all such conflict signified division in the ruling class proper.
This raises a problem which is central to our discussion – the
problem of leadership.

LEADERSHIP: THE GREAT FAMILIES

Leaving aside workers' revolts in the 14th century,[20] wherever
there was organized opposition, men from the great families
were likely to be found. Seldom was a plot hatched or a policy
successfully opposed without the participation of prominent
individuals. The man with a great family name was like a
magnet: he attracted or repelled the men and groups around
him. He galvanized action, that of the regime, or that of the
discontented. The popular movements of the 13th century
were often led by outstanding members of the aristocratic community – men driven by ambition and other motives too obscure for analysis. In working for the reform of the old
commune,[21] they seemed to go against their own kind. Des-
cended from the feudal nobility, from long-established consular families, or from other old families rich in lands and mercantile capital, such men enjoyed the greatest reputation and
authority: e.g. the Torriani in Milan, the Spinola and Doria
in Genoa, the Scaligeri in Verona, the Rivola in Bergamo, the
Torelli in Ferrara and the Salvani in Siena.

The presence of noblemen in the front ranks of the popular
opposition has occasionally aroused unnecessary surprise. But
though it was not fully in control of the public power, the
commune was oligarchically appointed. It was a defender of
rank. Against this background inherited authority was almost
a necessary condition for any man who wished to put himself
at the head of a movement of opposition. This was a deferen-
tial world where most men, being without political rights,
looked up to those at the head of the commune; a world

[20] As at Siena in 1371 and Florence in 1378.
[21] The so-called reforms were very often illusory, e.g., the results of the
Spinola–Doria regime in Genoa in the later 13th century: F. Poggi, 'Le
guerre civili di Genova dalle origini del comune al 1528', *Atti della società
ligure di storia patria*, LIV, 3, 1930, esp. pp. 47–57.

where certain houses looked like fortresses, where the extremes of wealth and poverty stood cheek by jowl, and where the signs of family authority were evident everywhere, being hemmed in by city walls and displayed by those who disposed of immense personal influence and bands of clients and armed servants. A powerful citizen sometimes commanded the obedience of whole peasant communities and possessed, down to the 14th century, the skills required for mounted combat.

Apart from the political pre-eminence, the commune's leading families always disposed of great wealth, which might be in lands, feudal rights, or – as in Pisa and Genoa – in maritime and commercial capital. It has been estimated that in the middle of the 12th century 80 per cent of Genoese trade with Syria was in the hands of five families, three of viscountal origins.[22] In the late 13th and early 14th centuries the co-operation of four great families (the Spinola, Doria, Grimaldi, and Fieschi) would have safeguarded the internal peace of Genoa.[23] Even in the 15th century, when Pistoia was under Florentine rule, the Panciatichi and Cancellieri could terrorize that commune at will. At Lucca in 1522 a single family of the oligarchy, the Poggi, started a civil war, rocked the city's constitutional foundations, earned hatred, death, and exile, and thereafter kept the oligarchy in a state of keen anxiety for years.[24]

The state was weak because the great families were strong. Part of the public power was in their hands. Permanently associated with the exercise of power – and when eliminated they were soon replaced by others who assumed the same role – these families had the character of semi-public entities. Such were the Tolomei, Salimbeni, and Malavolti in 13th-century Siena; the Da Lozzo, Carraresi, and Maccaruffi in Padua; the Langosco and Beccaria in Pavia; the Casalodi, Zanitali, and Buonaccolsi in Mantua; in Bologna the Buvalelli, Azzoguidi, and Gozzadini; and in Modena the Rangoni, Savignano, Boschetti, and Guidoni.

If the leading families in any of the great communes could have been brought together into a harmonious political unity,

[22] Vitale, *op. cit.*, p. 41.
[23] So I infer from A. Goria, 'Le lotte intestine in Genova tra il 1305 e il 1309', in *Miscellanea di storia ligure in onore di Giorgio Falco*, Milan, 1962, pp. 253–80.
[24] M. Berengo, *Nobili e mercanti nella Lucca del Cinquecento*, Turin, 1965, pp. 83–107.

as happened in Venice,[25] the state would have been united and
strong. In cities divided by inter-family strife, it was as if each
of the major families of the oligarchy held a piece of the state.
The unity and power of the state depended on the unity of the
ruling families. When these families fell into violent conflict,
the state, in process of formation, fell apart. Opposition which
attracted the leadership of one or more of the great families at
once produced a crisis: in a sense the state was divided against
itself. When a leading family moved over to form or join an
opposition, it was, with the best intentions and all the right in
the world, on the verge of provoking a conflict which easily became civil war. Leadership inevitably devolved on the well-
born,[26] owing to their long contact with the bastions of public
power. A Pagano della Torre, a Corso Donati, or an Opizzino
Spinola might have about him the aura that sometimes goes
with outstanding leadership, but it was nothing mystical. It
was a combination of political skills, great riches, a tradition of
leadership, and above all power 'filched' from the state: all of
which gave leaders a vast network of influential contacts both
at home and abroad.

THE OPPOSITION IN OLIGARCHIES

At the end of the 12th century Italian cities were faced with a
rising popular movement. The commune was a narrow oligarchy and now the *popolo*, working through the nascent guild
and armed companies of the different neighbourhoods, began
to press for political representation. A formidable opposition
was developing outside the commune. Often the ensuing differences were resolved by violence: a sudden, tempestuous
pressure which made the old commune yield. The armed
companies, followed by the guilds of craftsmen and lesser
merchants,[27] then achieved representation in the communal
councils. In some communes the representatives of the *popolo*

[25] Although here too there were rivalries which scholars have often not
emphasized enough.

[26] Obscurely-born *signori*, like Jacopo d'Appiano (a notary) and Francesco
Sforza, were very much the exception.

[27] Lawyers, international merchants and bankers had already managed in
many cases to work their way into the commune. At Genoa and Pisa the
influence of the great mercantile and maritime interests had long been
considerable.

suddenly appeared before the *podestà* with summary demands. Their rejection was the sign for an uprising of the *popolo* and a storming of the government buildings. The government would fall and a new one, its social base reconstituted, would emerge. Now and then the *popolo* seceded from the commune altogether and formed a new one.[28] Soon a working arrangement would be negotiated between the two, resulting in a more comprehensive commune, though one still oligarchically appointed.

During the second and third quarters of the 13th century, the *popolo* in many communes obtained up to one-half the number of seats in the governing bodies. The legislative councils served at times as agencies for a constitutional opposition. This arrangement, however, turned out to be inadequate. Apart from the fact that these councils could be convoked only by the executive, which alone could present measures to them, they were forbidden to hold debates. Furthermore, they were not filled by general election of the commune but by appointment or highly restricted election. Members were appointed or elected by the outgoing legislature and/or the principal executive bodies. Again, since the *popolo* was soon brought under the control of the richest and most authoritative *popolani* and guildsmen, a new communal oligarchy replaced and in part absorbed the old one. The commune of the later 13th century, the *comune del popolo*, was dominated by this oligarchy, whose composition included a sector of the old ruling families – hardy survivors of the consular and 'podestaral' commune. Yet once more the broad front of the opposition began to take shape outside the commune. The result was that the 14th century saw an endless succession of revolutions, conspiracies, civil wars, and scenes of crowd violence, in Perugia, Genoa, Siena, Pisa, Lucca, Bologna, and Florence. In Siena, although one government (the Nine Governors and Defenders) ruled from 1287 to 1355, it had constantly to fight against conspiracies and from 1320 it employed a foreign magistrate, the *capitano di guerra*, 'provided with extraordinary powers for the detection and punishment of political crimes'.[29] In 1368

---

[28] Although actually the *popolo* had not previously held *de jure* a political share in the commune.

[29] Schevill, *op. cit.*, pp. 204–5; and P. Silva, *Il governo di Pietro Gambacorta in Pisa*, Pisa, 1912, pp. 101–3, for the equivalent Pisan magistrate.

D

alone four Sienese governments were overturned, each *coup* bringing a different social stratum, or a new combination of groups, to power: the *Dodicini, Noveschi, Riformatori* and *Monte dei Gentiluomini.*[30]

Siena's problem was in large measure that of other cities ruled by oligarchies: the problem of governments which excluded socially important groups from public life. Most oligarchies combined this problem with one which was a little less troublesome in Siena: the problem of the free-wheeling activity of powerful families, even when these were under a political ban. The gravity of these two problems goes to explain the great force of the opposition which stood outside the commune's political councils. A major family and a group of the discontented had but to join forces to present the commune with serious menace. In the face of such danger, any constitutional opposition which survived in the legislative councils became more and more faint-hearted, or simply dissolved. At that point political differences could take a violent turn.

In some respects it was in Florence that the opposition produced one of the richest histories. Even under the early Medici (1434–69), and again under the revived republic (1494–1512), the legislative councils often put up a stiff opposition to measures which had the support of the ruling group. This kept alive a 14th-century tradition.[31] At no point did the opposition in Florence have the legal margins to prepare for organized action in the legislative councils, where in any case debate was prohibited.[32] Yet it was by no means unusual for these councils to reject bills sponsored and strongly supported by the government. Care must be taken, however, not to misconstrue the forces behind such opposition. Like other municipal republics of the time, Florence always had an *inner* oligarchy: a

---

[30] W. Bowsky, 'The *Buon Governo* of Siena (1287–1355): a Mediaeval Italian oligarchy', *Speculum*, XXXVII, 3, 1962, pp. 368–81; D. Hicks, 'Sienese Society in the Renaissance', *Comparative Studies in Society and History*, II, 4, 1960, pp. 412–20.

[31] On which, see G. Brucker, *Florentine Politics and Society, 1343–1378*, Princeton, 1962.

[32] F. Rinuccini, *Ricordi storici dal 1282 al 1460*, ed. G. Aiazzi, Florence, 1840, p. clx, for an exemplary case involving three Florentine 'grand councillors'. Guicciardini held that 'free debate' in such councils 'is the principal instrument of sedition', in his *Considerazioni intorno ai Discorsi del Machiavelli*, Ch. II.

tough core of families at the centre of the larger oligarchy, this larger body being the commune itself. As long as the inner oligarchy was united, its will prevailed and any opposition was soon dispelled. But no sooner was the inner oligarchy divided than opposition in the legislative councils immediately sprang into action – a function of the disaffected part of the ruling group. The legislative councils reflected the degree of unity or division which characterized this group at any given moment; hence the most significant or meaningful opposition – opposition which presented true alternatives – was that which went against the *united* inner oligarchy. It was practically impossible for this opposition to acquire a legal status.

Accession to leading office in most communal oligarchies was controlled by elaborate methods of election and appointment. This aspect of statecraft has been all but neglected by students of Italian city states, though it deserves painstaking study.[33] For it was by a shrewd manipulation of appointments and election procedures that inner oligarchies retained control of key offices, imposed their will, or effectively intimidated the opposition in the communal councils. The Venetian republic had one of the most complex of all systems of appointment and election. As much complexity obtained in Florence, where the Medicean oligarchy showed a matchless virtuosity in its ability to get legislatures to approve of temporary plenipotentiary councils, to acquiesce in the manipulation of the pouches containing the names of men eligible for major office, and to consent to a system of balloting which became ever trickier, always to the advantage of the inner oligarchy. Now and then there were defections. But when two or three members of an executive council, where voting was normally secret, were so stubborn as to refuse their votes to a measure clearly favoured by the inner oligarchy, one of the tougher members might get up in council and propose a new but open vote on the matter, so that all could see who really desired the 'good' of the regime. The measure was thus driven through.

Venice was in some ways outside the political mainstream. The aspects that made government so unstable in other city states were less evident there. The Venetian state was more highly developed. It was a more formidable institution and its

[33] Of the sort given to sixty years of Florentine history by N. Rubinstein, *The Government of Florence Under the Medici (1434 to 1494)*, Oxford, 1966.

oligarchy was more united. No single family or small bloc of
families ever acquired enough influence in and around the
lagoons to disturb the organic link between state and oligarchy. Did it follow that the fortunes of the opposition in
Venice were more stable, that dissent had a sounder legal
status? The answer depends on how *opposition* is defined. If
we define it as resistance to bills proposed in the city's major
legislative body, the famous grand council, the answer is yes.
But if we define it as activity or opinion, organized or not,
directed against the composition of the oligarchy, the answer is
no.

As in Florence, so in Venice the right of legal opposition
belonged to the oligarchs alone, though even then it had to be
given expression in senatorial debate or by vote in the grand
council. Noblemen could criticize or differ from their government heads provided they did so in the legally constituted
bodies. Once criticism moved outside these bodies it acquired
a delicate, more uncertain status; and if efforts were made to
organize dissent, the executive might well pounce on the organizers and bring them to trial.[34] Political organization was
ipso facto a threat. In January 1433 thirty-seven noblemen
were denounced to the Council of Ten. They were charged
with having agreed in private to cast their ballots in favour
of one another whenever the grand council held elections for
leading office. Such an agreement smacked of conspiracy and
could provide the framework for an effective opposition. All
thirty-seven were condemned: the severest sentence put
Marco Cicogna under a ban for ten years and barred him from
all offices in perpetuity; the most lenient condemned three of
the thirty-seven to be barred from office for three years.[35] In
1457, when the Ten forcibly deposed the doge, Francesco
Foscari, they forbade all citizens, on pain of death,[36] to discuss
the subject. Thus there were limitations on legal opposition
even within the oligarchy: the Ten had but to declare a certain subject taboo, adducing their authority over state secrets
as well as in matters concerning the security of the state, and
that put an end to discussion.[37] How could legal opposition on

[34] Thus, e.g., the conspiracy of Bocconio in 1300.
[35] Romanin, *op. cit.*, IV, p. 170.
[36] M. Macchi, *Istoria del consiglio dei dieci*, Turin, 1848, No. I, pp. 265–6.
[37] G. Maranini, *La costituzione di Venezia dopo la serrata del maggior
consiglio*, Florence, 1931, pp. 476–77.

a truly important issue be effective or have any organized existence when the discussion of controversial subjects could be outlawed by the government?

When the Venetian grand council was 'closed' at the end of the 13th century, much discontent and opposition were aroused, issuing partly in the conspiracies of Bocconio (1300) and of the Tiepolo-Quirini group (1310).[38] Like other republican city states, Venice suddenly had to confront the threat of a burgeoning opposition outside its political councils. To meet this danger the oligarchy established the famous and dreaded Council of Ten (1310). Their task was to root out conspiracy and subversive discontent – indeed, any form of dissent which made the oligarchy itself the object of criticism. And opposition of this sort was a continuing problem, as revealed by the intense activity of the Ten. One of the highpoints of this activity came in 1355, with the discovery of the dramatic conspiracy of the doge, Marian Faliero, who had managed in great secrecy to organize a group of discontented commoners.[39] But a divided and factious oligarchy, the curse of other cities, was not so serious a problem in Venice. Here the state had much greater stability and the conspiratorial opposition was most feeble. We should not, however, exaggerate the degree of harmony in the Venetian ruling class. The events connected with Francesco Foscari's election to the office of doge, his relations with Pietro Loredan and later on with the Ten, show that the oligarchy sometimes harboured rival family blocs. In 1486, on the election of Agostino Barbarigo to the supreme dignity, evidence emerged of a secret rivalry between the city's very ancient and more recent houses – the *longhi* and the *curti*.[40] The *longhi* or ancient houses had done all they could to get one of their own members elected to the dogeship, monopolized by the *curti* since 1382. In 1450 sixteen of the leading *curti* houses secretly vowed to keep this dignity from ever being won by a member of the *longhi*. The secret rivalry between the two groups persisted until at least the time of Bar-

[38] H. Kretschmayr, *Geschichte von Venedig*, 3 vols., new edn, Stuttgart, 1964, II, pp. 71, 181–3.

[39] On which, see the excellent article by V. Lazzarini, 'Marino Faliero: la congiura', *Nuovo archivio veneto*, XIII, 1897, pp. 5–107, 277–373.

[40] Romanin, *op. cit.*, IV, pp. 420–1; Kretschmayr, *op. cit.*, II, pp. 367–8, 479, 653–4.

barigo's election and was carried over into elections for some
of the other principal offices.

Secrecy had its advantages after all, for the illegal opposition,
especially in cities under Venetian rule, might have acquired a
foothold as a result of the break which opened between the
longhi and *curti*. Milan and Florence would have looked on
with happy approval and support.

THE OPPOSITION IN SIGNORIES

For most central and north Italian cities, the political and
social struggles of the 13th century led irresistibly to the triumph of the *signoria*. Worn down by generations of civil strife,
oligarchies turned to a strong man, whose autocratic rule, for
all its shortcomings, seemed to promise a reign of civic order
and internal peace. This, at least, is the standard interpretation.[41] Yet the general convergence on signorial rule was
neither mechanical nor inevitable. Florence, though it had experienced an interval of veiled rule of this sort, passed over
into the 16th century as a republic; Lucca recovered from one-
man rule in the 15th century and survived with its oligarchical
government *a comune* down to 1799; Siena, but for the short
signory of the Petrucci (1497–1522), long retained its republican institutions; and Genoa had periods of republican recovery. On the other hand, some communes passed over to
signorial rule as early as the second quarter of the 13th century
(e.g. Ferrara, in 1222), although their internal affairs were far
less tempestuous than those of other cities which did not experience one-man rule for another century or more.

When a city state was brought under the rule of a *signore*,
the communal legislative councils soon remained almost alone
as the possible agencies of legitimate opposition. Headed by a
podestà or a captain of the people, preceding governments had
a marked collegiate structure. Neither *podestà* nor captain
could act in questions of state without consulting a formal
body of counsellors,[42] who were elected or drawn by lot and
whose appointment was the prerogative of the communal oli-

---

[41] As seen in F. Lanzani, *Storia dei comuni italiani dalle origini al 1313*,
Milan, 1888; N. Valeri, *L'Italia nell'età dei principati*, Verona, 1949; and L.
Simeoni, *Le signorie*, Milan, 1950.

[42] E.g., *anziani, sapientes, consiglio di credenza*.

garchy. Hence some dissent could at times find its way into the highest councils of the commune. The *signore*, however, appointed his own advisers, and while he might listen to conflicting advice, opposition was out of the question. There remained only the legislative councils to provide an institutional outlet for the opposition. Whether or not these in fact performed that function depended on the political strength of the new lord. In many cases the take-over by the *signore* occurred in an atmosphere of such violence, intimidation, or moral confusion, that the defeated opposition did not dare show itself.[43] The new ruler and his successors gradually sapped the independent vitality of the major legislative council: they brought its membership under their control, changed its composition, allowed it to assemble more and more rarely, and whittled away its remaining powers. Any opposition to this progressive usurpation was dismissed or suppressed; encroachment came about piecemeal and was often legitimized by the bestowal of an imperial *vicariato*. Care was taken to observe the external legal forms.

Casting a glance over the 14th and 15th centuries, we light upon instances of communal bodies which sued for the attention of the lord of the city and carried protests to him. The opposition here found a legal outlet, but it seems seldom to have been effective. In the early 1350s, when Bologna was under the lordship of the archbishop, Giovanni Visconti, many of the commune's middle and lower administrative posts were held by outsiders, mostly Lombards – appointees of the archbishop and his three major officials in Bologna. When the commune protested, reminding the archbishop that the right over all such appointments belonged to the great legislative council of 4000, Giovanni replied by modifying the authority of that body.[44] At Milan, in the first half of the 15th century, meetings of the old legislative council of 900 were so infrequent that lodging protests with the duke, so far as this happened, fell solely to the *consiglio delle provvisioni* – a council of twelve men charged with a certain sector of municipal affairs. In 1427 this council offered the duke, Filippo Maria

[43] As emphasized by G. B. Picotti, 'Qualche osservazione sui caratteri delle signorie italiane', *Rivista storica italiana*, XLIII, 4, 1926, pp. 7–30.
[44] A. Sorbelli, *La signoria di Giovanni Visconti a Bologna*, Bologna, 1901, pp. 190–8.

Visconti, a large sum of money to help to pay for war expenses. It asked, in return, for the right to administer the municipality's revenue. Another condition was that Filippo's courtiers be prevented from reaping private advantage from the public treasury. The duke refused to receive their representations.[45]

In the 14th and 15th centuries, the enduring spirit of the commune provided the most fitting climate for the maintenance of significant opposition in states under one-man rule. Most scholarly opinion has played down the surviving sense of the commune and the force of republicanism in 15th-century Italy. But it is difficult to reconcile this with the temporary re-establishment of the commune at Bologna (1428–9), with the dramatic establishment at Milan of the Ambrosian republic (1447), and with the tenacious loyalties which enabled this republic to fight against overwhelming odds for two and a half years. The last Florentine republic (1527–30) was to exhibit the same vigorous loyalties.

It may already be clear that the line between legal and illegal opposition was never distinct. Why this was so can be traced to the fact that the legal identity of the state was itself in doubt. As a result it was no simple matter for governments to distinguish between opposition which merely took the form of criticism, and opposition which ultimately was intended to overthrow the existing regime. For the same reason, it is wiser to deal here with the sort of opposition (conspiracy) which was frankly illegal and which jurists had no trouble in condemning.

Defined as organized secret activity which at some point depends on violence to achieve its ends,[46] conspiracy was the most desperate species of opposition. That it was common in the early history of signories was mainly a sign of two things: of the uncertain foundations of signorial power and of the narrow margin accorded to the play of legal opposition. The political rise of the *popolo* was in some respects a mass conspiracy, but serious analysis would doubtless do better to see it

---

[45] In the new history by a team of historians: F. Cognasso, C. Santoro, F. Catalano, etc., *Storia di Milano*, VI, Milan, 1955–6, p. 467.

[46] Limitations of space have prevented the treatment of industrial organization, such as the formation of workers' guilds in the 14th century. The commune considered these to be conspiratorial and they were universally outlawed. See the excellent study by W. Ullmann, 'The Mediaeval Theory of Legal and Illegal Organizations', *The Law Quarterly Review*, 60, July, 1944, pp. 285–91.

in terms of the vocabulary of revolution. Conspiracy against a given *signore* was always more focused; it might be the work of two or three men or of a small group; it was more organized; and its objectives, ideally, were far more limited and defined than any which might attach to a revolution.

During the late 13th and early 14th centuries, conspiracies against *signori* were often successful, owing partly at least to the unstable foundations of the new signorial power. Thereafter conspiracy was less often successful, the signory having developed more solid institutional bases. The trouble with most 15th-century conspiracies was that they were conceived or executed in a political and social vacuum: they failed to get, or realistically to envisage, any support from a strategic sector of the community. Such were the conspiracies of Stefano Porcari in Rome (1453), of Andrea Lampugnano and his two companions in Milan (1476), and of the Pazzi in Florence (1478).

What types or classes of opposition came under the heading of conspiracy? There seem to have been two: the sort which aimed at substantive political changes and that which merely contrived to exchange one *signore* for another. The murder of Giovanni Maria Visconti in 1412, carried out by a tiny group of ducal officials, was the result of a conspiracy which had no objectives beyond the profit of a few highly-placed soldiers and courtiers. Much the same may be said of the assassinations which racked the small despotisms of 14th-century Italy; they were the fruit of conspiracies often planned or carried out by close relatives of the murdered *signore*.

It is important to distinguish between conspiracies in which the political factor was foremost and those which aimed at the satisfaction of personal grudges and private ambitions. For if our interest be the study of political opposition, we should be ready to see that there is opposition so narrow and personal in its objectives that its political features are insignificant and almost accidental.

THE *FUORUSCITI* (POLITICAL EXILES)

The Italian city state provides no figure who better incarnates the organized opposition than the political exile (*fuoruscito*). From the 13th to the 16th centuries he is a central figure in

Italian politics. He is found on all the roads and in all the cities large and small. His civil status, never secure, points directly to the difficult legal circumstances in which political opposition took place. His social identity reveals, almost without our having to probe, the strong oligarchical bent of Italian municipal politics. Not the lowborn or humble *fuoruscito* but one from a pre-eminent and powerful family was the sort of exile who aroused the anxiety of the regime back at home. Such, for example, were the Rangoni and Savignano of Modena, the Da Lozzo and Maccaruffi of Padua, the Oddi and Baglioni of Perugia, or the Canetoli and Bentivoglio of Bologna. In critical times, these were men who could overturn city states.

When treating the 13th and 14th centuries, scholarship often refers to the 'internal' and 'external' commune. This distinction is revealing: *internal commune* – the party or faction in power, ruling over the city and its lands; *external commune* – the party living in exile, sometimes organized along communal lines, with its own officials, seal, a small army, and often taken up with the despatch of emissaries or the holding of formal consultations. In its highest and most developed form the external commune was in effect the government in exile. Literally, it was composed of many scores or hundreds of exiles from leading families, in addition to their followers, servants, clients, hangers-on, and so forth. Milan in the middle years of the 13th century and Genoa in the early 14th century confront an external commune which is able to raise small armies, to conquer territory claimed by the internal commune, to establish a network of diplomatic contacts, and to conclude treaties with *signori* and other city states.

Conditioned by tradition and practice, contemporaries associated much of the public power with the great families of the communal oligarchy. When a bloc of these families was driven or retired into exile, it was as if they went off with part of the commune. They carried off more than a trace of the public authority which normally fell to their lot. Indeed, their removal from the scene was in some ways more illusory than real. For leading exiles maintained secret contact with men at home. They knew what transpired in the communal councils. They were aware of the political virtues and weaknesses of the men who ran the internal commune. They sometimes had the allegiance of rural communities under the *de facto* rule of the home city. They often received crucial support, military and financial, from princes, local *signori*, or neighbouring city states. And by a shrewd articulation of policy, they could count on promoting division and dissension in the ruling group at home.

The external commune flourished in the 13th and early 14th centuries. It was then that the strife between parties, factions, and classes, in central as in northern Italy, unfolded along lines which enabled exiles to find their political correspondents in the forefront of communes in other cities and to enlist their aid. *Popolo* and *nobiltà*, Guelfs and Ghibellines, Aigoni and Grasolfi (Modena), Reds and Whites (Verona), Blacks and Whites (Florence), Raspanti and Bergolini (Pisa), Scacchesi and Gozzadini (Bologna): all these had their friends and counterparts in other cities. As long as exiles, albeit few and discredited, managed to recruit the support of a neighbouring *signore* or of another city, they were feared and fought. They disposed of the means to return home triumphantly or to impose a foreign ruler on their native city. From time to time, and as early as the second quarter of the 13th century, there were groups of *fuorusciti* who were not averse to putting their cities under foreign rule, provided they could thereby return home, vanquish their enemies, and obtain a share in the political spoils. This mode of activity was a fundamental factor in the rise of Italian despotism.

Towards the end of the 14th century the Italian states were undergoing an internal consolidation. Signorial government could look back to a distinct tradition and thus appoint or conduct itself with greater certitude. There was a striking growth in the power of the executive, manifest even in republics like Venice, Florence, and Siena. The executive was better able to deal with civil disorder, and party and class strife were much reduced. In all the major signories a particular effort had been made to eliminate factions and family blocs. Altogether, the direction of change was moving away from a political geography which had once permitted the linking of parties, classes and groups of *fuorusciti* in relationships that cut across communes. Governments which would commit themselves to the ideological views of exiles were getting to be a thing of the past. With some notable exceptions, passions for party and faction were being toned down. The era which had succoured governments in exile was in decline.

Yet these changes did not signal a decline in the use of exile as a penalty against political unreliability. Governments in exile passed. The exile himself crowds the roads down to the middle of the 16th century and at times is plunged back into the centre of politics. But from the end of the 14th century or thereabouts, his position and function begin to be different from what they had been in the great days of the external commune. Henceforth he becomes a pawn in the hands of other states. Unlike 13th-century *fuorusciti*, he seldom has vital contacts, political or social, with groups in his city which wait and work for his return so that they can leap into power. Conspiracies take on a literary flavour, issuing forth from books rather than politics. All in all, the state has tightened up. Public authority presents a more united front and is capable of greater coercion. Opposition is under a closer surveillance. Fewer men take political risks – far fewer; and the incidence of political exile is so much lower that it seems different in kind from that which had gone before. The *fuoruscito* of the Renaissance is often a solitary figure.

Why was exile the penalty so often favoured in the punishment of organized opposition? This question touches on most of the major points already discussed: the indeterminate identity of the state, the passionate allegiance to groups within the larger community, the stubborn and tenacious exclusiveness of the commune in all its manifestations, and the imponderable power of the great families.

Exile removed the opponent from the scene as prison did not. It removed him to a place where he could not directly exploit his rank or oppose and threaten an insecure government. But we have seen that *fuorusciti* could be equally dangerous abroad. Why, therefore, was capital punishment not constantly and universally imposed? It *was* imposed, but not systematically.[47] Though argument from public necessity could be adduced and sometimes was, the legal grounds for applying capital punishment in political cases were not yet clear. It is only in the 14th and 15th centuries that lawyers, arguing from Roman law, gradually gave currency to the concept of

---

[47] The outstanding example was Venice, where the penalty for serious conspiracy was nearly always capital punishment.

the crime of *laesa majestas* – a concept developed *pari-passu* with the emergence of the sovereign city state.[48] Again, mass execution rather than the exile of leaders would in many instances have aroused so much indignation and protest that public authority might well have been plunged into graver difficulties than those with which it had been faced. Perhaps, too, there was some feeling that in a reversal of roles the lenient would be treated with lenience.

The need to guard against strong public reactions indicates something about the instrumental value of public opinion: it reveals that volatile political behaviour, while often menacing to governments, could also serve as a check on them. The opposition of the *piazza* was not a force for disruption alone: it was also a positive factor in politics.

Despite the ardour of party and faction, the fear aroused by the instability of government, and the keen desire to eliminate opposition, some longing for the benefit of compromise remained and some hopes were placed in it. Otherwise, it would be difficult to explain the fact that large groups of *fuorusciti* were often given leave to return home, sometimes under conditions of extraordinary lenience.[49] No doubt every such instance had its own particular reasons, and moderation must at times have been dictated by fear or craft. But regardless of how we choose to assess the moments of calm and tolerance in Italian cities, the fact remains that to exile opponents, despite their known potentiality for mischief, or to license their repatriation, meant that some civility was a permanent feature in politics and that not all the routes to compromise had been closed up.

[48] C. Ghisalberti, 'Sulla teoria dei delitti di lesa maestà nel diritto comune', *Archivo giuridico*, CXLIX, 1955, pp. 100–79.

[49] E.g. the return of the nobles to Milan in 1257–8, the exile and pardon after a few days of forty Genoese Guelfs (January 1289), and the pardon of the Spinola clan of Genoa in 1311.

Michael Oakeshott

On Magna Carta*

J. C. Holt: *Magna Carta,* Cambridge University Press, London, 1965.

THE HISTORICAL UNDERSTANDING OF THE GREAT CHARTER, LIKE that of nearly every important event or occasion, has emerged gradually out of the quite different enterprise of assigning it a significant place in the legend of English life. This enterprise of constructing and confirming a social identity and consciousness by establishing a significant relationship between present moods and past events is a perennial practical necessity, and in respect of the Charter it has been pursued since the 14th century. And the 'retrospective modernism' (as Maitland called it) of 19th-century historians, in which the Charter appeared as the palladium of English liberty, may now be recognized, not as historical error, but rather as evidence of the imperfect emergence of an historical understanding from the conditions of this practical, political enterprise. But, the task of historical understanding having been embraced, it is not unexpected that it should have revealed itself in a peculiarly determined attempt to detach the Charter from subsequent events and to interpret it severely in its 13th-century context.

The first version of this interpretation still contained relics of the legend-making enterprise: the baronial opponents of King John, deposed from their legendary role of champions of liberty, were merely cast for another role, that of self-seeking dissidents and the opponents of administrative efficiency. But that this first version should have concentrated upon the 'feudal' and the 'legal' character of the document was evidence both that a serious attempt at historical understanding was at last afoot and that the enquiry had broken the surface of things at a certain point. Those who, in their early study of the matter, were directed (by such great teachers as Lapsley and Professor Helen Cam) to Petit-Dutaillis, to Maitland, to Kate

Norgate, and to McKechnie, will remember the almost dramatic dissolution and reconstitution which what they had learned at school (or even from the indispensable writings of Stubbs) suffered.

From this beginning, the story of the historical understanding of the Charter during the last half-century of scholarship, has been one of endless and fascinating elaboration. The last relics of 'retrospective modernism' have been detached from it to compose a history of their own. The 'context' in which the Charter is read has been extended and immeasurably deepened; it has been pushed back into early Norman England, it has been enlarged to include 12th-century Europe, and its convolutions have been tirelessly explored. It has ceased to be predominantly 'feudal' and 'legal'. The Charter of 1215 has been recognized as a political document, its occasion as a piece of politics, and the quality of its thought as that which belongs to men engaged in political discourse and negotiation – imprecise, but with the characteristic imprecisions of an historical situation. Generalities have been replaced by specificalities, actual discontents, and their magnitudes have been distinguished. Named persons, with discernible characters, with individual interests and the usual mixture of motives, and named properties, have taken the place of 'the barons', their fiefs and castles, and rights. A situation composed of complicated tensions has replaced the old simplicities. England has emerged as having a political geography not less significant in the early 13th century than in the 17th century. And from it all a new outline, composed of more appropriate general statements, has been made to emerge – an outline in which, often, the exclusive utterances of earlier historians are given a new and relative significance. In short, this whole passage of the past has become historically more intelligible, and the process in which this has been achieved is a remarkable example of historical thought.

This, of course, has been the work of many minds and springs, in part, from record evidence having taken the place of that of contemporary chronicle; and, like all enterprises in historical understanding, it is unfinished – not merely because there are enquiries still to be satisfied but because its greatest gift is that of making us capable of entertaining and assimilating new representations of it and of the whole period to which this occasion belonged. Professor J. C. Holt has made his own distinguished contribution to this achievement, but his book is also a critical review of how this matter of scholarship stands at present. Its design is admirable, its command of detail remarkable, its argument clear, and the reader is given the immensely pleasurable experience of being in the presence of a first-class historical intelligence. It has something to say about the myth and about the place the Charter came to occupy in the minds of later generations of politicians and lawyers, but its main concern is with the Charter of 1215 itself, with the circumstances which generated it and with the quality of its thought.

Professor Holt presents the Charter of 1215 to us, not as a legal document, nor as a treaty, but as a political programme, the product of six-months negotiation between the king and the barons. It is a piece of political thinking all the more interesting because it escapes the speculative doctrines about government with which medieval academics were concerned (and which we all too often mistake for the sum of medieval political thought), and reveals practical men grappling with a practical situation with the aid of ideas which sprang directly from their experience.

The general conditions of the occasion were common to many of the realms of medieval Europe; they might be said to be the conditions in which political rule emerged from the technical despotism of 'lordship'. The chief peculiarities of the situation in England sprang from the circumstances of the Norman conquest, the nature of the baronage and the command which John's forebears had succeeded in establishing – all of which told against the king's opponents.

The immediate circumstance which provoked the barons to initiate the negotiations was the increasing arbitrariness of royal importunity. Perhaps no item of John's conduct was identifiably *ultra vires*, but the exigencies of foreign war had led the king to embark upon a policy of exploiting to the utmost the vagueness of the law (e.g. of descent and tenure) and the sources of feudal revenue, of disposing of his capital assets for ready money and of selling whatever immunities his subjects were anxious to acquire. These, in themselves, were disrupting activities, particularly when they came near to making allegiance a saleable commodity. But what made the situation worse was the absence of any settled rates for feudal aids, scutage, etc., and the absence of any settled price for privileges and immunities. It was government by bargain on the occasion and often by bargain with individuals. In short, what provoked the protest was uncertainty, not manifest illegality. And the immediate circumstance which compelled a reluctant king to enter into these negotiations was the need of funds (made desperate by the collapse of his adventures in France) and the perception that he had pushed a not inconsiderable number of barons to the edge of their loyalty – beyond the point at which they might still be silenced by individual concessions and rewards. Indeed, on 5 May 1215 the negotiating barons formally withdrew homage and fealty.

The subject of the negotiations was this whole method of ruling in which the routine exercise of justice and the enjoyment of the rights of lordship had become subordinated to the pursuit of royal policy. They were focused upon specific confusions and uncertainties. On the surface the parties debated administrative practices and even principles of alleged law; underneath, each party was seeking hidden advantages or escapes from the fulfilment of forced concessions. It was all on the borders of an unadmitted political novelty.

And the Charter itself? It was 'nothing but a vast communal privilege for which the King's subjects paid, not now by the offer of vast sums or the surrender or subjection of their lives and property, but by the restoration of their allegiance upon agreed terms'. Its imprecisions and vagueness made it possible, but they also made it impossible of application. But if what followed immediately was war and not peace, a beginning had been made of the introduction of a greater degree of law, order, and certainty in the tenurial relationships between Crown and vassal, in the duties of rulers and the obligations of subjects. It was remarkable that the unresolved tensions of the following decade did not destroy the realm.

This incident has some interesting features for those concerned with the adventure of governing and being governed. It was an occasion when, with a certain latitude, something which may be called 'opposition' emerged; and it is worth while to consider the quality of that opposition and what it was that was being opposed.

No government, not even the mildest, can expect to escape

the attention of malcontents who believe themselves to be ill-served or who think they could do better; and some governments invite rebellion and overthrow. But 'opposition', properly speaking, is something more sophisticated than either mere dissidence or insurrection. It assumes a distinction between 'ruling' and 'opposing', and it never presumes to the office of ruler. It can exist only where there is a legitimate government recognized to have authority to 'rule', and the activity of 'opposition' entails an unshaken allegiance to this government. It is possible only when it is recognized to have an authority of its own -- an authority to 'oppose' but not to 'rule'. And it will be most useful where it is a standing institution and not merely an *ad hoc* device provoked by an emergency.

It is not surprising that an institution of 'opposition' should have been thought a valuable insurance against rebellion on the one hand and autocracy on the other, or that it should have been believed (as Machiavelli believed) that it is a necessary condition of 'liberty'. But in fact, wherever 'opposition', properly speaking, has appeared it has first emerged as a residuary office performed by those who by historic circumstances have had the necessary independence and power and who have acquired the authority to perform it. That is to say, 'an opposition' is a political convention (often, but not always, appearing as a surrogate for insurrection) which requires certain conditions for its emergence.

In many respects the barons of early 13th-century England were ill-equipped to *rebel* against the royal government. Unlike the feudatories of France, they were not great, semi-independent lords of compact territories. Their holdings were compromised by intrusive particles of the royal demesne, and the realm had become an organization, not of baronial fees, but of counties, in which the royal sheriff was superior to the aristocratic bailiff. The time had long passed when they could (as they did in Stephen's reign) effectively regard their allegiance to the king as terminable if he exceeded whatever they chose to interpret as the limits of his authority. The only centre of powerful independence, and thus of possible rebellion, that remained was the marcher territory. But what they lacked in power to rebel effectively they made up in experience, and their authority to 'oppose' was a plausible extension of their right to be consulted and to consent in matters that concerned themselves and their property.

There was not, perhaps, very much to distinguish this occasion from the numerous 'rebellions' suffered by John's predecessors, and the situation was colourably one in which rebellions might be justified on the recognized principles of serious royal misdemeanour. But there was something to distinguish it, and the ambivalence of the situation is reflected in the ambivalence of the historian's language. The resisters of 1215 may be called an 'opposition' because they never denied the authority of kingly government; because their intention was not to overthrow John's government, or even to control it, but to correct it; because what they resisted was not items of conduct but a whole method of governing; and because what they sought for themselves they unavoidably sought for all – their relation to those who owed them duties was inextricable from their relation to the king. But the art of 'opposition' was in its infancy, and the conditions of its practice had not fully emerged. Negotiators who had no recourse but to withdraw their allegiance were quasi-rebels; clubs were trumps.

The object of the 'opposition' is instructive. The discontents provoked by governments recognized to be legitimate are, commonly, that they are capricious, oppressive, over-demanding, extortionate; that they exceed their known rights; that they fail to protect their subjects from injury; and that they pursue interests which are detrimental to their subjects. And, in one degree or another, all these discontents were felt by those who forced negotiation upon John.

Based upon the territorial power established by William I, and aided by an immense increase in administrative skills, the king had done everything that wilful and activist governments are apt to do. He had pressed the sources of legitimate revenue to their limits, he had lived upon the edge of legality, he had controlled his more powerful subjects by putting them into debt, and he had treated his subjects as objects of policy. But the situation was far from clear-cut. There was the confusion about rights and duties characteristic of a community where the intimations of political rule had appeared over the horizon, but where 'lordship' remained the familiar authority; there was the confusion between the king as the source of justice and the king as the conductor of policy; and, in addi-

tion, there was the confusion which sprang from John's in-
clination to govern by individual bargain and to buy allegiance with the penalties he extracted from offenders.

The 'opposition', no doubt, were averse from paying taxes;
but they were not a set of mere *poujadists*. Their protest was
directed first, against the uncertainty, the undefined character
of their obligations and the unsettled price to be paid for the
enjoyment of their rights; and secondly, it was guided by their
perception that the administration of justice, and the order of
the realm (the conduct of which was a major source of revenue
to the king), was being corrupted by being subordinated to the
king's need for funds to conduct foreign adventures. That the
wealth of a land should be exploited to support policy is something which every land ruled by adventurers has to suffer; but
that the administration of justice should be subordinated to
the profits it yields is an intolerable offence to good order. And
the difficulty of the opposers' situation was how to protest
against this without involving themselves in a more questionable protest against the rights of royalty themselves.

Frank O'Gorman

Party and Burke: The Rockingham Whigs*

HISTORIANS OF 18TH-CENTURY ENGLAND ARE COMING TO RECOG-
nize that the Rockingham Whigs played a significant role in
the establishment of 'party' and 'opposition' as political instruments in the life of the nation but they remain divided over
the precise contribution which the Rockinghams made to the
evolution of the party system.[1] On close analysis the party appears to be profoundly divided over some of the most fundamental political issues of the time. Its attitude towards the
American colonies was at best ambiguous and unsatisfactorily
thought out. It was deeply divided on reform. All too frequently its parliamentary performance was inept, its members
absent and its public credit low. In office, the Rockinghams
were unable to effect lasting political changes and were never
able to survive for more than a few months. Because most historians have concentrated their studies on these aspects of
Rockinghamite history they have tended to neglect, indeed
almost to dismiss, the party ideology which emerged during
the 1770s and have remained indifferent to the institutional
changes which occurred a little later. Only when the theoretical and institutional developments have been analysed and
their significance assessed can a balanced view of the Rockinghams emerge – and thus a more valid picture of party development in the later 18th century.

Indeed, as historians continue their researches within the

[1] The favourable assessment of A. S. Foord (*His Majesty's Opposition, 1714–
1832*, Oxford, 1964) should be compared with the somewhat jaundiced attitude
of J. Brooke (*The Chatham Administration*, 1956) and the cautiously non-
committal approach of I. R. Christie (*The End of North's Ministry*, 1958).
The account of the Rockinghams in L. B. Namier and J. Brooke, *The House
of Commons, 1754–1790*, H.M.S.O., 3 vols, 1964, is a more satisfactory,
though incomplete, sketch of the opposition to North.

* Vol. 3, no. 1, Winter 1968.

political framework established by Namier a generation ago
and while they employ the methodological techniques and
conceptual tools fashioned by that great historian, it becomes
increasingly clear that the 18th-century political system under-
went great changes during the latter half of the century. The
so-called 'classical balance' of the constitution of the earlier
period could not possibly endure the strains and stresses to
which it was subjected during the reign of George III. The
role of the monarchy itself became a political issue for the first
time in almost half a century. Its prerogatives were increasingly
called into question and their application by the monarch
himself subsequently declined. These powers passed into the
hands of a cabinet whose membership acquired a coherence
and its procedures a momentum of their own. While great
issues aroused an increasingly literate and sophisticated public opinion, national affairs began to make their appearance
in the constituencies to weaken the hitherto firmly based local
nature of British politics. The system of politics itself became
the object of the several reform movements which characterized the English scene at this time. Such developments are
by now familiar to all students of the period. What needs clari-
fication amidst these simultaneous and interacting trends is
the status of the Rockingham Whigs as a party and their relationship to these wider movements in British society. To
what extent can the Rockingham party be regarded as an improvement upon earlier forms of political connection and
with what justification can historians speak of 'the rise of
party' in Britain in this period?

Earlier in the century 'party' and 'opposition' had been ambiguous and ill-formed elements in political life. It was for
long unthinkable, in some sense unconstitutional, for members of opposition to force themselves on the king. And to oppose measures for the sake of opposing them was thought to
introduce divisions and dissensions into Parliament which
destroyed its role as a deliberative assembly and made it difficult for members to exercise their own judgement on particular measures.[2] Yet the 18th-century attitude to opposition was

[2] See the interesting paper 'On Opposition' by Speaker Onslow in *H. M. C.
Onslow*, pp. 458–73. For an interesting discussion of the theoretical difficulties
of oppositions, see Foord, *op. cit.*, pp. 103–9.

somewhat more complex and subtle than has sometimes been allowed.

Connection with the reversionary interest was not the only, and probably not the major, factor which facilitated the practice of opposition in these years.[3] The much-vaunted contemporary antipathy towards party and opposition began to lapse after 1730 when Jacobitism tended to lose its political influence.[4] The long ministry of Walpole almost inexorably bred an opposition which, disunited in many particulars though it was, attained a certain coherence and consistency of personnel. Against the practical manifestations of the development of parliamentary opposition can be set the beginnings of the theoretical enquiry into the nature and functions of opposition which acquired its impetus from Bolingbroke and its elaboration in the hands of Burke. Notions of party government and legitimate opposition could scarcely be reached until contemporary attitudes towards party were effectively challenged. Edmund Burke attempted to provide the Rockingham Whigs with a philosophy and a distinctive ideological basis. Not that his ideas were entirely novel.[5] What lends his theories particular importance is the fact that his *Thoughts on the Cause of the Present Discontents* (1770) were actually intended to provide the Rockinghams with their own creed and justification. Shortly before publication, Rockingham expressed the hope that the pamphlet would 'tend to form and to unite a party upon real and well founded principles'.[6] The party leaders clearly felt the need to present to the public (and to their own supporters) a vindication of the rectitude of their recent public activities and an expression of the uniqueness of their own party.

[3] Mr Owen argues (*The Rise of the Pelhams*, p. 63), that the importance of the heir-apparent cycle may have been exaggerated. Fewer than 20 M.P.s were attached to him (*ibid.*, p. 79) and most opposition members had no connection with him at all.

[4] P. Campbell, 'An Early Defence of Party', *Political Studies*, III, pp. 166–7; C. Robbins, 'Discordant Parties', *Political Science Quarterly*, 73 (1958), pp. 505–29; J. Owen, *The Rise of the Pelhams*, pp. 62–3.

[5] For Burke's debt to earlier Whig theory, see Foord, pp. 311–15.

[6] Rockingham to Burke, 15 October 1769, *The Correspondence of Edmund Burke, 1768–74*, ed. L. Sutherland, Cambridge University Press, 1960, p. 92. See also Rockingham's letter to Burke of 4 November 1769 (*ibid.*, p. 104): 'I know pretty well from conversations I have had with several – that the Idea totally corresponds as much with their *present sentiments*, as it does with all their *past conduct*.'

This can only be done by shewing the ground upon which the Party stands, and how different its Constitution, as well as the persons who compose it are from the Bedfords and Grenvilles, and other knots who are combined for no public purpose; but only as a means of furthering with joint strength, their private and individual advantage.[7]

Drafts of the work were passed around the leading members of the party until Burke could proudly state: 'It is the political Creed of our party.'[8] As such, the pamphlet, indeed, Burke's thinking in general on opposition, did not provide an exhaustive and systematic elaboration of its possibilities. Nevertheless, there is much interesting material to be gleaned from the *Thoughts* which demonstrates his concept of an opposition's role and aims.

'PARTY' AND 'OPPOSITION'

Burke identified party with opposition. Not only did he commend the Rockingham opposition as the only party in opposition but he saw that any opposition must be a united party. The party must be united in its fundamental principles because the normal course of public business depended on 'some great *leading general principles* in Government' and thus men of the same party might be expected to be of the same opinion 'at least nine times in ten'.[9] Opposition need not be restrained by timidity in its proceedings. It had a clear political objective to pursue and should follow 'every just method to put the men who hold their opinions into such a condition as may enable them to carry their plans into execution, with all the power and authority of the State'.[10] But this raised further problems. Burke realized that the Rockinghams were too few in number to stand alone in office and he was perforce driven to admit the necessity of 'healing coalitions' so long as they were not led or outbalanced 'in office or in council, by those who contradict

---

[7] Burke to Rockingham, 29 October 1769, *ibid.*, pp. 100–2.

[8] Burke to Shackleton, 6 May 1770, *ibid.*, p. 136. In spite of the strictures of J. Brooke (*The Chatham Administration*, pp. 233, 275–6), there are remarkably few instances of party men repudiating Burke's views.

[9] *The Works of the Rt. Hon. Edmund Burke*, 2 vols, 1834, I, p. 152. *Thoughts on the Cause of the Present Discontents.*

[10] *Ibid.*, p. 151.

the very fundamental principles' of the party and provided
that the coalitions did not bring with them 'the unreconciled
principles of the original discord of parties', that is, the King's
Friends.[11] Nor should the coalition accept that cabinet offices
should be equally shared. The opposition should aim at 'having the great strongholds of government in well united hands
... the great offices of deliberation and execution'.[12]

This is not to say that Burke was expounding anything like
the 19th-century theory of alternative governments. Still less
can he be depicted as the prophet of the modern two-party
system. He was, in fact, distressed, when, in the last decade of
the century politics came to be polarized between the ministry
and the Foxite opposition 'and that there appears a sort of
necessity of adopting the one or the other of them, without
regard to any public principle whatsoever. This extinguishes
party as party.'[13] What, then, is the nature of Burke's concepts
of party and opposition? He did not envisage them as permanent elements in the political life of the nation. Indeed his
concept of opposition is, like Bolingbroke's, somewhat self-
destructive for when the 'Present Discontents' had finally
been cured by the admission to office of the virtuous men of
the Rockingham party, there would be no need of opposition.
Party was simply an efficient instrument for curing temporary
ills in the nation.[14] Thus Burke's doctrine of opposition is
neither a political doctrine nor a fully developed body of
ideas.

In truth, Burke was not concerned with pioneering a novel
system of constitutional practice. He did not think about politics in terms of party and opposition. His initial postulate was
that politics concerned morality. Therefore much of his discussion of the 'Present Discontents' rests upon a moral basis
and his denunciations of the court system are charged with
ethical imputations. Thus the 'precipitate degeneracy' of public life could only be checked by 'an habit of life and communication of counsels with the most public spirited men of the

11 *Ibid.*
12 *Ibid.*, I, p. 119. *Observations on ... a Late State of the Nation.*
13 Burke to Fitzwilliam, 2 September 1796, Wentworth Woodhouse MSS.
Burke I. Sheffield.
14 'It is not every conjuncture which calls with equal force upon the activity
of honest men; but critical exigencies now and then arise ...' *Works*, I, p. 152.
(*Thoughts ...*)

age'.[15] On a more profound level, however, lay Burke's conviction that it was a moral imperative to uphold the form of
government established by the revolution settlement. The
principles and methods of the King's Friends were going far
towards bringing it into disrepute among the people. It was
the sacred function of the aristocracy to preserve the fruits of
the revolution and Burke, of course, believed that the Rockingham Whigs had inherited this trust. Their party was the refuge
of 'the ancient and tried usages of the kingdom' and here Burke
intimates his awareness of an immemorial and prescriptive
constitution which it is sacrilege to touch.[16] Ultimately, it was
upon considerations such as these that Burke rested his theory
of opposition and party.

The fact that Burke was occupied with the moral function
of party meant that he gave insufficient attention to problems
of practical politics and constitutional experiment. Logic, for
example, was clearly leading him to divest the crown of its
prerogative of appointing ministers yet he never faced the
problem squarely. Far from accepting that there must be an
inevitable conflict between a party administration and the
crown, Burke blandly assumed that the court would soon learn
the error of its ways and surrender without demur the exercise
of its prerogatives to the Rockingham party.[17] Although he
advocated party principles he put forward no alternative party
programme. Still less could he conceive of the possibility that
the party should be strengthened by efficient organization or
by new institutional and financial procedures. Although he
was interested for a time in forging a connection between the
Rockinghams and the merchants of the City of London[18] he
could not envisage that the party might strengthen itself on a
nation-wide level by the creation of links between itself and
the people. Indeed, although he might assert, in the 1770s, that
government rested upon the consent of the people, he was
fiercely suspicious of public opinion. His position is best epito-

[15] *Ibid.*, I, p. 120. *Observations on . . . a Late State of the Nation.*

[16] Burke to Weddell, 31 January 1792, *Correspondence of Edmund Burke*,
eds. Earl Fitzwilliam and Sir R. Rourke, 4 vols, 1852, III, p. 388; *Works*, I,
pp. 220–1, Letter to the Sheriffs of Bristol, 1777; J. A. Pocock, 'Burke and the
Ancient Constitution', *Historical Journal*, III, no. 2, 1960, pp. 125–43.

[17] *Works*, I, pp. 152–3, *Thoughts . . .*

[18] L. Sutherland, 'Edmund Burke and the first Rockingham Ministry',
English Historical Review, XLVII, pp. 46–70.

mized in his speech on Economical Reform in 1780 when he
told the Commons: 'I cannot indeed take upon me to say, I
have the honour *to follow* the sense of the people. The truth is,
I met it on my way, while I was pursuing their interest according to my own ideas.' This suspicious attitude to the people
followed perhaps from the aristocratic nature of the Rockingham party and Burke's essentially modest place within it but
it was grounded, too, upon his doctrine of representation,
which, in its turn, rested upon Burke's attitude towards
government and society. Not only was the House of Commons
a representative assembly. As he wrote in the *Thoughts*:

> The King is the representative of the people; so are the Lords;
> so are the Judges. They are all trustees for the people, as well
> as the Commons ... A popular origin cannot therefore be the
> characteristical distinction of a popular representative, this
> belongs equally to all parts of Government, and in all forms.[19]

Burke argued that forms of government and political practice
evolve through the ages to accommodate the temper, the social
and civic habits of the people and the social structure of the
nation. He wished to restore the 'ancient and tried usages' of
the constitution through the interposition of party, not to
change those usages by allowing the people to participate
directly in politics. Public opinion might occasionally serve to
support and justify the conduct of the opposition but there
need be no necessary connection between the two. Party was
a security for the rights of the people. Burke had thus no intention of bringing the people within the ambit of party and
opposition.

THE INFLUENCE OF CHATHAM

By identifying party with opposition, Burke identified opposition with a concept which was not only socially exclusive – and
thus static rather than dynamic – but politically distinctive.
Most contemporary politicians would have rejected Burke's
doctrines, ill-formed and tentative though they were. The
loyalist notions of Lord North and his friends represented the
older 18th-century attitude towards politics and, ensconced
in power, they naturally felt no pressure to reformulate or

[19] *Works*, I, pp. 140, *Thoughts* ...

even to examine those beliefs and practices. But Burke's ideas
were not even typical of 'the Opposition' of the 1770s. For the
prestige, though not the numerical parliamentary following, of
Lord Chatham made his ideas something of a force to be
reckoned with in contemporary politics. Their very incompatibility with those of the Rockingham Whigs goes some way
towards explaining why the two wings of the opposition to
North were rarely able to co-operate. Chatham himself was a
man who did not suffer 18th-century politicians gladly. He always wanted the first, and preferably most conspicuous, place
for himself. He refused to help the Rockinghams during their
short-lived ministry of 1765–66 although they went out of their
way to please him by way of personal favour and in their public policy.[20] And although it may be an exaggeration to speak
of a Chathamist philosophy of politics, his ideas and behaviour
suggest a certain consistency. Superficially, his political attitudes seem to amount to a projection of his own personality.
One of his cardinal beliefs was that planned combination in
politics was always to be avoided. On particular measures, on
which politicians were agreed, they might concert their efforts
but once the issue had passed there must be no standing commitment between them. Chatham accepted the 18th-century
platitudes concerning the conscience of the individual politician and his right to retain his freedom of action and thought.
Burke, on the other hand, assumed that combination was not
only desirable but inevitable in the common run of politics.
But Chatham, like Burke, never went so far as to divest the
monarchy of its prerogative of appointing ministers. Once
they were appointed however, Chatham demanded the full
exercise of the prerogative in subsequent appointments and in
the formulation of policy. In a sense he went further than
Burke in this respect, but he seems to have envisaged this not
in general political terms but in terms of his own use of power.
Burke believed that a party ministry would take power from
the monarchy. Chatham was simply too proud and self-willed
to allow a rival authority to challenge his own. His beliefs,
whatever their motivation, did not die with him. They were
adopted by Shelburne and inherited by Pitt the Younger and
thus they proved to be a force in politics at just that time when

[20] Burke remarked that the ministry 'was removed upon a plan settled by the
Earl of Chatham', Works, I, p. 75: A Short Account of a Late Administration.

Burke's doctrine of party was struggling to gain acceptance.
Because they were far less obnoxious to the king than the
Rockinghams' faintly antimonarchical sentiments, George III
was forced to acquiesce in their adoption. Thus Chathamite
political notions, translated into practice, proved to be incompatible with the beliefs and practices of the Rockingham
Whigs.

Personal factors counted for much, too. Shelburne had been
an ally of the detested Bute in 1762, a sin never to be forgiven
by any Rockinghamite. The personal animosity which persisted between himself and Fox was particularly bitter.[21] The
co-operation between the Rockingham and the Shelburne
Whigs on issues such as the Petitioning Movement, when Shelburne had wished to go much further along the road to constitutional reform by advocating the reform of Parliament as
well as Economical Reform, only served to reveal further discord between the two groups in the late 1770s. All the more
galling for the Rockinghams, then, that when North's ministry
fell, necessity brought them into office in uneasy alliance with
Shelburne. The king would not have Rockingham alone in
1782 and Shelburne knew that he could not stand without the
Rockinghams. There was in fact a wide measure of agreement
between the two groups – on Economical Reform and American independence they stood together. Yet differences in their
fundamental attitudes to politics persisted. Although contemporaries tended to interpret the constitutional crisis of 1782 as
a struggle between the king and the Rockinghams over the
prerogative of appointing ministers, the Rockinghams were, in
fact, reluctant to press this issue too far. They allowed the king
some room for manoeuvre and hence Shelburne became the
joint head of the administration with Rockingham. The Rockinghams, indeed, were outnumbered in the cabinet by a combination of Shelburne Whigs and King's Friends.

It was not long before angry disputes erupted on matters of
policy and constitutional practice. The Rockinghams were
suspicious of Shelburne's proximity to the king and they took
umbrage at his apparent willingness to distribute offices without reference to his cabinet colleagues. Shelburne told Leeds
that he 'could not bear the idea of a *round-robin* administration, where the whole cabinet must be consulted for the dis-

[21] J. Norris, *Shelburne and Reform*, London, 1963, pp. 8, 96.

posal of the most trifling employments'.[22] Shelburne did not
share the Rockinghams' solicitousness for cabinet solidarity,
the value of which Burke had recognized and which the structure of the Rockingham–Shelburne administration had so
patently violated. The death of Rockingham on 1 July 1782
gave the king his opportunity to name Shelburne as First Lord
of the Treasury but one may well doubt if the administration
would have lasted much longer had the Marquis lived.
Though Fox and several Rockinghams resigned, the party
survived intact but it was clearly unable to force the king's
hand again. In plain terms, a majority of members in Parliament were prepared to support the minister of the king's
choice. Clearly, the Rockinghams, in their hour of victory, had
depended for their survival in office upon the king's temporary
acquiescence and upon the life of their leader rather than
upon any self-sufficiency of their own.

BURKE'S DISAPPOINTMENT

Burke's plan for a party administration had clearly not been
fulfilled. The failure of the Rockinghams to achieve a numerical dominance in Parliament and their timidity in allowing
themselves to be outbalanced in the cabinet had led to the
disaster of July 1782. Chathamism had proved to be more successful in practice than the party notions of the Rockingham
Whigs. For much of their failure the Rockinghams were themselves responsible. Throughout the 1770s Burke strove in vain
to rouse them to greater efforts and to make a party of them.
His disillusion wth them antedates their unhappy involvement
with the Petitioning movement, the emergence of Fox as the
darling of the radicals and the beginnings of a division in the
party over parliamentary reform in 1780.[23] His disapproval of
the 'broad-bottom' ministry of 1782 was merely the culmination of many years of despair.[24] Willingness, he once complained 'only defeats its own purpose when given too long and

[22] *The Political Memoranda of Francis, Duke of Leeds*, ed. O. Browning,
1884, pp. 190–1.
[23] Cf. N. C. Phillips, 'Edmund Burke and the County Movement', *English
Historical Review*, LXXVI, pp. 254–78.
[24] Burke to Pitt, Autumn 1794, *Stanhope's Miscellanies* (2 vols., 1861,
1864), I, pp. 45–8.

too liberally'.[25] Disappointed by the failure of the party to
follow up the *Thoughts* 'by a continued succession of papers,
seconding and enforcing the same principle' he advised Rockingham that 'the more you are confined in your operations by
the delicate principles you profess, the more necessary it becomes to push with the utmost vigour the few means you have
left to yourselves'.[26] What Burke really wanted was

a settled plan of our own, founded in the very essence of the
American Business, wholly unconnected with the events of the
war, and framed in such a manner as to keep up our Credit and
Maintain our System at home, in spite of anything which may
happen abroad.[27]

Burke's pleas usually fell on deaf ears. And so the appeals to
Rockingham recur:

My great uneasiness is about our own Corps, which appears to
me in great danger of dissolution. Nothing can prevent it, in my
opinion, but the speedy and careful application of your Lordship's
own peculiar, persuasive and conciliatory manner in talking over
publick Business and leading them [the Rockinghams] into a
proper line of conduct.[28]

In Burke's eyes, the Rockinghams failed to live up to the
ideals and aspirations which he had placed before them. The
lazy aristocrats of the party, with whom Burke's influence has
probably been exaggerated in the past, were threatening the
very existence of their own party by their supineness and indifference. And any analysis of the Rockinghamite opposition
to the ministry of North must, in general, bear out Burke's
own unhappy conclusion.

THE ROCKINGHAM PARTY IN ACTION

The Rockingham party which emerged from the ruins of the
old Pelhamite connection in the early 1760s was in many ways

[25] Burke to Baker, 12 October 1777, *The Correspondence of Edmund Burke,
1774–1778*, ed. G. Guttridge, 1961, p. 389.
[26] Burke to Rockingham, 29 December 1769, *Correspondence of Edmund
Burke*, ed. L. Sutherland, pp. 175–6.
[27] Burke to Rockingham, 6 January 1777, *Correspondence of Edmund Burke*,
ed. G. Guttridge, p. 311.
[28] Burke to Rockingham, 11 January 1773, *Correspondence of Edmund
Burke*, ed. L. Sutherland, p. 411.

similar to other parties of the decade. They all developed aspirations and rudimentary organizations which were not unlike those of the Rockinghams. But, with the exception of the
non-party Chathamite group, the Rockinghams alone survived
in opposition during the 1770s. During these years in the wilderness of opposition they not only retained their following
and maintained their connection, but they demonstrated a
compelling awareness of their own distinctiveness. 'I think we
and *we only* of all the parts now in Opposition are so on system
and principle.'[29] They realized that they ought to remain faith-
ful to the policies which they had adopted during the ministry
of 1765–6. 'We should constantly look back . . . and adhere to
the same line in future.'[30] Their solidarity, some would say
cliquishness, was demonstrated during the negotiations for the
reconstruction of the crumbling administration of Chatham in
1767 when, although willing to co-operate with other connections in office, they demanded that Rockingham should
lead the new ministry. The fact that there was now no heir to
the throne around whom the constituent elements in opposition could gather militated against any union of that opposition. The great issues of the time, Wilkes and America,
aroused passions and raised principles which found politicians
divided among themselves. North's success in attracting the
Bedford and the Grenville Whigs into the ministry left the
Rockinghams stranded in opposition. Now they were the only
connection of any size remaining outside the political consensus which North had achieved and, to underline their
distinctiveness, the party doctrine of Burke put them beyond
the political pale.

Although the political attitudes which the Rockinghams
adopted during the American War might have been deemed
unpatriotic, there was now little resistance, even from minis-
terialists, to the presence and to the activities of a systematic
opposition within Parliament. It was even conceded that opposition might have a useful function to perform within the
existing constitutional framework. Thus the Rockingham
party did not feel constrained to conceal its opposition to
ministerial measures by feelings of delicacy for public opinion.

---

[29] Rockingham to Dowdeswell, 20 October 1769, Rockingham Papers,
Sheffield City Library, *q*. Foord, *op. cit.*, p. 315.
[30] *Ibid.*, not quoted in Foord.

They fought sincerely, albeit for long, hopelessly, to make executive actions responsible to Parliament. They maintained a stable following and refused to enter office without conditions.[31] They demanded that their claims to a party ministry should in some measure be accepted by the king. This meant the Treasury for Rockingham, and wide discretionary powers over appointments to the cabinet and even to the Household. It even meant changes of policy – on Economical Reform and America. George III was emphatically self-righteous in his rejection of the Rockingham programme and continued to regard them as little better than a self-seeking faction.

Indeed, although they were fond of wearing their party label, the Rockinghams continued to betray more characteristics of the typical 18th-century connection than of the modern political party. Although there was a 'Whipper-in' at Westminster there was as yet neither a party whip nor a central party office.[32] Burke acted the part of party secretary at times but his activities were not placed upon a solid institutional basis. At the general elections of 1774 and 1780 there was no concerted opposition campaign. Each patron still preferred to handle his own electoral affairs. Such coherence as the party enjoyed stemmed very largely from the extensive and interrelated patronage of the Whig grandees.[33] In Parliament, the opposition utilized the typical 18th-century minority devices. They never hesitated to divide the House – this was a public pledge of their own opinions and an inducement to party members to register their attachment to the party. They moved amendments to the Speech from the Throne with increasing confidence and frequency, contested elections for the Speaker's Chair (an initiative which former oppositions had not usually attempted) and proposed legislation of their own in an unprecedented manner.[34]

These were developments of degree rather than of kind. They should not be allowed to conceal the very real weak-

---

[31] For their loyalty and consistency in the face of ministerial inducements, see I. R. Christie, 'The Marquis of Rockingham and Lord North's Offer of a Coalition', *English Historical Review*, LXIX, July 1954.

[32] Foord, *op. cit.*, p. 344.

[33] Nevertheless there was a considerable number of members whose attachment to the party was voluntary and based on principle. See I. R. Christie, *The End of North's Ministry*, pp. 107–8, 210–12.

[34] Foord, *op. cit.*, pp. 353–6.

E

nesses of the party for which the Rockinghams were themselves responsible. Few of the lords of the party had real political ability and it was in the hands of this small group of men
that political decisions rested. (Large groups of advisers were
feared on the grounds that they only introduced divisions into
the party.) Each summer the party grandees would retire to
their estates and behave as though the party did not exist.
Communications during the long summer recesses were usually fitful and sparse. Such organization as the party actually
possessed only operated during sessions. Policy would be hur-
riedly elaborated at the last minute on the eve of the opening
of Parliament, the detailed work usually falling on men like
Burke and Dowdeswell whose opinions did not always prevail.
Party policy, such as it was, might not be communicated to
the ordinary party member and, because discipline was lax,
he was frequently not to be found in his seat. Attendance was
usually poor and the minority division figure sometimes
dropped to a ludicrously small total, especially towards the end
of sessions.[35]

Awareness of their own weaknesses sapped the morale of
the Rockinghams and many of the older members found little
virtue in keeping up the hopeless struggle.[36] It was but a logical
step to secede altogether from Parliament (another typical and
traditional minority device), a ruse which the Rockinghams
tried in 1772 and 1776. It misfired badly. The party was never
agreed upon the policy of secession; Lord North's business was
facilitated, public opinion was not impressed and the opposition drifted back to its seats in confusion and despair.[37] Factors
such as these simply added to already existing divisions in the
party and only served to exacerbate them.

It is scarcely surprising, then, that the Rockinghams largely
failed to make effective political capital out of the issues which
tormented the governments of the day and which destroyed
that political unanimity which the 18th century revered so
highly. Before 1776 some had favoured, some had opposed,
coercion of the Americans. Yet this was mere disagreement
over the application of the Declaratory Act of 1766. But after
Saratoga even the Declaratory Act was itself called into ques-

---

[35] Namier and Brooke, *The House of Commons*, I, p. 74.
[36] Foord, *op. cit.*, pp. 342–3.
[37] *Ibid.*, pp. 359–60; A. Olsen, *The Radical Duke*, Oxford, 1961, pp. 35–6.

tion. In the following years (1777–82) the party gradually and painfully brought itself to recognize the inevitability of American independence. Whatever the merits of this policy it did the Rockinghams no public good at all. For its success it depended on the failure of British arms and thus the party could with some justification be depicted as an unpatriotic faction. Nevertheless the party did show a sense of reality in acknowledging the necessity for American independence and it was one of the main planks in the Rockingham platform in 1782. On the American issue, at least, when the policy of the king and North had collapsed, there was no alternative but to throw government into the hands of the opposition.

THE PARTY AND THE REFORM MOVEMENT

The reforming movements which sprang to the surface of English life during this period presented the Rockinghams both with glittering opportunities and crippling problems. There was a very real element of reforming opinion within the party itself and the sudden outbreak of reforming agitation in the country both during the Wilkes affair and during the Petitioning Movement inevitably struck a chord in the hearts of reformers within the party. Rockingham badly needed public support if his party were ever to appear other than an aristocratic clique and here was an opportunity to widen the base of the party's following and to attract the support of that public opinion from the want of which the party had suffered so badly. For their part, the reformers in the country needed the local and territorial influence which the Rockingham lords enjoyed to raise the petitions and organize the movements which would exert such pressure on Parliament as to prevent resistance to their demands. Yet the Rockinghams and the reformers proved to be uncomfortable bedfellows. The reformers were well aware that the Rockinghams' commitment to reform was less genuine than their own and that the aristocrats wished to use the movements for their own purposes, to moderate their demands, especially over parliamentary reform, and to restrain the reformers. The newer reforming movements in the country learned to distrust the Rockinghams, who henceforward became indifferent to schemes of constitutional reform since these threatened to strike directly

at their own extensive borough influence. Even worse, the reform issue gave rise to divisions within the Rockingham party
itself. While the party as a whole stood by its policy on economical reform it was divided on parliamentary reform. Fox
and his *coterie* went to extreme lengths on their advocacy of
such proposals while Rockingham, Portland, Burke, and most
of the other leaders, save Richmond, came out against any such
policy. Thus the Rockinghams fell between several stools.
They neither established a solid body of support in the
country nor won the confidence of the reformers. They
offended the king and much loyalist opinion without doing
themselves any permanent good inside Parliament itself. Their
involvement with the reformers both demonstrated and exacerbated the basic lack of unity in the party which was to
persist for many years.[38]

Fundamentally, the role of the Rockinghams in the political
life of the 1770s demonstrates their failure to adapt themselves
to the changing nature of politics. In truth, they were not a
product of the newer forces coming to the surface. In many
ways they were suspicious and even frightened of them, and
they were unable to come to terms with them. Their status
as an aristocratic party and their implicit assumption of the
Burkeian doctrine of representation account for this failure.
They only attempted to use these newer movements in so far
as it suited their own purposes, within a political framework
which they did not wish to upset but only slightly to modify.
While some developments in the doctrinal and procedural
elements of opposition are discernible there was thus no
fundamental change in its nature.

If its proceedings in opposition indicate the severe weaknesses of the Rockingham party, its policy in the few short-
lived ministries in which it participated between 1765 and
1783 illustrates something more of the limitations which sur-
rounded party activity and party politics in the later 18th
century. At first sight, the Rockinghams seemed to wish to
impose stringent conditions upon the king before they would
serve him. In 1765 they insisted upon the exclusion of Bute
and his followers from the ministry, demanded the repeal of

[38] For a full discussion of relations between the Rockinghams and the
Radicals, see I. R. Christie, *Wilkes, Wyvill and Reform*, London, 1961, and
G. Rudé, *Wilkes and Liberty*, Oxford, 1962.

the Stamp Act and the Cider Tax and insisted that General
Warrants be condemned by a resolution of Parliament. In
1782 they demanded that the king should promise not to veto
American independence, and Economical reform. Moreover,
their insistence on a 'clean sweep' of even minor office-holders
in both the Rockingham–Shelburne and the coalition
ministries of 1782 and 1783 gave the greatest offence to the
monarch.

At the same time none of these administrations were 'party'
ministries in the strict sense of the term. The first Rockingham ministry of 1765 left Lord Northington in the cabinet as
Lord Chancellor and other politicians outside the Rockingham connection were not excluded from positions of power
and influence. Reference has already been made to the fact
that the Rockinghams were actually in a minority in the
cabinet of 1782 and the coalition cabinet of 1783 found seats
for men like North himself, Stormont, and Carlisle. Thus,
while the Rockinghams were ready to alienate the monarch
in their attempts to impose conditions upon him, they failed
to form exclusively party ministries. They thus allowed George
III a freedom of manoeuvre which bore bitter fruit for them
in the long term. They were prepared to push their party
principles so far as to render impossible any prospects of cooperating with the monarch but not far enough to safeguard
their own positions and the survival of their ministries. In
addition, they were inadequately prepared to exercise
supreme power in the state. Few of the leaders of the party
were men of real ability and fewer still had any experience
of the art of government. They proved totally incapable of
dealing with unexpected contingencies such as the death of
Rockingham in July 1782. There was no natural successor to
Rockingham in the party and the death of its revered leader
found its members at a loss as to how to deal with the crisis.
When George III took this opportunity of naming Shelburne
as his first minister, several of the Rockingham Whigs in the
cabinet, but not all, resigned. Only later was a new leader
elected but it was, in fact, Fox who engineered the election of
Portland, largely to serve his own ambitions for Portland was
a man who would succumb easily to his personal arts. While
the party was seemingly content to stagger on, unprepared
for the contingencies of political life, it was deficient, too, in

what might have been expected to be one of its first priorities, its parliamentary position.

Although the Rockingham connection survived Rockingham's death, with remarkably few defections, few, if any, attempts appear to have been made to reinforce or enlarge its numerical following in the lower House. Thus, after the appointment of Shelburne, the party was unable to force the king's hand again. It was this harsh reality which led the Rockingham, or Portland Whigs, as they had now become, into their coalition with North. Much can be said in defence of the coalition. Fox did not mind – as Rockingham had not minded in 1780 – joining forces with North as long as most of the cabinet offices were to be in party hands. North doubtless joined Fox, swallowing the indignity of such unequal terms, because he saw that if stable government were to be carried on then he must ally with somebody. If he did not ally with Fox then Shelburne must. However unlikely this prospect, both Fox and Shelburne had uttered ominous threats to impeach North in recent months. In addition, North saw his 'party' melting away around him and, out of office, it would continue to diminish. Once the American War was at an end, the major source of difference between the Portland and Northite groups may be said to have passed away.

Yet, when all the mitigating factors have been considered, there remains the hard fact that in assenting to the coalition, the Portland Whigs were guilty of factious opportunism in choosing to co-operate with a man whom they had consistently belaboured for twelve years, not merely for his American policy but for the very system of government which had prevailed during his ministry. The quest for office overbore the demands of party consistency and party exclusiveness. Similar short-term and self-interested motives predominated in the connection which Fox established with the heir-apparent in the summer of 1782. By this time there was no pressing need for the opposition to proclaim publicly its loyalty to the dynasty. Nor did the prince act as a 'focus of unity' for the party. On the contrary, the connection proved to be more trouble than it was worth. The party members were always divided on the desirability of championing the cause of the prince's debts and George III was still further provoked by the activities of poli-

ticians whom he felt, not without justification, were responsible
for encouraging the dissipation of his son and heir.

CONCLUSIONS

While it remains valid to speak of 'the rise of party' in these
years we should recognize that concepts of 'party' and 'opposition' evolved slowly and developed gradually. If Burke had
succeeded in laying the foundations of a specific party ideology
to which the vast majority of the Rockingham party lent its
approval, he had failed to push his theories to their logical
political conclusion. Although he identified 'opposition' with
'party' and outlined clear political objectives which the Rockinghams ought to pursue, he was unable to envisage 'party'
and 'opposition' as permanent factors in politics and thus he
failed to pose – let alone solve – some of the most important
problems which an 18th-century opposition had of necessity
to face. While outlining some of the claims, conditions, and
demands which the opposition should make of the monarch,
he was clearly incapable of finding a solution to the problems
raised by the almost inevitable royal hostility to the Rockingham party. Still less could he conceive of financial and institutional developments which might strengthen the party on the
electoral level and which might serve to build up its parliamentary following.

Thus the Rockingham opposition displayed many of the
traditional weaknesses of 18th-century oppositions. Although
one might allow them the title of the first modern political
party, in view of the advances they made on the activities of
earlier oppositions and in view of their indisputable uniqueness among the political connections of the second half of the
18th century, they remained essentially an aristocratic party,
failing to put to good effect the advantages which they enjoyed
and the opportunities with which they were confronted. Their
inability to survive in office for more than a few months at a
time was partly the consequence of the contemporary political
structure. Without the confidence of the monarch and without
an overwhelming parliamentary following, they were the victims of political circumstances over which they could exercise
very little influence. They were, in fact, unready to conduct
anything resembling a 'party' administration and it is, to say

the least, doubtful whether this would have been possible at the time. They were unable to live up to their own estimation of themselves, partly because it was impossible, partly because their own conduct, rooted in the traditional factional mentality of all 18th-century oppositions made it unlikely that they would have been able to transform the political world around them.

Yet 'party' and 'opposition', by their very ambiguity, remained flexible and adaptable notions. The period after 1784 witnessed no further ideological developments of these two concepts. What was needed was a strengthening of the opposition in the face of the almost unassailable ministry of the Younger Pitt. While Edmund Burke retreated further away from the position of influence which he had once enjoyed the function of party reconstruction fell into other hands. Men like William Adam, into whose activities historians have only recently begun their researches,[39] began the essential and long-overdue task of establishing party institutions which laid the party's activities upon a secure financial, propagandist and methodical basis. This second stage of 'the rise of party', with the beginning of national opposition election campaigns and the decline of the influence of the individual patrons within the party, facilitated and developed opposition practices. Yet it was a natural extension of the activities of the Rockingham Whigs and, while it went some way towards repairing the deficiencies of the Rockinghamite opposition it was established upon the foundations which they, and, in particular, Edmund Burke, had laid.

[39] For this topic, see D. Ginter, 'The Financing of the Whig Party Organisation, 1783–93', *American Historical Review*, LXXI, January 1966, and my own *The Whig Party and the French Revolution*, 1967.

H. J. Hanham

Opposition Techniques in British Politics: 1867–1914*

WHEN WALTER BAGEHOT FIRST PUBLISHED HIS *English Constitution* in 1865, it was already possible to regard 'Her Majesty's Opposition' as an established part of the constitution. Indeed, Bagehot regarded it as an essential concomitant of cabinet government, and remarked that a 'critical opposition is the consequence of cabinet government'. Already the folklore of politics was full of apposite quotations from statesmen of the old school about the virtues of an opposition, although perhaps only Disraeli and Derby were prepared to accept the doctrine, attributed to George Tierney (1761–1830) that 'the duty of an Opposition was very simple – it was to oppose everything and propose nothing'.

The chief characteristic of the relations between government and opposition in the middle sixties was, however, that opposition was essentially a parliamentary phenomenon. Leading politicians, it is true, sometimes made speeches in the country, and issued addresses at election times, but for the most part the struggle between the ins and outs was carried out within the House of Commons. Statesmen like Lord Palmerston, Lord Russell, and Lord Derby made little attempt to whip up popular support for their measures outside parliament. They relied on their principal supporters in the House of Commons and the country to do this for them in the localities. Hence, the apparent passivity of Whigs and Tories in comparison with Radical agitators like John Bright who chiefly relied on extra-parliamentary support. Not that at that period opposition was very effective even in parliament. Within the House of Commons the organization of opposition was often slack. Cross voting was common, and during the ascendancy of Lord Palmerston the government often received support

* Vol. 2, no. 1, October 1966–January 1967.

from all parts of the House except the opposition front bench.

The rivalry between Disraeli and Gladstone – both became Prime Minister for the first time in 1868 – gave a new impetus to the idea of a straight confrontation between government and opposition. Disraeli's attacks on the first Gladstone government became a model for all subsequent leaders of the opposition, and the swing of the pendulum which marked the elections of 1868, 1874, and 1880 established in the public mind an expectation that government and opposition should normally succeed one another in office. The importance of the opposition is spelt out at length in the text books of the time, which have, indeed, a surprisingly modern ring. Alpheus Todd in his *Parliamentary Government in England* sets out the functions of an opposition as follows:

The opposition exercise a wholesome influence upon parliamentary debate, and upon the conduct of the business of the crown in Parliament, for they are the constitutional critics of all public affairs; and whatever course the government may pursue, they naturally endeavour to find some ground for attack. It is the function of an opposition to state the case against the administration; to say everything which may plausibly be said against every measure, act, or word of every member of the ministry; in short, to constitute a standing censorship of the government, subjecting all its acts and measures to a close and jealous scrutiny.[1]

The main features of the Gladstone–Disraeli period, however, were (a) the strengthening of party ties brought about by the polarization of politics into two camps – the reforming liberals and the more moderate conservatives – and (b) the development of effective rival party organizations in the country to match the party phalanxes in the House of Commons, chiefly as a consequence of the extension of the franchise to the urban working men by the Reform Act of 1867. Disraeli's last years (he died in 1881) also saw the development of new forms of opposition from outside the two major parties: from the Irish Nationalists after 1876, and from the so-called Fourth Party in the parliament of 1880–5, each of them committed to obstructing the business of parliament. The great period of the minor parties was not, however, to reach its climax until the Liberal Unionist Party (1886–1912), the Labour Party (1900

1 Alpheus Todd, *On Parliamentary Government in England*, 2nd edn, 2 vols, 1887–9, II, 415–16.

onwards), and the Irish Nationalists co-existed side by side.

Much of the most permanent of these developments of the 1860s and 1870s was the gradual extension of the parliamentary parties into the country by way of propaganda campaigns, the creation of local party organizations, and the development of national party machines. For this extension of the parliamentary parties into the country had the effect of dividing every community into adherents of the conservatives or the liberals. Henceforth, the dichotomy between government and opposition existed at the grass roots as well as at the centre.[2] Rival liberal and conservative clubs were set up all over the country to act as political centres like the rival Reform and Carlton clubs in London. Even the technique of parliamentary debating acquired a new vogue in the localities and local 'parliaments' were established in nearly every major town.

LEADERSHIP

Benjamin Disraeli was the first man to perfect the role of leader of the opposition and Gladstone was a godsend to any political opponent. The odd thing to modern eyes about the two men was their curiously old-fashioned approach to the techniques of leadership. Neither approved of a party leader stumping the country (Gladstone's Midlothian campaign was conducted while Lord Hartington and Lord Granville shared the leadership of the Liberal Party). They normally made their public appearances in parliament or before their constituents – Disraeli at Aylesbury market, Gladstone first in South Lancashire, then at Blackheath, and subsequently at Midlothian – rather than before great popular audiences with which they were unfamiliar. Both men from time to time made exceptions to this rule – Disraeli notably in speeches at the Crystal Palace and at Manchester – but they were uneasy about doing so. Certainly as party leader neither man would take part in a popular agitation. Nor would Gladstone and Disraeli give a clear lead to their party on the full range of public issues. At election times they confined themselves to an address to their constituents, which might or might not be taken up by their followers. The object of the party leader was to provide an

[2] For politics at the grass roots, see H. J. Hanham, 'Politics and Community Life', *Folk Life*, 1966.

election cry (Gladstone advocated the disestablishment of the
Irish Church in 1868 and the abolition of the income tax in
1874) not to provide a party programme.

Inevitably both Gladstone and Disraeli saw the House of
Commons as the main sphere of political operations. It was in
the Commons that ministers could be questioned and discredited, where the diminishing prestige of the government
could be measured by the record of the division lists. And it
was in the Commons that speeches were best reported, since
each of the main newspapers maintained a body of high-class
reporters on the premises. It is significant that in that most
famous of all speeches by a leader of the opposition, Disraeli
drew attention to the record of the government in its parliamentary context:

As time advanced it was not difficult to perceive that extrava-
gance was being substituted for energy by the Government. The
unnatural stimulus was subsiding. Their paroxysms ended in
prostration. Some took refuge in melancholy, and their eminent
chief alternated between a menace and a sigh. As I sat opposite the
Treasury Bench the Ministers reminded me of one of those marine
landscapes not very unusual on the coasts of South America. You
behold a range of exhausted volcanoes. Not a flame flickers on a
single pallid crest. But the situation is still dangerous. There are
occasional earthquakes, and ever and anon the dark rumbling of
the sea.[3]

Disraeli chose to attack the follies of the government rather
than to stress the programme of the Conservative Party for the
very simple reason that the Conservative Party as such had no
programme. Official party programmes were a relatively late
development. The programmes offered to the electors by
Joseph Chamberlain in 1880 and 1885 were essentially unofficial and the first party programme as such was the National
Liberal Federation's Newcastle Programme of 1891.[4] Even
then the party leaders and the party managers had grave
reservations and Herbert Gladstone as Liberal Chief Whip did
his best to disembarrass the Liberal Party after 1895 of the
policies it put forward in the elections of 1892 and 1895. The
old dictum that it is the function of the opposition to oppose

[3] W. F. Monypenny and G. E. Buckle, *The Life of Benjamin Disraeli, Earl
of Beaconsfield*, 6 vols, 1910–20, V, pp. 190–1.
[4] On this see, A. L. Lowell, *The Government of England*, 2 vols, N.Y.,
1924, I, pp. 534–6.

and not to put forward alternative policies remained current orthodoxy down to the First World War.

Disraeli was not the only party leader who came to the fore as a critic rather than as a constructive statesman. Party leaders chosen when their party was in opposition were almost invariably chosen for their persistence in opposing the policies of their opponents in the House of Commons. Arthur Balfour was, indeed, driven to resign the conservative leadership by the general feeling that he was ineffectual as leader of the opposition in the House of Commons, however good he may have been in office. His successor, Andrew Bonar Law, at once brought a new aggressiveness to the office, and was indeed attacked for overdoing his criticism.

Bonar Law was technically simply leader of the Conservative Party in the House of Commons and leader of the opposition in the House of Commons. As such he ranked below Lord Lansdowne, the conservative leader in the Lords, and had no automatic claim to become Prime Minister when the conservatives returned to power. This was entirely in accordance with precedent: between 1876 and 1880 Lord Granville in the Lords and Lord Hartington in the Commons had led the liberal opposition; between 1881 and 1885 Lord Salisbury and Sir Stafford Northcote were joint leaders of the conservative opposition; in 1886 and 1892–95 Lord Salisbury led the opposition from the Lords with a front-bench spokesman in the Commons as his right-hand man; and for a time after 1895 Lord Rosebery and Sir William Harcourt led the liberal opposition. In such circumstances there could be no clearly designated leader of the whole opposition, although established House of Commons custom led the press to write of the leader of the opposition front bench in the Commons as leader of the whole opposition.

THE HOUSE OF COMMONS

The procedure of the House of Commons was extremely lax until the great series of reforms which began in 1882 gradually took effect.[5] Until then it was extremely hard for the govern-

---

[5] Cf. Edward Hughes, 'The Changes in Parliamentary Procedure, 1880–1882', *Essays Presented to Sir Lewis Namier*, ed. by Richard Pares and A. J. P. Taylor, 1956, pp. 289–319.

ment to be sure of getting through its programme and individual members could entirely disrupt the business of the House. The possibilities for obstruction were vividly demonstrated in the parliaments of 1874–80 and 1880–5, first by the Irish nationalists Joseph Biggar and Charles Stewart Parnell, and subsequently by Lord Randolph Churchill and his three colleagues in the so-called Fourth Party. Ministers were harassed, and the House was kept sitting night after night. It was not until one leader of the House of Commons (W. H. Smith) had been so worn down that he died from the effects of constant attendance on the government front bench, and the Irish Nationalists had broken in two on Parnell's death, that pressure in the Commons began to relax in 1892.

For a long time before obstruction was a serious threat to the pasage of government business, the timetable of the House had been arranged by the Whips on each side of the House. Ministers and the leader of the opposition in the Commons were indeed content to leave a surprising amount to the two Whips' offices. The order of speaking in the House was usually fixed by them in advance; so was the time for divisions (other than those snap divisions that were rather disapproved of); and so was the attendance of ministers and members. The assumption was that barristers and others engaged in regular avocations must be free of demands from the House until their business for the day was over, that country gentlemen must be able to return to their homes for the meeting of county committees and quarter sessions, and that a reasonable allowance must be made for hunting men and others whose attendance was for voting, not for speaking. As a consequence, the Whips developed a complicated timetable which depended for its success on government and opposition working closely together. From time to time, it is true, there were complaints from backbenchers that the system worked unfairly. One of the outspoken back-bench conservatives in the parliament of 1874, 'Big Ben' Bentinck, complained that only those nominated by the Whips were called upon to speak in the House, and demanded that the Speaker should no longer call members from the Whips' lists.[6] The Speaker agreed to abandon the practice of using these lists, but the arrangement was too con-

[6] G. H. Jennings, *An Anecdotal History of the British Parliament*, 1880, p. 439.

venient for the majority of members to be abandoned so lightly. Without a list members might wait for days not knowing when they would be called. So the lists quickly came back. Attacks also came from the opposite quarter. There were regular complaints from country gentlemen that they had to attend for divisions when they might be racing or hunting or managing their estates. Sir John Dugdale Astley, for instance, grumbles in his autobiography that parliament would have been unbearable were it not for the 'snuggery' maintained by the Serjeant-at-Arms for members who couldn't bear the House of Commons.[7]

The onset of obstruction posed very awkward questions for the opposition. Should the opposition still continue to act in the traditional way, accepting a large measure of responsibility (through the Whips) for the arrangement of the parliamentary timetable, or should they make use of the new weapons forged by the obstructionists? This was the root cause of the differences between the conservative leaders and the Fourth Party in the parliament of 1880–5. Sir Stafford Northcote, the conservative leader in the Commons, was an advocate of the old-established system of consensus management of the House. Parnell's Irishmen he regarded as vulgar hatchetmen from the Far West, who were a present nuisance, but would in time be civilized. For Northcote, the leader of Her Majesty's opposition had a duty to facilitate the passage of measures necessary for good government. By contrast Lord Randolph Churchill stood for the rougher tradition that it was the duty of the opposition to oppose. For him anything that would embarrass the government should be fully exploited. His object was not to facilitate the passage of necessary legislation but to bring the government to its knees. Like Parnell and his followers Churchill was ready to make use of any weapon to achieve this end.

The vital importance of the Whips as the managers of parliamentary debates meant that the selection of a Chief Whip was a matter of first-rate importance. Both liberals and conservatives preferred an aristocrat or a country gentleman or a wealthy manufacturer's son for the purpose, because such men combined high social standing, wealth, and a suave upper-class manner which was difficult for boorish provincials to resist.

[7] Sir J. D. Astley, *Fifty Years of My Life*, n.d., Ch. XXIV.

In normal times oppositions relied less on special techniques
to wear down the government than on the ebb and flow of
opinion in the House. Right down to the First World War the
House of Commons thought of itself as a club where the rulers
of the country met to discuss the country's business, rather
than as a debating chamber, continental style. Those who attended regularly – usually no more than a bare majority of
members – gave as much attention to the tone of the House as
to the business it transacted. Some ministers were constantly in
trouble because the House did not like them: others always
had an easy time because the House trusted them. Some opposition members were effective because it was generally agreed
that they talked good sense, whereas others were disregarded
because they were thought to be of little account. Thus Ellis
Ashmead-Bartlett who was effective on the public platform in
lambasting the government, was totally ineffective in the
House of Commons, first as a backbencher and then as a junior
minister, because his pomposity and futility led to his being
regarded as a buffoon. Nor were successful ministers always
good as opposition spokesmen.

The main charge brought about by the gradual tightening
of the parliamentary rules of procedure which began in the
1880s was a steady increase in the number of party divisions.
This was the inevitable consequence of allocating the great
majority of parliamentary time to government business.[8] It
was a change welcomed by the Whips on both sides, because it
made it easier to keep their men in order. Now that it was
possible to present members with a clear choice between voting for or against the government, members naturally stuck
to their party colleagues. This reduced the chances of a break-
away by small groups, diminished the influence of pressure
groups and served to make life in the House a little more
tolerable. The growing tightening of party discipline in debate
was, however, to some extent counteracted by the steady increase of the importance of parliamentary questions. When
Gladstone and Disraeli were in their prime parliamentary
questions were relatively uncommon, and it was not until the

[8] For government control of the Commons, see Peter Fraser, 'The Growth of
Ministerial Control in the Nineteenth-Century House of Commons,' *English
Historical Review*, LXXV, 444–63, and Lowell, *Government of England*, Ch.
XVII.

beginning of the 20th century that the parliamentary question came into its own.[9]

As the number of party divisions in the House of Commons increased, the pressure on the Whips to put up a good showing likewise increased. Newspapers commented on variations in the vote from one division to another, and a specially bad showing usually produced a rocket from the party leader. In this situation the opposition Chief Whip was often more vulnerable than his opposite member on the government benches. Except by chance governments were rarely defeated in divisions because their supporters wanted to keep the government in office and had to answer to their constituents for any failure of duty. Members of the opposition, by contrast, expected to have more free time, and were harder to keep up to the mark. The best that could be hoped for was a good attendance at certain times on certain days. Even this was difficult to manage. In the 1892 parliament, for instance, we find the opposition Chief Whip commenting 'The fault I have most to complain of is that while the men come here every day and are in force from 5 to 7 and from 10.30 to 12 they are apt to run away to dinner sometimes unpaired and if paired to come back 20 minutes after their pair has expired.'[10] Increasingly, opposition in the House was becoming a matter of turning out the big battalions on certain state occasions.

EXTRA-PARLIAMENTARY OPPOSITION

After the Reform Act of 1867 the liberals and the conservatives set out to establish in the country a comprehensive network of local party associations and of local party clubs.[11] The object was twofold — first to confer legitimacy on the work of the existing local organizations of the party by opening them (at least on paper) to all comers, and secondly, to provide centres of initiative for party activists and their sympathizers. As a result the party divisions in every local community were quickly extended downwards from the local magnates and professional men who traditionally chose parliamentary candi-

[9] D. N. Chester and Nona Bowring, *Questions in Parliament*, Oxford, 1961.
[10] Aretas Akers-Douglas to Lord Salisbury, 19 May 1893, quoted in Viscount Chilston, *Chief Whip*, 1961, p. 247.
[11] For details, see H. J. Hanham, *Elections and Party Management: Politics in the Time of Disraeli and Gladstone*, 1959.

dates to working men marshalled in working men's liberal or conservative clubs. Under the influence of Joseph Chamberlain's 'Birmingham caucus' the level of political participation in the local associations quickly increased until by 1885 both parties had come to expect what is by mid-20th-century standards an astonishingly high degree of activity and enthusiasm from the party activists. This impetus was kept up on the conservative side by the Primrose League into the nineties, when the level of popular interest in parliament and in politics gradually began to decline. By then, however, the new norms of political behaviour had been firmly established.

The chief activities of the new local organizations may be briefly summarized as follows:

(1) To provide centres of initiative from which to organize contests in national and local elections.
(2) To keep party feeling alive in the localities by political and social means.
(3) To evolve local leaders.

The result was to produce a permanent liberal *versus* conservative confrontation in the localities which had to be kept alive from London.

The national party headquarters expected the local associations to follow the clash of parties at Westminster and to provide noises offstage where appropriate. The supporters of the government were expected to stage meetings where resolutions of confidence could be passed with acclamation: the supporters of the opposition were expected to stage meetings of protest. To keep the localities informed of what was required of them, the party headquarters developed special publicity services which were the direct ancestors of the present party literature services. On these they spent increasingly large sums of money starting from a few cheap pamphlets in 1868, running through a series of speeches by the party leaders, and culminating in the systematic issuing of propaganda material that began in 1885. Here the pioneer work was the annual *Constitutional Year Book*, first published by the Conservative Central Office in 1885, which continued down to 1939. This was supplemented by the Edinburgh-produced *Campaign Guide*, which was by 1900 a substantial octavo volume full of facts and figures. Even this was not considered enough, however, and the conservatives also published a number of stout volumes covering all the questions of the day.

These literature services were designed to fan the flames of partisan warfare already kept alive by the local press, which, quite as much as the national dailies, kept political controversy going. Indeed, if one wants to discover what the struggle between government and opposition meant for the mass of electors one has to turn to the local papers. Practically everywhere both liberals and conservatives had access to at least one local paper. In most towns there was a liberal paper and a conservative paper, and papers from neighbouring towns were taken in as well. Many of these papers ran at a loss and were subsidized by their supporters, just as conservative or liberal clubs were subsidized. Most of the small-town papers relied heavily on the national dailies for inspiration. But even this had its advantages for the parties, because the very local papers tended to select material for their leaders from the more partisan national journals, chiefly the *Daily News* on the liberal side and the *Standard* or *Morning Post* on the conservative.

The work of the local associations and local newspapers was supplemented by oratorial forays. For the most part these were organized by the party headquarters to suit local needs. MPs, budding lawyers, and paid speakers were despatched all over Great Britain to spread the orthodox views set out in the *Campaign Guide* and other party compendiums.

The party leaders were divided as to whether or not the parliamentary struggle should be carried into the local councils. In many boroughs municipal elections had been contested on party lines for a generation before 1867, but the party leaders regarded the extent of party involvement in local elections as essentially a local affair. As a result many of the local leaders kept out of municipal politics and by 1868 the quality of councillors had often fallen very low. In Nottingham, for instance, we are told that the candidates nominated 'are generally of opposing politics, but they are not persons of influence or position in the town, and the contests of late years have subsided into a struggle between persons in the lower rank of life who have accumulated a little prosperity, and who wish to obtain a position in the town'.[12] Both Joseph Chamberlain in Birmingham and John Gorst, the first head of the Conservative Central

[12] Cited in Hanham, *Elections and Party Management*, p. 387.

Office, set themselves after 1870 to raise the tone of municipal
politics, and to encourage the leading local party magnates to
play an active part in contesting municipal elections. The
object was partly to clean up local government, partly to keep
the local party organizers on their toes. And both parties in the
next thirty years put a good deal of money into fostering in the
bigger towns ward clubs which could be used as centres of
initiative in municipal and school-board elections, as well as in
parliamentary elections. None the less, the level of party activity in municipal elections remained very variable.

The party leaders were but little interested in local elections
before the creation of the county councils in 1889. The party
managers might think in terms of turning each local council
into a local replica of the House of Commons with the whole
apparatus of government and opposition, but the party leaders
were not convinced that such a change was either possible or
desirable. The publicity which attended the elections to the
new London County Council and other county councils gradually shook them out of this complacency. It was generally felt
that the liberals, without publicly committing themselves to
do so, did try to make party capital out of the election, and that
a good many conservatives had followed the liberal example,
even where the parties called themselves progressives and mod-
erates. As the *County Council Magazine* put it, 'At the first
election under the Act, partisanship has governed the voting
in five cases out of six.'[13] About the same time the national
press began to take a new interest in municipal politics and to
publish lists of party gains and losses. This practice was there-
upon also taken up by the party managers and the conservative *Handy Notes on Current Politics* (vol. 1, pp. 147–8) published a complete list of party gains and losses in 1890. By 1894
Lord Salisbury was at last willing to bow to the inevitable. In
a speech at Queen's Hall in Langham Place on 7 November of
that year, he ruefully conceded that the conservatives had been
mistaken in believing that London County Council elections
could be fought on non-political lines. The time had now come
to fight all local elections on party lines and 'from the highest
to the lowest, to act as a party, and to vote so that our principles
shall prevail, as in the elections of members of Parliament'.
Even after 1894, however, there was a good deal of feeling that

13 *County Council Magazine*, vol. I, p. 65.

it was not quite right to contest local elections on party lines.

The uneasiness about contesting local elections on party lines, which *The Liberal* was attacking, has of course continued down to our own day. Yet in practice, a large proportion of councils has always been run on Westminster lines with a government of 'ins' controlling the aldermanic benches, the mayoralty and the key committees, and an opposition of 'outs' condemned to a minor role. Nobody expected Joseph Chamberlain to share his power in Birmingham with declared opponents, because he stood for a ministerial-style forward policy. Only, as in Manchester, where real power lay with officials, were local councils run by consensus, with the places of power shared among the parties.

ISSUES

There is a widespread belief that Gladstone's Midlothian campaign marked the high point of political awareness in modern Britain. Whether this was in fact the case has still to be investigated in detail, but the Midlothian campaign is the obvious starting point for any discussion on the role of issues in opposition. Gladstone's own position at the time was an anomalous one. He was not leader of the Liberal Party or of the opposition in either house of parliament – that was the function of Lords Granville and Hartington – but he spoke as if he were leader of the opposition, and the Midlothian campaign of 1879–80 was staged by the liberal Chief Whip in the Commons, W. P. Adam, on the assumption that Gladstone would be the next Prime Minister. As a result, Gladstone's assault on the Disraeli government was accepted by the majority of people at the time as the work of the *de facto* leader of the opposition.

The Midlothian campaign carried to its logical conclusion Disraeli's attack on the Gladstone administration of 1868–74. Whereas Disraeli had confined himself to a number of isolated public addresses, followed up by provings and buffetings in the House of Commons, Gladstone opened an all-out attack on the government, designed to secure maximum publicity for a series of speeches which built up cumulatively a case against the conservatives so overwhelming that the electors would be convinced that the conservatives were wrong, both morally and politically, in practically everything they had been doing.

This was politics in the grand manner, and men responded with extraordinary enthusiasm.

Gladstone's 1879–80 Midlothian campaigns made such a dramatic impression on the general public – some regarding it as a sort of messianic visitation, others as the devil's own work – that many contemporaries were inclined to regard it as a once-only performance. Yet this was to underestimate its importance. For the campaign was supported and underpinned by an unrivalled series of liberal pamphlets which set the standards to be followed for the next generation. There was, indeed, never to be anything again quite as effective as *The Approaching General Election: a Political Catechism Containing an Endictment and a Programme*, generally attributed to W. T. Stead, for appealing to the non-conformist conscience. It contains for instance such period pieces as

Q. – What has been its [the government's] Foreign Policy?
A. – Minding other people's business and neglecting its own; employing England's might and treasure to support foreign tyrants; plundering the weak, cringing to the strong; alternately 'swaggering and sneaking', and varying bluster and buncombe by bloodshed and Secret Agreements.
Q. – What is the Afghan War?
A. – The modern version of Naboth's vineyard, with Lord Salisbury as Ahab, and Lord Lytton as Jezebel. A scheme of conquest begun in deceit, executed by violence, and crowned by a great disaster.

One has here the direct ancestors of those splendid opposition posters and pamphlets of the 1906 election dealing with Chinese slavery and the other iniquities of the Tory government.

Where the Midlothian campaign failed was in the follow-up. The reforms promised by W. T. Stead and other pamphleteers were too often stillborn. Gladstone and Stead wished to make parliament work more efficiently. In fact, between 1880 and 1885 it was so frequently brought to a standstill that the entire legislative programme was disrupted. Worse still, the liberal government, so far from bringing peace and an end to colonial wars, soon became embroiled in one of the worst of imperialist wars in the Sudan. Finally, when Gladstone had disentangled himself from these embarrassments, he plunged his party into the disastrous divisions which followed his conversion to home rule.

The great problem for us is to decide whether the Mid-lothian campaign (or the 1906 general election campaign for that matter) made any real difference to the result of the elections which followed it. Most contemporaries were sure that it did, but later observers have not been convinced: A. L. Lowell, the American political scientist, gave more weight to the near-mechanical oscillation of the parties from election to election than to campaigning zeal,[14] and more recent studies have also tended to play down the consequences of campaigning.[15] If men are to be persuaded to change their minds, it must be over a relatively long period of time and not during the short space of a single election campaign.

Emphasis has therefore shifted away from campaign issues, to the cumulative effects of minor shifts of loyalty and interest in the life of a parliament. Or in other words from the spirited campaigning of Gladstone to the relentless exposure of government failures by Disraeli. Disraeli, it is now clear, learned on the opposition benches that most governments destroy themselves and that a successful opposition can do little more than accelerate the process. Cartoonists who showed Disraeli and Gladstone as two pugilists were nearer the mark than those who emphasized the overriding importance of ideas and lofty moral aspirations. Essentially, politics, then as now, was about whether or not governments could in the end do what they had promised to do.

14 Lowell, *Government of England*, vol. II, pp. 104 f.

15 J. P. B. Dunbabin, 'Parliamentary Elections in Great Britain, 1868–1900 . . .', *English Historical Review*, LXXXI, 82–99, and Hanham, *Elections and Party Management, passim.*

Richard Hofstadter

On the Birth of American Political Parties*

William Nisbet Chambers: *Political Parties in a New Nation: The American Experience, 1776–1809*. Oxford University Press, New York, 1963, 231 pp.

MODERN DEMOCRACY WAS CREATED BY THE COMPETITION BE-tween political parties and is unthinkable without them. Since, as Professor Chambers contends, the modern political party, strictly defined, was originally an American device, the importance of his subject, early American party development, is patent. Of course, much hangs on how we define a political party, and if we make the definition loose enough, the American parties of the 1790s had their obvious predecessors in English history. The author asks that we think of political parties as 'broadly based social structures that perform crucial political functions in a regularized manner'. Put this way, the party must transcend the largely personal alliances of factional politics based upon the 'connections' familiar to the 18th century. They are 'something more than mere aggregations of men who share certain points of view, such as the Whig and Tory persuasions of 18th century England were'. By the terms of this definition, 'such parties did indeed emerge first in America,' Chambers concludes, 'and they were the earliest examples of their kind'. Needless to say, they owe some debt to the long process of parliamentary development after 1714, through which a legitimate opposition was at last made possible in British politics, but the extent of this debt is obscure. In any case, the United States, by the beginning of the 19th century, was engaged in a very avant-garde experimentation with oppositional politics. The phrase, 'His Majesty's Opposition' was first used, in a spirit of levity, in the House of Commons in 1826 by Sir John Cam Hobhouse; at that point the Americans

* Vol. 1, no. 1, October 1965.

had had more than a quarter of a century of fitful experimentation with partisan opposition, and their two-party politics was
even then, after the lapse of a decade, being resuscitated. If the
modern procedure for a change of ministry in Britain may be
dated from 1830, the first American precedent for the transfer
of power from government to opposition dates from 1801. If
one is concerned with the development of the popular party
and mass participation in an orderly political system, the
avant-garde character of American party development is more
striking. Popular participation in American politics, based
upon a broad suffrage and intensified in those states of the
union where party competition was keen, frequently reached
remarkable intensity well before the Reform Bill of 1832
achieved its modest changes.

But Chambers is only incidentally interested in questions
of priority. His primary concern is with how the American
two-party system originated and developed, and with what conditions make a legitimate opposition possible. However we are
to assess the emergence of the two-party system in the United
States, it was not a response to political theory. *Am Anfang
war die Tat*. The Founding Fathers did not create the first
modern political parties because they saw the value or necessity of such agencies or understood their functional role in a
modern democracy. Their achievement was well in advance
of their theory, and indeed stood in contravention of it. In
common with many political theorists of the 18th century,
they thought of the political party – when they thought of it
at all – as a nuisance. They spoke often of the 'pernicious' or
'mischievous' spirit of party or 'faction', and its main function
in their political thinking was as one of the various manifestations of human corruption that have to be held in check. In
The Federalist, James Madison defined faction as 'a number
of citizens, whether amounting to a majority or a minority of
the whole, who are united and actuated by some common impulse of passion, or of interest, adverse to the rights of other
citizens, or to the permanent and aggregrate interests of the
community'. He thought of party spirit as one of the diseases
incident to republican government, one of the costs of freedom, and he took it to be one of the primary purposes of a
sound constitutional system to check the ravages of this disease.
His view of the matter was echoed by many contemporaries,

among them Jefferson and Washington. There are a few intimations in the political discussion of the 1790s that some men
had a glimmer of the possible functional role of a two-party
system, but they are exceptional.

Quite aside from their theoretical hostility to parties, the
Americans had no historical models of successful party politics. English politics, despite its party labels, gave them no
example of a working party system, and their own provincial
pre-Revolutionary politics (with the possible exception of
Pennsylvania) went little further in this direction; it was in
the main a matter of shifting factions, family cliques, intermittent caucuses, ruling social élites, or clannish juntos.

But this prevalent suspicion of faction or party stood at odds
with many of the realities of American life – the extraordinary
suspicion of authority, long since noted by Burke and others,
and now intensified by the experiences of the Revolutionary
era; the Anglo-American heritage of freedom and dissent,
which, flawed though it was in legal usage, cried out for extension; and the heterogeneity of interests and centres of power,
which had to be pulled together by some effective machinery of
accommodation if there was to be any nation at all. Perhaps
the most remarkable aspect of the American politics of the
1790s was the rapidity with which opposition emerged and
with which it foreshadowed the future two-party pattern. The
policies of the Hamiltonian system were profoundly provoca-
tive, and it soon became apparent that opposition to an entrenched, brilliantly led, and (under Washington) prestigious
administration would be vastly more effective if it were united
in a single opposition party. The new government began its
operations in 1789, party divisions were apparent to contemporaries by 1792, the electorate had its first chance to choose
between competing presidential nominees in 1796, and in the
election of 1800–1 the opposition had already ousted the
Federalists and had peacefully taken power.

When Hamilton brought the Federalist party into being, he
did not consider that he was organizing a political party; he
was organizing a government, forging an administration out of
the herd of leaderless men that constituted the Congress, and
formulating a policy that would strengthen the state. But this
very policy, though it had the intended effect, was also highly
controversial, and it set the terms for a polarization of political

sentiment. In rallying behind Hamilton's policies the Federalists themselves achieved a rudimentary party which had considerably more firmness than any of the old-fashioned factions – a stable structure with an active and cohesive leadership, performing the functions of nominating candidates and defining policy, of explaining this policy to the electorate, and developing a coherent view of political issues, a fighting creed. It was not a popular party – the task of devising such an organization fell to the Jeffersonians – but rather, in Chambers's terms a plebiscitarian party; that is, it was based upon an acceptance of the necessity of explaining and justifying its actions to a broad electorate whose approval and ratification it hoped to win. Its philosophy was not a popular or ultra-democratic one, and its efforts to broaden its mass base were too little and came too late.

Historically speaking, the normal way of governments in dealing with opposition is, regrettably, simply to suppress it. In this respect the Federalists, so far as theory and intention are concerned, were little better than par. When their opposition began to form, they did not characteristically say: We are a party in power, and they are a legitimate party of opposition who will one day be in power. Their disposition was, rather, to say: We are a government, and they are a disruptive and potentially seditious body of malcontents with a distinctively foreign allegiance, who would bring us all to ruin. This manner of thinking, of course, became dominant after the party contest was intensified by divisions of sentiment that grew up after 1793 in the wake of the French Revolution. (There can hardly be better testimony to the fundamental significance of the Revolution for the 18th-century mind than the fact that the Americans, who were of all people most objectively situated to remain aloof from the ideological debate aroused by the Revolution, became completely immersed in it.) The Federalists' conviction that the opposition was subversive found its legal embodiment in the Sedition Act of 1798, which had the approval of every leading member of the party except John Marshall (who opposed it on grounds of expediency and not of principle). In the election of 1800 the Sedition Act was used as a partisan weapon, but the machinery of prosecution was feeble as compared with the size and heterogeneity of the country. The counter-attack against the measure, as Chambers puts it, 'had evoked the young nation's developing liberal spirit, and it gathered support. It insisted again that a lawful opposition must be permitted to live and act, and this very insistence helped the nation to move from fear of opposition to acceptance of it. It thereby also helped the new polity to survive as a free republic.' With the failure of the Sedition Act, opposition had an unquestioned foothold.

This does not mean that the Jeffersonians, upon taking power, were more than a shade better disposed towards the legitimacy of the Federalists than the Federalists had been disposed towards theirs. It was their belief that the constitution had been violated, that the government had been led away from its true principles, that would-be monarchists had been selling out America's interest to Britain. The very attempt of the Federalists to stifle criticism led to the feeling that reciprocity would not be undeserved. But though the Jeffersonians did not accept the functional role of opposition, or reconcile themselves to its persistence, their conception of how to deal with it was more benign. They did not attempt in a comparable degree to silence criticism by law. (So far as the Federal government was concerned, this self-restraint was entailed upon them by their own constitutional pronouncements; but they were not equally committed to refrain from using the state governments as a weapon against Federalist 'sedition' and they did not altogether dispense with the common-law approach to seditious libel.) As a popular party with a greater following and superior organizational skills, they had a stronger and less objectionable weapon with which to dispose of opposition: they could realistically hope to overwhelm the Federalists with numbers, absorbing the more moderate Federalist elements into their own party and reducing the stubborn remainder to political impotence. In short, their aspiration was to destroy opposition through their own political effectiveness, not to accept its permanence as a fact of political life; and this, almost as much as the conception behind the Sedition Act, was alien to the philosophy of the two-party system.

Thanks to the political ineptitude and the factionalism of the Federalists, the increasingly sectional limitations of their party, and their opposition to the war of 1812, the Jeffersonians had their way. Opposition first waned, then disappeared. The two-party division was followed by a period of one-party domination. But the Republicans had found themselves obliged to continue enough of the original Federalist fiscal policies so that the terms of the first party quarrels became obsolete. Federalism died not because of suppression but partly because what was most valuable in its inheritance had been quietly incorporated into the political framework and the policies of its opponents. By the same token the Jeffersonians justified themselves as a successful opposition by refraining from excessively violent or disruptive assaults upon the structure erected by their predecessors.

When American political leaders once again set themselves to the task of recreating a two-party system in the 1820s, their work was no longer so difficult as it had been a generation earlier. The Federalists and Republicans had left an unforgettable model of viable two-party competition and sound examples of party structures, and the lessons of experience became cumulative. As Chambers observes, the second generation of party builders 'knew what modern parties and a party system could be ... and they had no doubt of the virtue of party ... The new American nation had proved that it could survive and "promote the general welfare" as a stable, modernized democracy in the liberal tradition.' It was ready once again for full-scale party rivalry, this time between parties both of which aspired to be, and were, popular parties.

In his attempt to explain the conditions that made a legitimate opposition and the two-party system possible, Chambers enumerates most, if not quite all, of the propitious factors in the American situation. One of the first of these was a broad consensus on fundamental political rules. Despite their misunderstanding of each other's intentions, both sides adhered to a common republican and liberal Lockean philosophy and shared a strong commitment from the beginning to constitutionalism in general and to their own constitution in particular. Property was broadly diffused, and even such incidents as the Shays Rebellion of 1787–8 and the Whiskey Insurrection of 1794 were efforts by small property owners to protect their property rights, not assaults upon the validity of ownership. Even on economic policy, a rough consensus was reached at a fairly early point, despite the original acrimony over Hamilton's policies. Even before they took office, the Republicans had given up hope of drastically reversing Hamilton's policies ('What is practicable,' Jefferson characteristically wrote, 'must often control what is pure theory'), and their main efforts in domestic policy were directed towards a temperate roll-back of his expenditures and a gradual reduction in the national debt. Of some importance here is the fact that the adoption of the constitution was followed by a period of prosperity and general well-being which worked against political extremism. It was important too that the presence of plural centres of power under the federal system made oppression difficult, and extreme policies had to be weighed carefully against the risk of breaking up the union. To a degree, even the threat of particularism could be made functional to the union. Finally, one must add to these considerations the fact that political leadership rested largely in the hands on both sides of members of a ruling élite who were accustomed to managing affairs and to dealing circumspectly with each other even before the union was formed, an élite whose members had had in common a profoundly affecting revolutionary experience.

During the past ten years the early formation and development of political parties and institutions has been the object of a good deal of new and rewarding scholarship. In many ways, Professor Chambers's book is the most significant. It attempts, more than any other, to stand above the cluttered and confusing details to arrive at an overall view of the political process, to trace systematically the stages of party formation, and to analyse the character of the emerging party structures. More than any other book of comparable brevity, it puts the American experience into a theoretical framework.

Silvano Tosi

Italy: Anti-System Opposition Within the System*

THERE IS NO NEED, PERHAPS, TO REPEAT THAT AS IN OTHER European countries, and especially France, but not in Great Britain and the United States, the most characteristic feature of Italy's contemporary political life is the fact that within its liberal-democratic political system the main opposition is carried on by a party or parties which deny in principle the structure and purposes of the liberal-democratic state, and the values of electoral representation and its institutions. The interchange between government and opposition in countries like Great Britain and the United States is centred around the agreement between the parties to play fair and to acknowledge the rules of the parliamentary process as the permanent basis of the country's political life. But the communist parties, and in the countries where they still exist the fascist or neo-fascist parties, reject these principles and proclaim that when they come to power they will replace them by forms of 'direct' or 'all people's' democracies. This ideological argument about the respective merits of the purely political or parliamentary and the social-economic centralized forms of democracy is at the core of the doctrinal discussion between the communists and the neo-fascist parties, and the other Italian parties.

But in practice, and so long as the anti-parliamentary parties do not obtain the power to alter the foundations of the present system, how does such an opposition work with and within the system? It is on this question, and especially on the underlying one of how the anti-system opposition influences the system that these notes will concentrate.

'Influence' in this context is taken to mean the continuous and pervasive action of the anti-system parties to adjust, alter

* Vol 2, no. 1, October 1966–January 1967.

and disturb from within the programme and policies of the
government in which they take no official share, and which
indeed they attack frontally, but upon which they can still
have a direct and deliberate effect. This is attained by institutional as well as by political means and procedures and it is
under these two headings that we shall look at the problem of
the influence of the Communist Party on the present policies
of the Italian government. Some more critical students of
Italian contemporary politics hold that communist influences
on governmental policies have become stronger since the
socialists entered the governmental coalition. The emotional
and ideological residual influence of the Popular Front mentality, the continuing collaboration of socialists and communists in the trade unions and the impact on the socialist
rank and file of the fact that for the first time in the political
history of Italy their party has come, even if only in a coalition,
to power, might, according to some students of Italian contemporary politics, open the socialist flank of the government and
of the parliamentary majority to a certain kind of communist
influence. This idea cannot be entirely dismissed as there are
inevitably old links between some sectors, organizations and individuals in the two working-class parties of Italy. But to take
this as the only explanation of how the anti-system opposition
actually collaborates with, and within, the system, and of how
some mutual adjustments of programmes and practical views
are achieved, would leave one with far too partial a view of
the entire operation. For its profound and real causes lie in
the provisions, and the current interpretation, of the constitution and of the electoral law, and in the deformation of the
party-system at work in Italy (*partitocrazia*).

THE INTERPRETATION OF THE CONSTITUTION

An outline of the function of the opposition in the Italian
constitutional system cannot overlook the specific conditions
laid down by the main laws of this system. The Italian Republican constitution does not establish, or visualize, a parliamentary regime of the classic British type, in which the binomial
relation between government and opposition covers the entire
area of active political initiative. In the Italian system, the opposition is not one main party which, while criticizing and

endeavouring to amend the legislation and policies of the government in power, challenges the latter with a view to succeeding it, and prepares itself as a 'shadow cabinet' for the responsibilities of power. And neither the government nor the cabinet is the unique seat of the executive.

To deal first with this aspect. According to the Italian constitution, there are two organs which exercise direct control over the government and its actions. One is the President of the Republic. The other is the Constitutional Court. Unlike the President of the USA, the head of the Italian state is not the head of the executive; but he exercises a greater influence than the British sovereign on the government's actions and decisions. He has the right, after consultation with leaders of the political parties and with other personalities, to designate the president of the Council of Ministers, and the right to dissolve parliament. He has some control over the bills and laws sent to him for his signature, and he can exercise his influence by means of his right to send messages to Parliament on certain occasions. In its turn, the Italian Constitutional Court has the authority, like its counterparts in other Western constitutions, to pronounce on the legitimacy of legislative acts and on the conflicts between the agencies of the state; and to pass judgement in cases where individuals feel themselves to have been injured in the exercise of the rights granted to the citizens by the Constitution.

Thus, in the Italian constitution, the government is controlled in some of its basic activities by the President from above, and by the Constitutional Court as the supreme expression of the judicial power, quite independent of the executive power. These relationships, together with the responsibility of government to parliament, are the very foundation of the constitutional system of Italy. But one of the peculiarities of the Italian variation on the classic constitutional system lies in the fact that the holders of these supreme positions, the President of the Republic and five of the fifteen members of the Constitutional Court, must be elected by specially large quorums of the two chambers of parliament, the Chamber of Deputies and the Senate, sitting together. The requirement by the constitution of a specially large quorum, and the fact that in both chambers the Communist Party controls a substantial part of the final vote, renders it inevitable that some

F

form of compromise should be reached, before the election, on the persons who will be elected to fill these posts – a compromise in fact between the parties which fully acknowledge the legitimacy of the regime, and the parties which regard it only as an obsolete form which obstructs the establishment of the socio-political system they propose in its stead.

Should the candidate for the presidency of the Republic be a personality particularly suspect to the Communist Party for his general principles and his attitude towards that party, his election could be endlessly delayed, or indeed totally obstructed, and in any case the entire functioning of the system could be impaired. The candidatures of some, usually two, of the fifteen judges of the Constitutional Court are supported, if not actually sponsored by the opposition. The president and the judges thus elected must afterwards be impartial to the point of taking into consideration, in their deliberations as supreme guardians of the system, the points of view put forward by the anti-system opposition.

Elections to the organs of regional administration could provide a further opportunity for the anti-system opposition to strengthen its influence. These regional administrations were provided for in the constitution of 1948, but so far only four have been established in peripheral regions. The left-wing parties have been very vocal in their demands that regional administrations should be set up in all regions with a consequent economic and administrative decentralization. The merits and demerits of decentralization cannot be discussed here. But what must be stressed is that should an anti-system opposition gain control by means of elections of the organs of regional government, it could super-impose on the perennial conflict of views and attitudes between central and regional centres of power, the ideological conflict between the central, parliamentary regime, and the local, or regional organs of direct administration. In such a situation use could also be made of the provisions in the constitution for popular legislative initiative (granted to 50,000 electors at least) and for the referendum to abrogate laws, which can be proposed by 500,000 electors.

Generally speaking, however, the main source of power of the anti-system opposition, as a parliamentary opposition, derives from the proportional representation system of the

Italian electoral law, and the advantages it gives to a parliamentary minority. The Italian multi-party system would be destroyed if the majority system were to replace proportional representation – presumably only two major, bloc parties would be left facing each other. The effect of majority electoral representation on the anti-system opposition would be to reduce the number of communist mandates and to annihilate the Neo-Fascist Party. But when in 1953 an electoral reform was proposed, which was intended to produce a solid majority, within the system of proportional representation, by correcting it through a *'premio di maggioranza'* (a premium in seats allotted to the party or coalition of parties which had won more than 50 per cent of the votes in the elections) a communist campaign against the proposed law, nicknamed by them the *'legge truffa'* (the fraud law) was successful. The democratic coalition led by de Gasperi was unable to obtain an absolute majority in the election and since then all projects intended to correct the proportional system have been abandoned. The present Italian electoral law allows the political parties to measure with a fair approximation their real strength in the country; but it does not allow any of them to form a government by itself, nor does it even allow the democratic parties together to form a sufficiently solid and lasting coalition.

But perhaps the most characteristic controversy about the Italian constitution of 1948 and its impact on the political life of the country, and especially on the role and status of the anti-system opposition within the system, is that deriving from the interpretation of articles 1 and 49. The former states that: 'Sovereignty belongs to the people who may exercise it in the forms and within the limits of the constitution.' Article 49 reads: 'Every citizen has the right to associate freely in parties in order to contribute by democratic methods to the determination of national policy.' Article 1 offers a radical innovation on the traditional principle of the representation of the people. In the Italian constitution sovereignty does not 'emanate' from, or 'derive' from the people, in accordance with the classic definition of sovereignty in liberal democratic theory and constitutions, but *belongs* to the people as much by birthright as by exercise. This affirmation serves to legitimize such instruments of direct democracy as exist in the present Italian regime. Moreover this interpretation of article 1 can be supported according to how article 49 is interpreted. What is, in this context, the 'national policy' which all citizens may contribute to determine through political parties?

The reply of the opposition, both in its parliamentary and extra-parliamentary activity and in theoretical works by many of its authors, is somewhat involved. The constitution, they say, has rejected the absolute authority of the will of the majority – which is taken to mean the general will. On the contrary, in their view, the constitution recognizes the validity of the will of the majority and of the will of the minority – both wills being the expression of the same sovereign source of power, the people, and thus both equally qualified to take part in determining 'national policy'. The Italian democratic state thus does not rest ultimately on the will of the most numerous, but on the will of all, which amounts to the will of all the parties. To be sure, only the majority party or parties would be qualified to form the government, but this is interpreted as a matter of method, a technicality, since the government can only take decisions and administer within the framework of the 'national policy'. The only government which can be regarded as having true constitutional legitimacy would be a government which succeeded in expressing in its activity the demands of the minority, the 'will' of the opposition. Further arguments in favour of such an interpretation are drawn from the fact that since the constitution requires a higher quorum of votes on such special occasions as the election of the head of the state, the revision of the constitution, or the election to certain high offices it evidently intended a distinction to be made between the usual administrative tasks of government and the broad decisions of 'national policy'. For the latter, the consensus of both the governmental majority and the opposition minority is required.

But interesting as this interpretation of the constitution may be, it is nevertheless false, since it makes the constitution say what it does not in fact say. One of the main provisions of the constitution is that the Council of Ministers is responsible for 'the general policy of the government', which must be approved, after the President has appointed the cabinet, by parliament, that is by the majority in parliament. The policy-making factors are therefore the government and the parlia-

mentary majority which endorses the programme and policies
put forward by the government. In the opinion of the most
authoritative Italian jurists, the expression 'national policy'
thus used in the text, and in the context of the constitution,
refers to the prejuridical moment in the origination of policies,
and serves to legitimize the role of political parties in the
Italian regime. The parties can propose alternative national
policies. But the government in power is free to take or not to
take into account these proposed policies when it presents its
programme to parliament, to which it is exclusively responsible, and from which it expects a vote of confidence.

The role of the opposition, therefore, remains in the Italian
constitution and political life, as in other parliamentary countries, that of checking and criticizing the legislative and administrative action of the government, and of competing for
power through the established electoral procedures. As in all
parliamentary regimes, there is no way of escaping the conclusion that the opposition is in opposition because it has not
secured the majority of votes which would have enabled it to
form the government. And the minority's main function is to
express by constitutional means, its dissent, and to persuade
the electorate to opt at the next elections for the alternative
solutions which it proposes and on which it bases its 'national
policy'. In so far as the opposition is credited with a constitutional role other than the above, it does not derive from a non-
existent and assumed identity between the general policy of
the government, and the 'national policy' as expressed by all
the parties, but from the formal constitutional provisions
which require the participation of the minority in the formation of certain constitutional organs, or in the discussion of
certain issues.

But as long as the basic mechanism of the entire political
system of a country is centred around the principle of electoral representation, institutionalized in constitutional procedures, with political parties competing freely for power, all
those who participate in the working of the system must recognize its consequences for the part which they themselves play
in it. The longer, and the more smoothly the institutions of
political democracy function, the clearer it becomes that they
carry with them their own logic which dispels the ambiguities
of those parties which, while using these institutions, distrust

and undermine them and claim openly that they should be
replaced by, or refurbished into, organs of direct or popular,
non-representative administration. One of the most striking
difficulties which faces communist parties today, in power and
in opposition, is precisely how to bridge the gap between their
former monolithic political doctrine and the more pluralistic
views which they clearly see now that they must accept, if they
are to be considered as modern political organizations, fit to
govern in the complex societies of today. It is interesting to
note that the two communist parties with the largest electoral
following, the French and the Italian, are now, from a doctrinal point of view, though perhaps for tactical reasons, the
furthest advanced towards recognizing the need to maintain
the multi-party system within any kind of social political system. This of course presents them with endless doctrinal contradictions and internal polemics, on which, however, these
notes will not digress.

On the contrary, leaving aside the vicissitudes of the internal ideological evolution of the communist parties in a
multi-party system, these notes should concentrate on the evolution of the multi-party system itself in Italy.

THE NEW LINE OF THE ANTI-SYSTEM OPPOSITION

The history of political life in Italy since the end of the Second
World War and the restoration of the multi-party political
system shows with some clarity the evolution of the concept of
opposition and of its role within that system.

The opposition had no influence, not even indirect, in the
making of Italian politics in the years of the first republican
legislature (1948–53). That historical period, dominated by
Alcide de Gasperi's strong personality, and characterized by
the absolute majority which the electorate gave to the Christian Democrats in the House of Deputies, came nearest in
Italian political life to what is known as the 'cabinet system'
and to the British two-party system. The democratic parties,
united in the Christian Democratic coalition government,
kept the Socialist and Communist Parties out of the sphere of
policy-making, since their robust combined majorities gave the
government a broad basis for its policies and legislation. Each
of the parliamentary parties which joined in the coalition

government was able to express its views in the making of the government's policies, yet these parties found sufficient common ground between them to present a common front in opposition to the more radical programmes of parties not included in the coalition. Parliament assumed the aspect at this time, as was remarked by an observer, of a frontier in a civil cold war. If there were not in fact only two parties, there were certainly two party groups. But the coalition, and the particular relationship between political forces on which it was based, dissolved finally after de Gasperi's death; it was already doomed before, ever since the proposed electoral reform law (the so-called fraud law) failed in the elections of 1953. From that date one can follow the evolution of the new influence of the anti-system opposition on the policies of the system.

From this time on both the monarcho-fascist opposition, which in any case carried but little political weight, and the far more effective and important section of the anti-system opposition represented by the Communist Party and large sectors of the socialist movements, began progressively to abandon their support of revolutionary or insurrectional programmes and methods. Togliatti, the able leader of the Italian Communist Party, realized that the consolidation of the Italian democratic state, internally through its obvious economic and social recovery, and externally through the Western defence system set up by NATO, rendered its collapse and the emergence of a revolutionary situation more and more improbable. He also realized that the parties previously united in the de Gasperi coalition were now unable to find an adequate common electoral basis, and that the Communist Party had now been given an excellent opportunity to attempt a 'legal' entry into the citadel of power. The policy of what the French communists call *noyautage* (infiltration) and of penetration of the institutions of the parliamentary state by legal means then began in earnest.

In Parliament, the *introuvable* majority of the House of Deputies, produced by the 1953 elections, enabled the anti-system opposition to get out of the corner into which it had been driven and to get into the middle of the policy-making ring. First it was the turn of the monarcho-fascists to negotiate terms for the support which they agreed to provide, to enable the Christian Democrats to form their minority government –

an alliance which proved precarious and short-lived. But the
communists and the socialists made most use of this opportunity: they were helped by the impact of Stalin's death, and
of the 20th Party Congress with Khrushchev's secret speech,
which led to a psychological breakdown of the frontiers of the
Cold War. By parliamentary manoeuvres and bargains, the
anti-system opposition achieved its first great victory with the
election of Gronchi to the presidency, since they succeeded in
imposing on the Christian Democrats the candidate who was
not their first choice. And there is no denying the influence of
President Gronchi in the shaping of new orientations towards a
left of centre grouping as against the right of centre grouping
which followed on de Gasperi's death; and it was the case that
this new orientation favoured the further increase of the influence of the communists and left-wing socialists on political
life.

But there was more to come. While the Christian Democrat
Party was paralysed by internal dissensions and the impossibility of obtaining a working parliamentary majority, the communist and left-wing–socialist opposition (the Italian Communist Party and the Italian Socialist Party were still united
by the pact of unity and action) seized the initiative in the
legislative and policy-making field, and urged the divided and
hesitant parliament to adopt measures which should have
been passed long before; and which, though they belonged to
the programmes and ideas of the democratic parties, were now
transformed into successes and achievements of the anti-system
opposition. Thus, to take an obvious example, the Constitutional Court provided for by the constitution in 1948 had not
yet by 1956 been set up. The socialist–communist opposition
took the initiative on this issue, and met with a warm response
from the electorate, irritated by the endless delays of the
Christian Democrats. Although it may have been a paradoxical situation to see the anti-system opposition fighting against
the government for the setting up of one of the most fundamental institutions of the regime, and although it was slightly
farcical to hear the communists dropping Karl Marx in favour
of Benjamin Constant, the fact remains that this was an outstanding success for the opposition. More than anything else
the struggle waged against the obstructionism of the government on this very issue of setting up the Constitutional Court

has served to build up the myth of the Communist Party as the guardian of the constitution — a myth which still survives.

A further phase opened with the coming into existence of the centre–left coalition and the concentration of the anti-system opposition on the denunciation and discrediting of the social classes from which the Christian Democrats draw their main support. As far as the centre–left coalition is concerned, it must be said that its leaders have not, at least as yet, proved capable of using the historic meeting between socialists and catholics to devise a new, organic constitutional policy. Catholics and socialists, the two forces which had both been alien and hostile to the formation of the liberal state of the Risorgimento — and the post-Risorgimento — when faced with the task of proposing new policies for the new political and social structures, have not shown themselves able to cope with the great problems of an efficient modern democracy. The executive power is weaker than in the past because of dissensions and factionalism within the forces of the majority; legislation is haphazard and inadequately prepared; the administration suffers from the intervention of pressure groups, sometimes assisted by the political power-holders, which the bureaucracy has not the strength to resist.

It is in these conditions that the communist opposition has concentrated on the indictment on moral grounds of what can be called the democratic political class of Italy. Parliamentary enquiries, press campaigns, vast stirrings of public opinion on the question of the *mores* of this class have marked this period. Sensational trials and resounding sentences have helped more than anything else to illustrate the charges made by the anti-system opposition against the system society. It would not be true to say that this reflects any penetration of the judiciary by the communist opposition. The communists do not have a great number of sympathizers or adherents among the Italian magistrates and judges. It is true, however, that denunciations by communists (and by anyone else) of certain aspects of bad administration and behaviour has induced a large number of the judges to apply the provisions of the penal laws against some activities of the political class, and particularly of the public corporations sponsored and controlled by the political forces of the majority. Again, the credit for this very necessary campaign for better morals in the higher circles of Italian political society went to the communists, and served to increase their popularity.

But, one may ask, why is it that while this new, and in a sense ambiguous popularity of the anti-system opposition is increasing, there is not a marked difference in terms of political results or in terms of reorientation of public opinion? Where are the great triumphs and successes of the opposition? The answer probably lies in a different sphere from the electoral results which determine the composition of parliament. It lies in the decomposition from within of parliament itself, described by the graphic term *partitocrazia*. *Partitocrazia* does not mean only the increasing assumption of constitutional authority and political power by the leadership of the political parties. This is a phenomenon which is not confined only to Italian parliamentary life, but is perhaps more highly developed in Italy, because, by reason of the small electoral majorities, the extra-parliamentary centres of the parties exercise tighter discipline over the parliamentary groups. But in the sense in which it is more frequently used now, *partitocrazia* means almost the opposite of the preceding interpretation, namely the process of the breaking up of the parties into smaller and less co-ordinated groups, the unchecked struggle of party factions, the capricious alliances between the dissenting minority wings or fringes of one party with one or more similar splinter groups in an opposing party; above all, the phenomenon of the *franchi-tiratori* (snipers), those dissenters within the majority party, who, protected by the secrecy of the vote, direct their fire against the government, and secretly collaborate with the opposition. The *franchi-tiratori* present one of the most characteristic features of the contemporary Italian political scene. *Partitocrazia* therefore is responsible for the weakening from within of the parliamentary parties, so much torn by disruptive cross-currents that they have not enough unity to provide a strong political direction. It is indeed a case of the snake eating its own tail. But it is above all this aspect of *partitocrazia* which renders possible the official initiatives of the opposition. These begin, typically, as minority proposals, pass through what has almost become a pattern of parliamentary intrigue and confusion and end as legislative acts passed by triumphant majorities, in which the votes of the opposition combine with those of dissenters from within the government majority.

Such techniques have been used in vital elections, such as those of President Gronchi and President Saragat. But one should not overlook the fact that they prevail also in the daily course of legislative activity. The vigilant and disciplined opposition succeeds in imposing its own formulations and amendments in the bills brought before the Chamber, which are voted by the kind of haphazard coalitions described above. In the long run this tends towards a systematic alteration of the initial projects of the government – which are in any case not drafts originating from the government itself, but the result of compromise and bargaining with extra-parliamentary organizations. Though not strictly constitutional, such consultation has almost become 'institutionalized', notably with regard to the trade unions. The inferiority complex from which the Italian executive suffers, thanks to the lack of unity among, and within, the parties which support it, has led the executive to adopt the practice of consulting the unions on legislative projects affecting the economic and social life of the country. The bill presented to parliament is what the government has salvaged from its own plan after such consultations. The stronger the trade union, the more influence it exercises during these informal consultations; and the strongest union is the CGIL, the Communist Labour Union. Thus communist influence on legislation is exercised in two stages: communist-dominated unions can bargain with the government during the process of informal consultation with government agencies or departments; and subsequent modifications can be pushed through the Chamber by majorities influenced by communists in the various ways described above. The extent of communist influence on legislation and decision-making is therefore greater by far than might appear on the surface – and while this can be seen to some extent as a process of mutual adjustment and integration within the system, it should also be seen, with greater concern, as a continuous drifting and disorientation of the democratic political forces.

And what of the non-communist opposition? The role of the monarchist and neo-fascist parties is now but slight, and as political phenomena they are in decline. The only important non-communist opposition is the Liberal Party which

could play a large part, both because it can claim full democratic legitimacy, and because its arguments are reasonable.
Yet, oddly enough, the liberal leaders have adopted a position
which reduces the efficacy of their political action almost to
nothing. Unlike the communists, who have deliberately put
aside any maximalist claims, and appear in the guise of a constitutional opposition with no other aim than that of improving the existing system of government, the Liberals have
adopted, in opposition to the policy of the centre–left, an attitude of theological struggle which automatically puts them out
of the running. Hence communist initiatives, introduced in
accordance with the most correct parliamentary orthodoxy,
achieve their object, while the liberal arguments do not succeed in breaking through into the decision-making process. It
may be added that the Liberal Party has not been able, or
willing, to profit from the Anglo-Saxon example of creating
free private associations, such as cultural pressure groups or
other interest groups or leagues of private interests which it
might well have formed. The Liberal Party has considerable
electoral strength, but it carries no political weight in parliament because it is not backed up, as many would have wished
it to be, by an effective and articulated opinion freely linked
with the policy of the party. It is true that the independent,
non-party press, with its great organs of information, is almost
all liberal in inspiration, but in the absence of a network of
clubs the political influence of this press is almost entirely
wasted.

In conclusion, the anti-system opposition in Italy is strong
and influential because the government and the majority are
weak. And they are weak because of an erroneous interpretation, in the French tradition, of constitutionalism; because of
the electoral system; because of the lack of political morality in
the administrative personnel; and because of the lack of cohesion in the political movements which form the majority.
There is consequently a divorce between the 'legal' country
and the 'real' country, which leads the latter to adopt increasingly an attitude of protest. In saying that the anti-system
opposition is strong, we refer really to the communist opposition. It has overcome the setbacks of de-Stalinization, and the
ideological breakdown of Marxism; it has shrewdly taken on
the aspect of a radical bourgeois movement, and taken over

the shafts from the non-Marxist opposition's quiver. The part played by the communist opposition is revealed partly in the constitutional mechanisms, which require its assistance in order to function at all, and partly in communist penetration into the legislative or decision-making process, either by means of the trade unions or through their own deputies.

Gerhard Lehmbruch

The Ambiguous Coalition in West Germany*

ON 1 DECEMBER 1966 THE BUNDESTAG ELECTED THE CHRISTIAN democrat leader Kurt Georg Kiesinger as head of a government formed by christian democrats (CDU) and social democrats (SPD), by a majority of 340 (out of 496) members.[1] The liberals (FDP), with 49 members, were pushed aside into opposition. For the first time since 1930 the social democrats entered a German central government, not as the result of an electoral victory but at the conclusion of an inner crisis within the hitherto existing majority. The CDU whose prestige was badly damaged by this crisis continued to provide the chancellor. This helps to explain why some 60 members of the coalescing parties voted against the candidate. Public opinion oscillated between feelings of relief because of the end of a period of insecurity, and feelings of discomfort in view of an experiment which seemed unorthodox and hazardous. The disputes around the *grosse Koalition* (great coalition) thus revealed the ambiguity of conceptions of parliamentary government as they had developed since the establishment of the Federal Republic.

The constitution-makers of Weimar, in 1919, thought it essential that a strong and stable executive should be vigilantly controlled by a parliament representing all shades of public opinion. Stability of the governing body was to be guaranteed by a popularly elected president (an *Ersatz-Kaiser*) on the one hand and a strong, politically moderate centre group in the assembly on the other.[2] This pattern was, of course, quite

[1] The members for West Berlin, where votes are counted separately, not included.

[2] Cf. Gustav Schmidt, *Deutscher Historismus und der Übergang zur parlamentarischen Demokratie*, Lübeck and Hamburg, 1964, esp. pp. 155–84, 212–20 (on the political ideas of Meinecke and Troeltsch).

* Vol. 3, no. 2, Spring 1968.

inconsistent with the idea of alternative government represented by British traditions. In a country which had just experienced revolutionary class conflict and was marked by
religious and regional heterogeneity, the system of alternative
government was regarded as inappropriate.[3] Moreover, this
concept ran counter to German ideological traditions which
regarded party conflict as prejudicial to consensus rather than
as a prerequisite of liberal government.

Among the factors which contributed to modify this state
of public opinion one may point to changes in West Germany's
party system after the Second World War; to the fusion of
political catholicism and protestant conservatives within a
single political movement, the CDU, and to the subsequent
decision of the SPD not to join a coalition with the christian
democrats but to stay in opposition (at first in the bizonal
Economic Council in 1947, and then in the newly elected
federal parliament in 1949) – a decision which fitted
Adenauer's strategic concept as well as that of Kurt Schumacher. The party system, which before then had formed a
rather complicated pattern of overlapping affinities and shifting majorities, became strongly polarized, and federal elections
took the form of a contest for power between two rival blocs,
with a progressive concentration of votes on the two large
parties. While at first the CDU advanced much more than did
the SPD and obtained an absolute majority of seats in 1957,
the steady increase of social democratic strength nevertheless
maintained hope alive in the left that the opposition party
might finally gain a decisive electoral victory.

It is true that, except for the third *Bundestag*, formation of
a government always implied a coalition. But this was increasingly perceived to be a somewhat abnormal situation, a regrettable deviation from government based on 'unequivocal
majorities'. Traditional admiration for the British pattern of
parliamentary politics grew in intensity as the system of alternative government, once a rather academic idea, began to seem
to offer a realistic chance of political and constitutional development.[4] This applied, of course, to the perceptions of the

[3] See, for example, Max Weber, *Gesammelte politische Schriften*, 2nd edn,
Tübingen, 1958, p. 372; Richard Thoma, 'Das Reich als Demokratie', in:
Handbuch des Deutschen Staatsrechts, Tübingen, 1930, vol. I, p. 195.

[4] This was helped by the evolution of the party system in the *Laender*. The
CDU–SPD coalitions, which (generally with the support of other, minor

170 GERHARD LEHMBRUCH

political system among the élite; but at the same time, mass opinion polls pointed to a growing understanding of the functions of party conflict and of parliamentary opposition. Correspondingly, the idea that large or all-party coalitions should be preferred as representing a higher form of consensus was abandoned in ever larger sectors of public opinion. This explains why the Austrian coalition of conservatives and socialists (knowledge of which was in general rather superficial) was generally regarded as highly objectionable; it was referred to slightingly as *Proporzdemokratie*.

These more recent constitutional conceptions were subject to a hard test by the decline of the fourth and fifth Adenauer cabinets and the Erhard cabinets. The crisis was due not only (as christian democrats would have one believe) to the oscillations of the liberal coalition partner; a major factor was the progressive erosion of authority within the CDU since Adenauer's prestige had been heavily damaged by his manoeuvres in the presidential election of 1959. The majority now seemed to be a rather loose federation of interest groups and party clans which had been integrated by a dominating leader, as well as by economic prosperity and by a political success which had permitted it to satisfy all major interests and thus to strengthen the party leader's authority. The stagnation in the domain of foreign policy since the end of the 1950s, then the stagnation of GNP and the budget crisis in the middle of the 1960s put an end to what might have been described as a 'Pareto-optimal' situation. That is to say, the government was faced with the necessity of making political choices which might frustrate several important groups, be it the refugees, or other opponents to any recognition of the *status quo* in German affairs, the farmers, or the groups interested in social

parties) existed in all the *Laender*, broke up successively, the last one (that of Baden-Württemberg) in 1960. Since then some *Laender* have seen the hegemonic rule of one of the parties; others (such as Bavaria, Northrhine-Westphalia, Hamburg, Lower Saxony) an alteration of CDU-led and SPD-led governments. On the other hand, it was significant that the formation of an SPD-CDU cabinet in Lower Saxony, in May 1965, preceded the crisis of the Erhard government. Since then the great coalition has been re-established in Baden-Württemberg, while in Northrhine-Westphalia the social democratic backbenchers thwarted the party leaders' project to form a government with the CDU and pushed the christian democrats into opposition with the aid of the liberals.

security. The government proved unable to make such choices because the majority lacked a firmly established structure of authority as well as cohesion in the ideological domain. The resulting *immobilisme* of the late Adenauer and Erhard governments created a situation which, in the logic of alternative government, could have been overcome only by a reversal of the parliamentary majority.

However, this reversal of forces did not occur. Neither the presidential crisis of 1959, nor the *Spiegel* affair of 1962, nor the resignation of Adenauer led to a decisive breakthrough of the socialist opposition. In 1961, the CDU lost its absolute majority, but mainly to the benefit of the FDP. In 1965 it succeeded in improving its position again. Even the agony of the second Erhard cabinet only strengthened extremist opponents, while the social democratic vote stagnated – or even regressed – in subsequent local elections. It began to seem doubtful whether, under existing institutional arrangements (i.e. under proportional representation) and under presumed middle-class prejudice against a Social Democratic Party lacking governmental experience and confirmation, any 'alternative' majority might ever come about. This stalemate was aggravated by the strategy of the FDP. Some sectors of public opinion expected it to render possible an alternative majority by changing its coalition partner.[5] But the liberal leaders felt that a majority of their electors would not approve of such a *renversement des alliances* in favour of the SPD. To be sure, they deliberately sought to preserve their identity within the coalition with the CDU, thus further contributing to the dissensions within the majority bloc, and finally undermined the Erhard cabinet by withdrawing the FDP ministers. But as the Liberal Party could not make up its mind to join the SPD in the election of a social democratic chancellor (i.e. to set in motion the procedure of the 'constructive vote of no-confidence' according to article 67 of the Basic Law) the only result

[5] The usual objection to this form of alternative government on a merely parliamentary (and not electoral) basis is that it might signify a sort of 'merry-go-round' without authentic political change. But while this objection may well be true for coalition reshuffling in the Weimar Republic or in the French Fourth Republic it overlooks the fact that in the Federal Republic the dominant party of the coalition would have changed, as would have most holders of ministerial office. This might well signify a major political upheaval.

of this withdrawal was to put the Erhard cabinet into the position of a minority government.[6]

Now it is significant that continuation of a minority government seems not to have been seriously considered.[7] To be sure, with the existing political constellation the elaborate constitutional provisions for minority government might possibly not have worked.[8] Moreover, if we correctly interpret the state of public opinion at that time,[9] a cabinet lacking the support of a parliamentary majority would probably have been rather unpopular. One might argue that a minority cabinet would have been more consistent with the ideal of alternative government than a great coalition because, in default of a working majority–minority confrontation in parliament, this expedient would still preserve the chance of political change. But this argument ran counter to another – and perhaps prevailing – principle of contemporary political thought in West Germany, namely, the high value placed on governmental stability. In 1966 even observers who had earlier considered an eventual CDU–SPD coalition as contrary to an important rule of the political game, felt some relief because this alliance might prevent a period of political instability.

JUSTIFYING THE COALITION

It is true that spokesmen of both great parties presented the 'great coalition' not as a rupture with the idea of alternative government but as an intermediate stage on the way to its achievement. The coalition was to be a provisional arrangement which aimed at creating the conditions of an authentic

[6] SPD and FDP tried to circumvent article 67 by passing a resolution of the (negative) *Bundestag* majority demanding that the chancellor should himself put the question of confidence according to article 68. This constituted an implicit vote of no-confidence but was considered unconstitutional by Chancellor Erhard.

[7] The FDP ministers were not replaced, and Chancellor Erhard stated his intention to secure a majority in parliament again.

[8] According to articles 68 and 81, a minority government may legislate with the support of the Federal Council, but, leaving aside the question whether a sufficient number of *Laender* governments would have lent their support to such 'emergency legislation', the procedure would have supposed the consent of the Federal President who was known to advocate the formation of a great coalition.

[9] In the absence of reliable empirical data we are reduced to conjectures which are based on more or less subjective impressions.

two-party system. Hence CDU and SPD agreed upon introducing some sort of majority representation beginning with the elections of 1973.[10] To put it more simply the leaders of both parties wanted to eliminate the uncertainty which the existence of the FDP brings into parliamentary life because of the alleged tendency of this party to trade its support in exchange for exaggerated concessions from the larger parties, and, in a more general fashion, arising from the bargaining processes inevitable in coalition. The promoters of the great coalition, the Social Democratic Party manager Wehner, the Conservative Catholic Baron Guttenberg, and the 'Social Catholic' Lücke, agreed on this point.[11] They agreed all the more since both parties expected to have a better chance to win a majority with an electoral law based on the principle of majority representation. With such an electoral law the CDU would probably have obtained an absolute majority in 1965 and would have escaped the necessity of an alliance with the liberals. On the other hand social democratic hopes of gaining an effective majority under proportional representation are rather slim in the near future, and even if the SPD won a relative majority of seats it would find it difficult to find a reliable coalition partner. But its actual numerical inferiority to the CDU might be compensated – at least with the classical single-ballot system of majority representation – by a bias in its favour arising from the overwhelming (and hence useless) christian democratic majorities in some parts of the country.[12]

Additional strategic considerations seemed to justify the great coalition as a transistory stage on the way to an authentic two-party contest. For the CDU, it might mean the opportunity to recover from the inner crisis of the previous years and thus to face the ensuing elections in a better condition. For some

[10] The CDU wanted to introduce majority representation for the elections of 1969. This was refused by the social democrats on the grounds that members actually sitting should not legislate on a question which concerned the eventual continuation of their mandate. Furthermore no agreement was made upon a specific system of majority elections.

[11] These three personalities already tried during the *Spiegel* crisis of 1962 to prepare a great coalition, but at that time the SPD refused to follow Wehner.

[12] Cf. Rudolf Wildenmann, Werner Kaltefleiter, Uwe Schleth, 'Auswirkungen von Wahlsystemen auf das Parteien- und Regierungssystem der Bundesrepublik', in Erwin K. Scheuch, Rudolf Wildenmann (eds), *Zur Soziologie der Wahl, Kölner Zeitschrift für Soziologie und Sozialpsychologie*, Sonderheft 9, Köln and Opladen, 1965, pp. 74–112.

SPD leaders, a coalition meant that the christian democrats
had ceased to regard the advancement of social democrats to
positions of governmental responsibility as (in Adenauer's
words) the imminent 'ruin of Germany'. The party got the
opportunity to prove its political maturity and governmental
capacity, and this was considered to be an important condition
in order to compete for power with equal chances of success. In
short, for many in the CDU as well as for the SPD leadership a
temporary alliance of both parties fitted well into their strategy
which in both cases aims in the long run at achieving a monopoly of governmental power for the whole legislative period.
Hence, the great coalition could be quite consistent with the
idea of alternative government.

Yet there are other motivations which, without being given
the same publicity, point rather in the opposite direction. This
is most clearly the case of those socialists who, in view of the
'waning of opposition in parliamentary regimes',[13] see in the
great coalition a pattern more adequate to the necessities of
modern democracy than alternative government. An important SPD member of the Bundestag, for example, argued some
years ago that − considering the concentration of political
power in the hands of the administration − a parliamentary
opposition no longer had the means to control the holders of
power efficiently, and that a coalition might re-establish some
sort of separation of powers in which parliamentary control of
the executive might gain new vigour. 'The existing power
cartel of parliamentary majority, government and administration would thus be overcome.'[14] The same author then
pointed to the fact that all-party government is an established
rule in West German local government. This brings us to an
important aspect of our problem: large sectors of the political
system preserve traditions of proportional participation which
date back to a situation when alternative government was a
notion alien to German political thought. The law provides
for proportional representation of political parties in local
executive authorities, while in parliament not only presidents

[13] See the article by Otto Kirchheimer, in *Social Research*, vol. 24, 1957, pp.
127–156.
[14] Ulrich Lohmar, *Innerparteiliche Demokratie. Eine Untersuchung der Ver-
fassungswirklichkeit politischer Parteien in der Bundesrepublik Deutschland*,
Stuttgart, 1963, p. 140. The author of this doctoral dissertation in sociology is
a member of the executive of the SPD parliamentary party.

and vice-presidents of the assembly but also those of specialized committees are elected by *Proporz* in virtue of the standing orders or of convention. The same is virtually true of the judges of the Constitutional Court. Public institutions of political education (such as the *Bundeszentrale fuer politische Bildung*, an agency under the administrative jurisdiction of the Federal Minister of Interior) are placed under all-party supervisory boards, and the supervisory boards of radio and television are formed by representatives of the political parties, large interest groups and churches in order to establish the political neutrality of these media.[15] Of course such institutional arrangements need not be incompatible with a competitive party system, as is demonstrated by the fact that local executive authorities in Great Britain (but not in France or Italy) are likely to be composed by representatives of the rival parties according to their importance in local councils. But in Germany they can be regarded as an older stratum of political culture in which party co-operation is viewed as a condition of impartial, hence just and rational decision-making,[16] which has only recently been partially overlaid by a stratum constituted of the above-mentioned trends towards alternative government. On the whole, the political system of West Germany may be characterized as a mixed system which combines elements of party competition and majority rule with elements of proportional division of influence and of bargaining, and its *Proporz* segments keep alive political attitudes which may regain preponderance on the level of national policy-making too.

The ambivalent motivation of the formation of the great coalition appears most clearly in another argument frequently put forward by its advocates: any government resting only upon a small majority in parliament and facing a strong opposition might be unable to carry out certain fundamental and

[15] The Federal Constitutional Court, in its decision condemning Chancellor Adenauer's attempt to establish a governmental television network, ruled that, as a consequence of the constitutional guarantee of liberty of the press, 'all relevant forces should be represented in the bodies governing radio stations'. (Judgement of 28 February 1961, in *Entscheidungen des Bundesverfassungsgerichts*, vol. 12, 1962, pp. 262 ff.)

[16] These traits of the political culture are dominant in Switzerland, and play an important role in Austria. Cf. Gerhard Lehmbruch, *Proporzdemokratie. Politisches System und politische Kultur in der Schweiz und in Oesterreich*, Tübingen, 1967.

drastic reforms which public opinion and political leaders tended to regard as urgent. These reforms presumably requiring a 'broad majority' might be, according to these arguments, the restoration of public finances, including the adjustment of relevant constitutional rules; constitutional amendments concerning 'common tasks' of Federation and *Laender* in areas until then under the exclusive jurisdiction of the latter (areas where the action of the *Laender* is considered to be insufficient or lacks co-ordination, as, for example, in aid to scientific research, urbanism, etc.); constitutional amendments on the role of executive and parliament and on civic rights during an eventual state of emergency; perhaps (but this was true only for some of the supporters of a great coalition) even a cautious revision of foreign policy *vis-à-vis* the Soviet Union and its East European allies. That these tasks could only be performed by a 'broad majority' is by no means self-evident. The political crisis was a crisis of the majority rather than of the state; there was no dramatic situation that called for some sort of 'national government'. In the past the socialist opposition had collaborated in such important reforms as the legislation on national defence. The aspirations for a government based on a broad majority may, however, be explained by the peculiar institutional and social conditions of West German politics.

First, as the projected reforms implied amending the constitution and hence necessitated a *Bundestag* majority of two-thirds, negotiation with the social democrats (who hold over 40 per cent of the seats) was inevitable and perhaps could be facilitated by giving them their share of governmental responsibility. However, such reasoning may be contested for it remains doubtful whether the SPD could use its key position to block constitutional reforms as long as it remained in opposition. Since the failure of Kurt Schumacher's intransigent opposition strategies most social democratic leaders were convinced that the electors expected them to conduct what has been called 'constructive' opposition politics. Refusal to co-operate in important political reforms might easily be interpreted as 'obstruction', an attitude unpopular with West German public opinion. Moreover, a strategy of co-operation and bargaining gave them the opportunity to exert strong influence on legislation. The turning point might be dated in 1956 when the SPD participated in the elaboration of legislation on national defence. In more recent times, the party has engaged in negotiations on constitutional emergency provisions. Indeed, in contrast with the increasing polarization of the West German party system, the *Bundestag* has developed a particular style of conflict management in which the distinction of governmental majority and opposition has largely been blurred and public contest of parties replaced by private bargaining among party leaders.[17] In historical perspective this trend towards increased inter-party co-operation in parliament could be interpreted as the prelude to co-operation in coalition government. But it may equally be argued that a great coalition was not necessary as long as pending problems could be resolved by bargaining in parliament.

Things were complicated, however, by the distribution of power within the federal system. Although it lacks the support of public opinion, West German federalism, by the fact that it is a stronghold of autonomous bureaucratic bodies, sets limits to the efficiency of majority rule and alternative government. Conflict management takes the form of tiresome bargaining among federal and *Laender* bureaucracies, party groups on the federal and on the regional level, and interest groups. Constitutional amendments concerning public finance proved difficult as long as a strong group of social democratic *Laender* governments acted in concert with stubborn christian democratic *Landesfuersten* to block the federal government's proposals.

Furthermore, the pluralism of interest groups seemed to raise serious problems for economic and financial policy decision-making. Neo-liberal ideology with its straightforward condemnation of 'pressure-group egoism' lost much of its persuasive power in the middle of the 1960s. But 'organized pluralism'[18] and some sort of *économie concertée*, as they had developed in other European countries, might be difficult to establish under the existing party constellations. Stabilizing the economy and developing a long-run fiscal policy necessitated, on the one hand, that the public authorities should co-ordinate their financial policy (Federation, *Laender*, and

[17] This point has been emphasized by G. Loewenberg, *Parliament in the German Political System*, Ithaca, N.Y., 1966, pp. 393–7.
[18] Cf. Robert Dahl, 'Epilogue', in Robert Dahl (ed.), *Political Oppositions in Western Democracies*, New Haven, 1966, pp. 395 ff.

municipalities) and, on the other hand, co-ordination of the
wage policies of management and labour was also required.
Given the distribution of power existing in the West German
political system, such action can be obstructed by coalitions
formed by opposition parties, autonomous political entities
such as *Laender*, and unions or other important interest
groups. It was tempting to speculate that, lacking the support
of a strong opposition in parliament, such obstructive coalitions
might henceforth become impossible. One should therefore
include the social democrats in the federal government in
order to bring about the collaboration of all relevant holders of
power.

TECHNIQUES OF COALITION GOVERNMENT

Whatever may have been the motivations of political leaders
upon entering on the coalition experiment – they had to count
with a widespread reluctance among the politically active
strata of the population. As opinions on parliamentary government had been strongly influenced by the generally unfavour-
able judgement of the defunct Austrian coalition, it seemed
necessary to forestall any assimilation with *Proporzdemokratie*.[19] Some important rules of conflict management adopted
by the CDU–SPD coalition must be understood against this
background for they constitute a deliberate effort to avoid the
grievances to which the Austrian coalition gave rise. In
Austria, as in West Germany, a fundamental difficulty lies in
the fact that the great coalition works within the constitutional
framework of parliamentary government, which places a high
premium on solidarity of government and parliamentary
majority, a solidarity guaranteed by a rather strong degree of
party cohesion in parliament. While in current conceptions of
parliament it is not so much parliament as such which controls the executive branch but a parliamentary opposition
which controls the government and its majority, in a coalition
this mechanism of control is evidently weakened.[20] It is true

[19] For an analysis of the Austrian coalition system, see Frederick C. Engelmann, 'Austria: The Pooling of Opposition', in Robert Dahl, *op. cit.*, pp.
260–83; Gerhard Lehmbruch, *op. cit.*

[20] The situation is different with the Swiss all-party government: the Swiss
tradition of the separation of powers can be – as has been demonstrated in the

that observers of the Austrian scene have pointed to the phenomenon of *Bereichsopposition* by which coalition partners control each other in their respective administrative *Proporz* domains;[21] but German public opinion has failed to perceive this element of the system. And in any case it cannot be denied that in Austria parliament had been deprived of all independent activity by the preponderance of the *Koalitionsausschuss* (coalition committee) and by the rigid rules of the *Koalitionspakt*. The coalition committee, formed by the principal party leaders in government and parliament and by leaders of the foremost interest groups (which in Austria are strongly tied to one or the other of the parties), was the actual decision-making body and elaborated the compromises which were binding on government and parliament. Only matters of secondary importance were left to the discretion of parliamentary committees. This led to widespread feelings of frustration in public opinion and even within the ranks of the coalition parties.

Coalition committees and formalized coalition agreements have been a rather familiar institution in German politics and have played an important role in some *Laender*.[22] But they were familiar to the initiated rather than to public opinion, for their existence was generally neglected by the press. Only in 1961 did a heated legal controversy arise on the constitutionality of the coalition agreement of the CDU and the FDP, especially on the role of the coalition committee which had been formed on the demand of the liberals.[23] Critics argued, for example, that such an institution infringed upon the chancellor's right to determine the general direction of policy

---

Mirage affair – sufficiently strong to counter-balance the effects of the partisan solidarity of parliamentarians and members of the executive.

[21] Cf. the articles by Kirchheimer and by Engelmann cited above.

[22] For example in Bavaria, where the heterogeneous coalition of the Hoegner cabinet, consisting of socialists, liberals, Bavarian particularists and the refugee party, was held together during its existence (1954–57) by a coalition committee in face of a strong christian democratic opposition. Formal written coalition agreements had already existed in the Weimar Republic.

[23] See, especially, Adolf Schüle, *Koalitionsvereinbarungen im Lichte des Verfassungsrechts*, Tübingen, 1964. On Austrian coalition pacts, see Gustav E. Kafka, 'Die verfassungsrechtliche Stellung der Parteien im modernen Staat', in *Veroeffentlichungen der Vereinigung der Deutschen Staatsrechtslehrer*, Heft 17, 1959, pp. 53–102; Rene Marcic, *Die Koalitionsdemokratie. Das oesterreichische Modell im Lichte der Wiener rechtstheoretischen Schule*, Karlsruhe, 1966.

(according to article 65 of the Basic Law). However, the committee failed to fulfil the hopes which the FDP had entertained that it might serve as a counterweight to the cabinet dominated by Adenauer (a function, by the way, significantly different to that of its Austrian counterpart). When the Kiesinger government was formed coalition spokesmen told the public that this time no formal coalition agreement had been concluded. Instead, the chancellor's governmental declaration to the Bundestag should serve as the fundamental document of the coalition. The practical difference seems to be negligible.[24] Of greater importance is the decision not to create a coalition committee. Of course this does not mean that Kiesinger can make use of his constitutional powers as Adenauer did. The determination of the general direction of policy, according to Vice-Chancellor Brandt's declarations to the SPD party conference of November 1967, could only take place by agreement between chancellor and vice-chancellor – a view which Kiesinger confirmed. The phrase of article 65 (*Richtlinien der Politik*) thus loses importance. When in January 1967 the chancellor blamed two cabinet members (a christian democrat and a social democrat) for having publicly disclosed legislative projects of their ministries, on which the cabinet had not yet come to a decision, he was in fact not determining policy but demanding observance of the rules of procedure concerning cabinet discipline.

Within the cabinet, guidance is in part exercised by small bodies in which both parties are represented. Chancellor and vice-chancellor may confer with each other, or together with two cabinet members who occupy important party functions, namely Wehner, vice-chairman of the SPD, and Heck, general secretary of the CDU. In matters of economy and finance, the collaboration of the social democratic Minister of Economy, Schiller, and the christian democratic Minister of Finance, Strauss, has been widely remarked; it played an important role in justifying unorthodox measures such as deficit spending and in restoring confidence within the business world and the general public. In some cases, compromises may be worked out

[24] In November 1967 the SPD objected to the demands of certain CDU leaders that majority representation should be introduced for the elections of 1969, on the grounds that such an objective had been fixed for 1973 only, and that this agreement could only be changed by formal negotiations within the coalition.

at the level of *Staatssekretäre*: the project on constitutional amendments for the state of emergency for example was worked out by Benda, parliamentary secretary of Interior (CDU), and Ehmke, permanent secretary (but a social democratic party nominee) of Justice. In such cases, of course, the project is finally agreed by the cabinet. Generally speaking, the cabinet seems to play an important role because influential – and sometimes rival – party leaders belong to it, such as Schröder and Lücke (CDU) or Leber (SPD), besides the personalities mentioned above. The chancellor thus cannot be much more than *primus inter pares*.

RELATIONS BETWEEN THE PARTIES

Chancellor and vice-chancellor, as leaders in the cabinet, are chairmen of their respective parties and thus continue a tradition established by Adenauer.[25] But this does not mean that, if cabinet leaders agree on a matter of policy, their parliamentary parties (*Fraktionen*) feel automatically bound by these decisions. The parliamentary parties, on the contrary, constitute a rather autonomous locus of power. This is in part due to the personalities of their chairmen, Barzel (CDU) and Helmut Schmidt (SPD), who are often considered as potential candidates for the chancellorship.[26] About once a week, there is an informal reunion of the cabinet leaders (Kiesinger, Heck, Brandt, and Wehner) with the two chairmen discuss current affairs. This body, known as the *Kressbronner Kreis*,[27] resembles in its composition the controversial

[25] Kiesinger, as Erhard before him, at first showed a certain reluctance to accept this supplementary burden but soon had to acknowledge that the logic of party government, as it had developed since 1949, required him not to allow anyone to use the party machine as a rival source of leadership power. On the other hand, Brandt may have committed an error of judgement when he claimed for himself the important portfolio of foreign affairs; this task absorbs him more than his position as party chairman really allows.

[26] In 1966 Helmut Schmidt renounced entering the cabinet because he failed to obtain the portfolio of first order to which he felt entitled. Barzel was, with Schröder, one of Kiesinger's rivals for the chancellorship; today he seems to have recovered from the disgrace into which he had fallen as a consequence of his manoeuvres against Chancellor Erhard.

[27] The first important reunion of these personalities took place in summer 1967 at Kressbronn, the chancellor's holiday resort on the Lake of Constance. It was then felt that closer contacts between party leaders would be necessary to improve the working of the coalition.

Austrian coalition committee. It cannot, however, take binding decisions because the party leaders do not feel free to
commit their *Fraktionen*; it fulfils a communication, rather
than a decision-making function. The decision to implement
coalition compromises must in general be arrived at within
parliament, by agreement among the *Fraktionen*. Their chairmen are in permanent and close contact with each other which
greatly facilitates negotiations. More important problems are
settled with the participation of some other party leaders and
experts. Major budgetary decisions on social security and
related matters, for example, were reached by an *ad-hoc* committee consisting of four leading CDU deputies (among them
three former ministers) and four of the SPD *Fraktion*, which
met on 24 October 1967. This agreement was then regarded
as strictly binding upon members, in committee as well as
in the plenum.[28]

Observers have sometimes deplored a decline of parliamentary influence which they attribute to the coalition.[29] Indeed, at the end of 1967 the parliamentary parties of the CDU
and the SPD accepted the governmental proposals for 'middle-
term budgetary planning' without major discussions or modifications. But the *Bundestag* has always been badly equipped
to develop initiatives of its own in budgetary matters, and it
would perhaps be premature to generalize from the case. The
obvious decline of parliamentary controversy and debate is
largely due to the importance of the private negotiations of
party leaders and specialists which, in itself, is not a new
element in German parliamentary politics – the new element
is rather the pooling of the already existing 'oligarchies' within
the *Bundestag* which has resulted from the coalition. This
does not mean that the role of parliament itself within the

[28] This was drastically demonstrated when the *Bundestag* committee on
finance had to revise its own amendment tending to limit a supplementary income tax to a period of four years. The CDU members of the committee, who
had voted with the liberals, argued in vain that they had not been informed
of the 'coalition agreement' of 24 October, according to which the tax should
be levied without any limitation in time. See 'Widerstand im Finanzaus-
schuss gegen die Regierung', in *Frankfurter Allgemeine Zeitung*, 14 November
1967 (D-Ausgabe), where the correspondent speaks of 'the coalition committee'.
(This is inexact in so far as the agreement was made by an *ad hoc* meeting of
party leaders.)
[29] See, e.g., 'Armes Parlament', in *Frankfurter Allgemeine Zeitung*, 9 December 1967.

political system is declining: while the parliamentary leaders endeavour to take a strong line with members, they have also not hesitated to demonstrate their independence in relation to the government.[30] And in this they take into consideration the mood of their rank and file. Sometimes a parliamentary party objects to a compromise worked out in the cabinet; then bargaining may begin again, this time *interfraktionell*, and eventually among parliamentary leaders and government.[31] Parliament thus serves as a locus of *Bereichsopposition*, with, for example, a centre–left coalition of social democratic and left-wing CDU members opposing governmental attempts to check the expansion of expenditure on social security, a strong CDU group opposing a more flexible policy in the relations with East European countries, and socialists backing the FDP counter-project concerning the state of emergency.

It has even been argued by some that with the great coalition the political system has been regressing towards an older form of parliamentary government in which the govern-ment is no longer the leader of the parliamentary majority, according to the doctrine of party government, but confronts the parliament in its totality – a confrontation which would bring to mind the constitutional framework of Imperial Germany. But this argument is likewise misleading: on the one hand it oversimplifies the relationship between cabinet and parliamentary majority under the Adenauer governments, which cannot adequately be described as 'cabinet leadership'.[32]

[30] The chancellor himself manifested his irritation when Helmut Schmidt insisted in public declarations on the subordination of government to parliament.

[31] In February 1967 the SPD objected to the government's decision to raise unemployment compensation by 10 per cent and demand a rise of 20 per cent. In a new coalition bargain with Barzel and the cabinet a compromise resulted which raised the compensation by 15 per cent. At the end of 1967 it became evident that the compromise worked out in the cabinet on constitutional amendments for the state of emergency had no chance of passing in parliament without important modifications taking into account the strong objections of SPD members. In January 1968 the government's project to impose taxes and *dirigistische* restrictions on private long-distance motor traffic (proposed by the SPD Minister of Traffic Leber) met with strong opposition within the CDU parliamentary party; a counter-project was proposed by christian democratic spokesmen.

[32] On this subject, see Jürgen Domes, *Mehrheitsfraktion und Bundesregierung. Aspekte des Verhältnisses der Fraktion der CDU/CSU im zweiten und dritten Deutschen Bundestag zum Kabinett Adenauer*, Köln and Opladen, 1964.

On the other hand it overestimates very considerably the independence of the *Fraktionen* of the majority in relation to the cabinet. Unlike the Austrian parliament, the *Bundestag* has preserved a remarkable degree of autonomy under the 'black-red' coalition; but as the coalition feels 'condemned to succeed' the solidarity of the coalition in parliament and government is in general rather high.

A second field in which the coalition diverges from its former Austrian counterpart is patronage. When the alliance was concluded in November 1966, its leaders denied any intention of establishing a *Proporz* with equal distribution of spoils. As, under the Adenauer and Erhard governments, many leading posts in the federal administration had been filled with sympathizers of the CDU and its minor allies, this meant in practice that the SPD gave up the demand for a major *revirement* in its favour. Seven out of eleven *beamtete Staatssekretäre* (permanent secretaries) in the ministries now headed by social democrats were replaced, but only some of the new nominees came from the party ranks. In the lower levels of the administration there were on the whole few changes (except, of course, in the personal staffs of ministers). The proportional staffing of a ministry by members of both parties was even more rejected, with the only exception of the Federal Press and Information Office.[33] Among the SPD rank and file this cautious policy has caused some discontent; but socialist party leaders have frequently avoided yielding to such pressures.[34] The nomination of parliamentary secretaries (*parlamentarische Staatsekretäre*) was a more controversial issue. Adversaries of such an institu-

[33] This agency is perhaps the most 'politicized' administrative body within the federal government. Consequently, the SPD demanded the position of deputy speaker of the government; but it nominated Konrad Ahlers, once the principal defendant in the *Spiegel* affair, who was not a member of the party. In January 1968 the SPD demanded the post of deputy chief of the Federal Intelligence Service (*Bundesnachrichtendienst*, a post it has held for a long time in the *Bundesamt für Verfassungsschutz* (Federal Office for the Protection of the Constitution) which fulfils the functions of a 'political police'.

[34] It should be added that there are rather few candidates available in the ranks of the SPD who are qualified for top positions in the federal administration. Qualified younger party members have generally preferred to enter the civil service of the *Laender* or municipalities governed by SPD majorities to the rather modest chances of a career at Bonn. Thus, when Klaus Schütz left his post of permanent secretary of the Ministry of Foreign Affairs (which he had held since the forming of the coalition) in order to become mayor of West Berlin, his successor was a diplomat without party ties, Mr Duckwitz, for no suitable SPD member could be found.

tion (the most important among them was chancellor Adenauer) had been afraid that it might become a favourite object of coalition bargains and that parliamentary secretaries coming from the ranks of another party than the minister might undermine the authority of the latter. Again Austria, where some ministries under the jurisdiction of one of the parties had been checked by a *Staatssekretär* belonging to the other party, provided a negative example. The Kiesinger government finally decided to conform to the British example in that parliamentary secretaries should serve as junior ministers to take some of the burden off the head of the department and at the same time to become acquainted with governmental affairs, and that they should belong to the same party as the minister and enjoy his confidence. Thus, in spite of some controversial aspects which still survive (especially in regard to the relationship between parliamentary and permanent secretaries), the coalition could not be blamed for practising *Proporz*.

THE PRICE OF COMMON RESPONSIBILITY

Some of the differences between the West German and the Austrian coalition systems are the result of deliberate political decisions. These decisions in turn arise from differences in the character of the respective party systems. While Austrian parties are still rather strongly antagonized by ideological conflict, the West German parties have advanced much further on the road to transforming themselves into 'catch-all-parties' which have abandoned much of their original ideological motivations.[35] In Austria party leaders and members perceived the system in such a manner that they felt the need for strong mutual guarantees against possible disloyal moves by the partner in the coalition. The rigid structure of the alliance, the centralization of decision-making within the coalition committee and the highly-developed *Proporz* patronage may be understood as substitutes for a lack of confidence in the rules of the democratic and parliamentary game. The future evolution of the Austrian system may lead to the strengthening of such confidence, just as happened in West Germany in the course of the past two decades. In Germany the rules of the

[35] For a critical analysis of this transformation, see Wolf Dieter Narr, *CDU–SPD. Programme und Praxis seit 1945*, Stuttgart, 1966.

game have proved to be quite efficient, and thus the CDU–SPD
coalition depends much less on a system of institutional, procedural and personal guarantees such as had developed in
Austria. The resulting greater flexibility of the German great
coalition signifies, however, that the co-ordination of political
forces is more difficult. The strong segmentation on party lines
so characteristic of Austrian social structure has no real equivalent in West Germany. This means that the vertical integration of interest groups into party 'camps', which made it
possible in Austria to check wage policies if the coalition
parties agreed, is of less importance in Germany. Hence co-
ordination is more difficult here, as is demonstrated by the
example of what has been called (by a barbarism of language)
konzertierte Aktion: spokesmen of the federal administration
(of the Ministries of Economy, Labour, and eventually Finance) meet at a round table with union and management
representatives. This procedure, which resembles practices
current in some Scandinavian countries, is much less formalized than that of the Austrian *Paritätische Kommission für
Preis- und Lohnfragen* which checked wage policies (and, with
less success, price policies) by agreement between unions and
employers with the assistance of the government.[36] In West
Germany the system of labour relations is much more complex,
and spontaneous co-ordination of the *Sozialpartner* accordingly
more difficult. These are much less subject to party leadership,
and besides industrial unions enjoy a considerable measure
of autonomy within the Trade Union Federation. Likewise the
co-ordination of public authorities has not been as successful
as some had expected. To be sure, the SPD no longer has an
interest in encouraging social democratic minister presidents
of *Laender* to resist the policies of the federal government; but,
on the other hand CDU minister presidents no longer feel
obliged to back the federal government for reasons of inner
party solidarity. Thus constitutional reorganization of public
finance and long-term financial policy have progressed no
further with the great coalition than they would have done
with a small coalition.

Generally speaking, those who expected that the great

<hr />

[36] On the Austrian case, see Herbert P. Secher ' "Representative Democracy"
or "Chamber State": The Ambiguous Role of Interest Groups in Austrian
Politics', in *Western Political Quarterly*, vol. 13, 1960, pp. 890–909.

coalition would facilitate more profound structural reforms have been disappointed. The Kiesinger government has certainly succeeded in several fields, but within the existing institutional framework, and only insofar as this framework (and the existing equilibrium of political forces) have left it latitude of action. The instruments of economic policy have been modernized, thus contributing a great deal to the overcoming of the serious economic recession of 1966–7. But urgent structural problems of the economy, the crises of coal mining for instance, have been dealt with in a rather dilatory manner. The dangerous state of public finance resulting from the inconsiderate policies of the Erhard cabinets has been remedied for the time being. But only modest progress has been made towards better long-term planning of public expenditure, which would involve decisions on political priorities and which should be combined with a modernization of budgetary procedure.[37]

For the coalition faces an important handicap owing to the ambiguous, not to say paradoxical, character of its aims. Such an alliance, if it is to function without serious friction, must be conceived of as more or less permanent. If, on the contrary, the marriage has been contracted with the intention of divorcing as soon as possible, each partner will try to establish his innocence in the rupture. The efficiency of the work of government and coalition is thus hampered by strong rivalries and animosities within the CDU and SPD and between several of their leading figures. Under these conditions it was unrealistic to assume that the great coalition would noticeably facilitate structural reforms. This would have meant to break up the complex and balanced network of veto groups which form the potential allies of either CDU or SPD in coming electoral contests. In a more general manner, the advocates of drastic reforms failed to assess realistically the conditions of a strategy of political reform in democratic societies with an advanced socio-economic system. Such reforms may become possible if a profound crisis leads to sudden shifts in the institutional and political setting and thus disorganizes (at least temporarily) the channels of access of veto groups – as hap-

[37] On the economic policy of the great coalition, see Hans-Hermann Hartwick, 'Konturen einer neuen Politik. Ein Jahr Grosse Koalition' in *Zeitschrift für Politik*, Band XIV, 1967, pp. 428–58.

G

pened in France during the summer of 1958, to take a more recent example. In Germany in 1966 this was not the case. There was, to be sure, a crisis of the majority; but since the CDU remained in office the existing political setting was only slightly transformed by the great coalition.

The entry of the SPD has however caused certain minor shifts in the equilibrium of forces and thus it has created conditions of gradual change in some fields. This has been most noticeable in the field of foreign policy. While under the Erhard cabinets conservative forces within the CDU (and especially within its Bavarian branch, the CSU) were strong enough to block those actions of West German diplomacy intended to restore normal relations with East European countries, these factions have now lost their power of absolute veto and can only exercise a delaying influence. Of course spectacular moves (which might perhaps sensibly improve the diplomatic position of the Federal Republic) are excluded in such circumstances,[38] but the range of West German diplomacy has been gradually enlarged though this may not have been clearly perceived abroad, the *Hallstein-Doktrin* has been relaxed, and if international recognition of the GDR is still refused this does not mean that the legal fiction of a 'Soviet Occupation Zone' lacking decisive attributes of sovereignty is still maintained. The desire to establish 'orderly' (*geregelte*), though not diplomatic, relations with East Germany which has been repeatedly manifested by certain (especially social democratic) spokesmen of the coalition responds to strong trends in public opinion.[39] It is true that this more pragmatic and flexible attitude has not yet produced all the results in the international field expected by the coalition spokesmen; but if a certain stagnation has been sensible since the establishment of diplomatic relations with Rumania, this is due not so much to internal as to external factors,[40] among them the failure of East German (and, perhaps, to a certain degree, of Soviet and

[38] Recognition of the GDR for instance.

[39] Opinion polls indicate an increasing agreement with a more accommodating attitude towards East Germany. And it is significant that many papers have abandoned the prevalent label 'Soviet Occupation Zone' in favour of the term 'German Democratic Republic' which had been taboo for a long time.

[40] Establishment of diplomatic relations with Hungary, which seemed imminent, as well as with Czechoslovakia and Bulgaria, has apparently been blocked by strong pressures from East Berlin and Moscow.

Polish) communist leadership to understand the mechanism of gradual change in the political system of the Federal Republic.[41]

One may interpret this example as follows: the shift of forces which occurred with the formation of the great coalition broke, to some degree, the deadlock of political forces which characterized the Erhard majority. Thus the impulse towards innovations was released in some domains. But it was limited by the fact that the hitherto dominant party still preserved its established positions of power, and by the continuing veto capacity of important groups, especially in those sectors of policy affecting the redistribution of national income. No important change has been attempted by the coalition parties in the system of social security or in agricultural policy or in regard to the problems arising from the growing concentration of industrial property and economic power. In these fields the existing equilibrium has been largely left untouched. There remain important issues where a certain fluidity in the situation should permit the coalition to introduce some change, for example in the field of transportation or in urbanization. Yet one may doubt whether the tensions between CDU and SPD will allow these opportunities to be seized. It may well be that the coalition, after having restored a certain stability to the economy and public finance, will be absorbed by the effort to stabilize itself; political innovation may then be sacrificed to the preservation of the equilibrium of hegemonic forces.

A condition of political innovation is the articulation of alternative policies, which depends on the degree to which political conflict is managed by public controversy. The West German political system, already before the formation of the great coalition, was characterized by a reduction of public de-

[41] The apprehension of conservative christian democrats that the more flexible attitude of the great coalition might lead to a progressive 'selling out' of traditional diplomatic positions is probably justified. If a majority of East German communist leaders fail to perceive these dynamic aspects of the present situation this is probably due to the ideological outlook of this élite group: having been raised in the tradition of conspiratorial societies, the older elements of party leadership are unable to understand the character of the political process within a system which cannot be sufficiently explained in terms of Leninist class theory. (This aspect has been stressed in the recent study of Peter Christian Ludz, *Parteielite im Wandel. Funktionsaufbau, Sozialstruktur und Ideologie der SED–Führung. Eine empirisch-systematische Untersuchung*, Köln and Opladen, 1968.)

bate. Since then the importance of discreet management of
party conflict by private bargaining has increased in spite of
the efforts to preserve some autonomy of parliamentary life.
There is of course a liberal opposition party which, by skilful
parliamentary moves, has recently succeeded in enlarging
somewhat the area of open discussion; but it continues to suffer
from internal dissensions and is therefore strongly handicapped for the crystallization of deviating political attitudes.
Trade union leadership too has preserved a certain autonomy
in front of the CDU–SPD alliance and has forced the social
democratic leadership to press for a public debate on controversial political issues.[42] Important independent newspapers,
by maintaining a critical attitude to the 'cartel' of the political
parties, have preserved elements of public discussion although
the vital importance of conflict over alternative policies for a
liberal democracy is not always understood in German journalism. All this prevents the complete depoliticization of the public but it does not solve the problem of how the voters can
articulate their discontent within the democratic system.

The revival of extremist movements on the right and on the
left acquires a particular significance in this context. Leftist
extremism, especially among students (where it takes the form
of a neo-anarchist protest movement against industrial society
in its 'capitalist' or Soviet communist form[43]) is clearly a reaction to the closed character of the political system which has
been accentuated by the formation of the great coalition.
Whether it will be able to crystallize discontent outside the
academic world remains to be seen. Yet rightist extremism,
which had been assumed to be dead, undoubtedly again constitutes a factor which cannot be neglected within the political
system. The 'National Democratic Party' (NPD) is not, as its
leaders would like to suggest, a mere conservative movement
but clearly continues the specific German tradition of the
extreme right. This does not mean that the proportion of

[42] One may doubt whether the discussion on constitutional emergency
powers, which had hitherto taken place in the privacy of 'expert talks', would
have been given public hearings in committee of the *Bundestag* if the
existence of a FDP counter-project and the tenacious opposition of trade
union spokesmen had not put strong pressure on the social democratic
leadership.

[43] The political ideas of the student protest movements are largely derived
from the Marxist-Freudian social philosophy of Herbert Marcuse. Its 'Maoist'
aspects seem to be more a matter of 'style' than of ideology or platform.

voters with explicit and consistent rightist-extremist orientations has increased. Their numerical importance, which had
continuously fallen since the beginning of the 1950s, is still less
than it was a decade ago, and dictatorship in its national-
socialist form as well as in principle is disapproved of by an
overwhelming majority of the electorate.[44] But this is not the
problem. The problem is rather that in Germany, as in other
Western societies, important numbers of voters hold inconsistent orientations, partly liberal and democratic, partly – as a
response to strains inherent in industrial societies – authoritarian, which, under specific circumstances, may be mobilized
for anti-liberal, authoritarian movements and eventually may
threaten the democratic system.[45]

In this particular case, the revival of extremism of the right
had begun before the formation of the great coalition, yet the
latter has been an important factor in the further development
of the NPD. Its breakthrough seems to be due, in the first
place, to a growing sense of insecurity, arising from a feeling of
diplomatic isolation within the international field.[46] This sense
of insecurity has apparently been reinforced by the erosion of
confidence in the political system during the long agony of the
Erhard majority. Discontent could only partially be crystal-
lized by the social democratic opposition: since the middle of
1966, the NPD progressed in regional elections at the expense

[44] This emerges from opinion polls and is acknowledged by th NPD leaders
who insist on their respect for the rules of the democratic game – an
attitude dictated not only by fear of a possible interdiction by the Federal
Constitutional Court but obviously also by the fact that many electors with
authoritarian opinions nevertheless continue to believe in these rules.

[45] This argument follows the hypothesis developed by Erwin K. Scheuch as
a result of his research on extreme rightist movements and, in particular, the
NPD. See Erwin K. Scheuch, unter Mitarbeit von Hans D. Klingemann,
'Theorie des Rechtsradikalismus in westlichen Industriegesellschaften', *Ham-
burger Jahrbuch für Wirtschafts- und Gesellschafts politik*, 12 Jahr, 1967, pp.
11–29.

[46] Among the elements causing this insecurity the most important are
probably the fading away of hopes that West Germany might find its place
within a European supranational unit (hopes that had been a surrogate for
the discredited German national idea) and the *cauchemar des alliances* resulting from increasing US–Soviet co-operation. This led to a loss of confidence
in the solidarity of the Western powers and accounts for the increasing
attraction of Gaullist arguments among the West German élite. They failed to
grasp that the French fiction of an independent national policy rests upon
particular conditions which do not exist in the case of Germany and that
the range of international activity of the Federal Republic is severely
restricted.

of the SPD still more than of the christian democratic and
liberal parties. As has been mentioned above, the resulting
stagnation of social democratic strength contributed to render
doubtful the possibility of an alternative majority under existing institutional conditions. In fact, the great coalition has
been a short-term response to extremist challenge. For the
time being, the economy and public finance could apparently
be stabilized; confidence in the political institutions seems to
have been restored to a certain degree, and feelings of insecurity have declined. There are reasons for thinking that the
extreme right vote will not sensibly exceed the level reached
in 1966–7 in the near future, that is, a proportion somewhat
below 10 per cent. This is not, of course, an abnormal percentage and would be quite innocuous under conditions of
internal and external stability. But this stability is by no means
certain and if new strains were to appear[47] the political opportunities for the expression of dissent within the framework
of liberal institutions and of a democratic party system would
be rather limited precisely because of the existence of the great
coalition. This has repeatedly been acknowledged by CDU and
SPD leaders: by forming their alliance, these parties have run
the risk of excluding any alternative democratic solution. They
are 'condemned to succeed together'.

Besides, even a modest NPD representation in the next
Bundestag, of, perhaps 8 or 10 per cent of the seats, might
create a rather difficult situation. Actually, an alternative to
the great coalition (e.g. a renewed CDU–FDP or a SPD–FDP
majority) is excluded for political reasons. After 1969, the great
coalition might remain the only possible solution for reasons
of simple parliamentary arithmetic, leading to a quite dangerous deadlock. The supporters of majority electoral representation – among them most important CDU and SPD leaders –
have thus a strong argument.[48] That such a reform would

[47] For example if the evolution of US–Soviet relations led to an increasing
isolation of West Germany.

[48] Prospects of electoral reform remain uncertain because majority representation in its classical form would work to the disadvantage of incumbent
deputies in both parties – christian democrats in urban areas, social democrats
in catholic rural districts, and so on. While the CDU could expect to gain an
absolute majority in 1969 with such a system, the SPD has more interest in
postponing the reform until 1973 and continuing the coalition until then.
This follows from the assumption of SPD leaders that the party's chances

almost automatically lead to an authentic system of alternative government – as some authors seem to assume on the basis of theoretical reasoning founded on the isolation of some variables of electoral behaviour – seems by no means certain. If one considers the remaining institutional and social conditions as well as the established customs for the management of political conflict, one may expect that many important issues will continue to be settled by negotiation among groups rather than by electoral contest and parliamentary majorities. The problem remains now to restore a certain equilibrium between the elements of bargaining and open contest within the West German system of managing political conflicts.

---

would be sensibly ameliorated by a period of participation in government which they hope would dispel the apprehensions of middle-class voters.

Kenneth R. Libbey

Initiatives, Referenda, and Socialism in Switzerland*†

POLITICAL INSTITUTIONS IN DEMOCRATIC STATES HAVE USUALLY
come into existence as the manifestation of a principle of
political philosophy or as the result of a compromise among
forces with different aspirations for the polity. Often both factors have been involved. Certainly the consequences for political behaviour of introducing any particular structure have
been of concern to its architects, but many of these consequences are unforeseeable and the actual impact of an institutional
change or the character of a formal role may in time become
quite different from that intended.

For a political actor, such as an individual, an interest group
or a party, formal structures are given attributes of the political
environment. Along with the more diffuse qualities of the
political culture, they constitute the framework within which
political actors must compete for influence over public policy.
This framework, both formal and informal, is uneven in its
effects on the fortunes of the various political forces. It favours
some approaches and some groups more and in different ways
than it favours others. The British Labour Party, with its concentrated voting strength, is disadvantaged by the single-
member district/plurality electoral system, while its counterpart in Germany is able to maximize its strength in a system of
proportional representation.

Each political actor must make use of the various features of
the political environment in so far as possible, and try to
attenuate the advantages which they afford to his adversaries.
This article will explore the consequences of some peculiar in-

* I would like to thank Professor Stephen Koff of Syracuse, Professor William
Keech of Chapel Hill, and Mr Charles-F. Pochon of Berne for their comments
on an earlier draft of this article.

† Vol. 5, no. 3, Summer 1970.

stitutions for the fortunes of the Swiss Socialist Party. At the same time, some more general observations will be included concerning the influence of these institutions in the political system. The perceptions of Socialist Party leaders were explored through the use of a questionnaire which formed part of a larger study of the party.[1] Response to the questionnaire was 45 per cent, including a comparable number from each of three categories: members of the Federal Parliament, other members of the party's Central Committee, and other cantonal leaders. The canton of residence of each respondent was also known, and the number from each canton corresponded roughly to the importance of the cantonal party to the national party.

Switzerland is undoubtedly the country in which the possibilities for the direct intervention of the people in the political process are the most extensive. One canton and four half-cantons have preserved the tradition of the *Landesgemeinde*, the annual assembly of all adult male citizens as supreme legislative authority.[2] Moreover, many smaller communities continue to hold communal assemblies to exercise the legislative function.[3] If these survivals of a less complicated era constitute only a marginal aspect of modern Swiss politics, the opportunity for the simple citizen to participate in public decision-making is nonetheless far-reaching and plays an important role in the life of the nation.

At the federal level, all proposed amendments to the Swiss constitution which are approved by the parliament must be submitted to a referendum. Such an amendment may be proposed as well by 50,000 citizens (constitutional initiative), either in the form of an edited text or as a statement of principle. In the latter case, approval by the people obliges the parliament to prepare a corresponding text and submit it to a second referendum.[4] The parliament cannot refuse to submit a constitutional initiative to the people, but it can present a counter-project, which sometimes results in the withdrawal of

[1] Kenneth R. Libbey, *The Socialist Party of Switzerland – A Minority Party and its Political System*. Unpublished PhD dissertation, Syracuse University, 1969.

[2] Glarus, Nidwalden, Obwalden, Appenzell Exterior and Interior Rhodes.

[3] Most communal legislatures, in fact, recognize the right of a citizen to speak up at their sessions.

[4] Georges Sauser-Hall, *Guide politique suisse*, Lausanne, 1965, pp. 121–3.

the original initiative by its sponsors.[5] All such changes in the constitution must be approved simultaneously by a majority of those voting and by a majority of the cantons. It is thus impossible for the large urban cantons to impose an amendment upon the smaller rural ones. A simple law passed by the Federal Parliament is not subject to a legislative referendum unless this is demanded by 30,000 citizens or eight cantonal governments within ninety days of its publication by the Federal Chancellery.[6] In such a case, only a simple majority of those voting is required to accept or reject the law. Decrees declared 'urgent', the federal budget and other financial credits cannot be so challenged, however.[7]

The extent of such interventions at the cantonal level varies considerably, but in general it is greater than in federal affairs. In some cantons, including the populous ones of Zürich, Berne, and Aargau, a referendum is obligatory for all laws passed by the cantonal parliament. This extraordinary reservation of authority to the people results in a half-dozen or more calls to the polls each year. The budget of those cantons is not subject to a referendum although those of their communities normally are. Appropriations are submitted to a vote if they surpass a certain amount. In other cantons, a referendum must be demanded by a number of citizens varying from less than 1000 to 12,000.[8] Again, appropriations above a specified amount may be automatically subject to a referendum although a number of cantons have abandoned this practice.[9] In addition, all cantons practise the legislative initiative whereby a number of citizens – sometimes higher than for a referendum – may propose a simple law or revision of a law to a popular vote. Again, the cantonal parliament has the possibility of proposing a counter-project, or simply recommending the acceptance or

[5] At the cantonal level, an initiative can be declared unreceivable if it is judged to violate the federal constitution. Since 1962, the Federal Parliament can declare an initiative void if its different points are not intrinsically related. Sauser-Hall, op. cit., p. 123.

[6] There has, in fact, never been a case of a referendum demanded by eight cantonal governments.

[7] Sauser-Hall, op. cit., pp. 119–20. Urgent decrees are valid for only one year if challenged by a referendum.

[8] Ibid., p. 119. The number has normally been doubled in those cantons which have introduced women's suffrage. See Jean Meynaud et al., Études politiques vaudoises, Lausanne, Études de science politique, 1963, p. 13.

[9] Neuchatel, on the other hand, introduced it several years ago.

rejection of the initiative.[10] No right of legislative initiative exists in federal politics.

The purpose of this study is to examine the consequences of these rights of popular intervention for the activity of the Socialist Party. One may make the general observation that the right of initiative is a cherished one for a progressive minority. It affords the party the opportunity to short-circuit a hostile parliamentary majority and take its case directly to the people. Since the factors which govern the decision of the voter in an election and those which are determining in a plebiscite may differ, the minority can hope to become a majority on the issue in question if its position is persuasive enough. The practice of the referendum, on the other hand, normally has greater appeal to conservative forces. Rather than introduce a proposal for governmental action, its function is frequently to disavow the measures which the parliament wishes to take, or to refuse the constitutional authority requested by the parliament for a certain kind of action.

One should hasten to add that this rule is subject to significant exceptions, however. It is possible for conservative forces to launch a constitutional initiative designed to have a restrictive influence on the government – the fixing of a ceiling on tax rates or the obligation to operate with a balanced budget, for example. The left, on the other hand, might conceivably challenge military policies with a referendum. In 1963, the Swiss people were called to pronounce upon a socialist initiative aimed at rendering a referendum obligatory for any decision to provide the Swiss army with atomic weapons. Moreover, a referendum demanded by conservative forces can in some circumstances have unexpected consequences. A referendum against the introduction of federal social security in 1947 was crushed by a majority of four-to-one with an exceptionally high rate of participation.[11] The programme received a popular acclaim in the plebiscite which undoubtedly has remained a factor in the succeeding revisions of it.

[10] Sauser-Hall, *op. cit.*, pp. 120–1.
[11] *Annuaire statistique de la Suisse*, Berne, Chancellerie fédérale, 1947, p. 484.

THE REFERENDUM – A BRAKE ON PROGRESS?

Traditional commentaries on the practice of direct democracy in Switzerland have frequently praised the manner in which the Swiss 'people' have 'wisely' used these instruments to prevent an undue public interference in their private affairs.[12] Such exercises undoubtedly constitute a temptation for the citizen to manifest a negative attitude towards the state. The authority of the state may be assimilated with other sources of authority in his life, and a referendum gives a chance to demonstrate his hostility. A further problem arises from the nature of the goods and services whch the state provides: they are invisible or semi-visible; they are indivisible as opposed to goods and services which can be possessed or received directly. The citizen as consumer may naturally give more attention to tangible consumption.

In the case of some persons, this reflex probably entrains a habitual rejection of projects of all sorts – the Swiss-Germans refer to this kind of voter as a *Neinsager*. It is likely that the importance of these electors is often exaggerated, however. A project which is seemingly harmless and is not opposed by anyone usually collects a negative vote of 10–25 per cent according to the region. Rural regions and certain cantons, such as Aargau, exhibit a larger proportion. But the core of resolved opposition is not by itself capable of repudiating a government's proposals. On the other hand, the reservoir of latent opposition among the public can be awakened without great difficulty. It is often sufficient for a single party, *ad hoc* committee, or in some cases a single newspaper, to furnish some reasons for opposing a measure and a negative majority can materialize. Moreover, certain kinds of propositions are susceptible of generating more natural opposition than others. The citizens of Valais have twice refused the purchase of electronic calculating equipment for the cantonal administration, despite the absence of organized opposition.[13] In the canton of Neuchatel, a proposal to increase the salaries of public service personnel aroused the opposition of 40 per cent of the voters

[12] For good examples, see William Martin and Pierre Béguin, *Histoire de la Suisse*, Lausanne, 1963, pp. 342–5; Sauser-Hall, *op. cit.*, p. 120; Georges-André Chevallaz, *La Suisse ou le sommeil du juste*, Lausanne, 1967, p. 64.

[13] *Le Peuple-La Sentinelle*, La Chaux-de-Fonds, socialist daily for French Switzerland, 26 October 1966.

although it had been approved unanimously by the cantonal legislature and had not brought forth a single written word of opposition.[14] The appropriation of important sums is also vulnerable in those cantons which practise an obligatory finance referendum.

Much legislation in the modern state is of restricted effect – it is designed to meet a specific problem or to benefit a certain segment of the society. A series of such measures taken together may cover a great deal of territory and be understood by a parliament to be a programme in the general interest. But any given one, subject to a referendum, can encounter the opposition of a majority who will receive no apparent benefit from the measure. For example, a project of aid to an industry of timber transformation in the mountainous canton of Grisons was challenged and defeated in 1956. A further problem in the case of many projects is the level of participation in the consultation, a factor which can vary enormously. A significant minority may have reasons to oppose a measure while the majority is simply acquiescent. The activated minority goes to the polls while much of the majority does not bother, and the government is defeated.

The institution of the obligatory finance referendum is especially attractive to conservative forces. It renders the parliament vulnerable to the anti-fiscal sentiments of much of the populace. Moreover, it permits the opposition to remain equivocal or in the shadows. It is not necessary to organize openly the collection of signatures and spell out the reasons for opposition. Instead, newspaper articles expressing certain doubts or cryptic comments about the project in question can appear, the rest being left to the imagination of the suspicious citizen. The government itself can be placed in a difficult position by such a strategy, because to campaign too vigorously for the approval of the proposal could simply magnify the importance of the opposition and increase the suspicion of the public. The obligatory finance referendum can in fact be an embarrassment for responsible political forces in general. The prestige of the political parties is not enhanced when their constituents reject projects which have been unanimously recommended by the parties. This is not at all uncommon, but the most celebrated case was undoubtedly the refusal of the citizens

[14] *Ibid.*, 17 October 1966.

of Aargau to approve the credits necessary to present a cantonal day at the Swiss National Exposition in 1964. The
canton was conspicuous by its absence. Such whimsical interventions by the 'sovereign' have led some cantons, such as
Geneva and Vaud, to suppress this institution. In others, such
as Berne, it would probably be impossible to induce the
electorate to surrender this prerogative.[15]

The opinions of leaders of the Socialist Party with regard to
the obligatory finance referendum are given in Table 1. It can
be seen that a majority of socialists believe this practice to be a
weapon in the arsenal of their adversaries. But this is noticeably less true in the cantons where it is in use than in those
where it is not. In the latter group, of course, a number of
respondents gave no opinion because of lack of experience
with this kind of referendum. But the institution did exist
previously in some of these cantons, and it earned a remarkably poor reputation among partisans of the left. In a number
of the other cantons, Berne for example, many socialists appear
to find that even if the obligatory finance referendum is not a
particularly desirable component of the political system, it can
be useful in obtaining concessions from the other major
parties, who also have favourite projects that must pass the
test of public approval. The Agrarian Party's interest in subsidies to agriculture and to the smaller railway lines in the
canton of Berne would be an example. It may be added that
some respondents did comment that this referendum is a
natural part of the people's rights. In the canton of Neuchatel,
where the obligatory finance referendum was introduced
several years ago on the initiative of the bourgeois parties, the
socialists have tried unsuccessfully to suppress it.[16]

It should not be assumed that the electorate regularly refuses
the laws submitted for its approval. In general the government
and parliament have a fairly good record in these votes, much
better than the sponsors of popular initiatives. Table 2 shows
that the government's position has more often than not been
upheld in referenda, especially since 1920. While its record is

[15] Its suppression in Vaud, supported by the left and generally by the radicals
but opposed by the right (Liberal Party), was achieved with a comfortable
majority. Only 30 per cent of the voters participated. Meynaud et al., Études
politiques vaudoises, pp. 33–5, 183–4.

[16] Le Peuple-La Sentinelle, 13 December 1967.

TABLE 1

Socialist Opinions of the Obligatory Finance Referendum

Would you say that the obligatory finance referendum is:

A. A valuable weapon for the right?
B. Useful also to the left?
C. A mutual burden?
D. A valuable weapon for the professional organizations but a burden for the parties?
E. Other.

Cantons where the institution is in practice: *	A	B	C	D	E	No Opinion	Number Received
Appenzell-Ext.	—	—	—	—	1	—	1
Aargau	2	1	4	1	1	1	6
Grisons	1	—	—	—	—	—	1
Neuchatel	4	—	3	—	—	1	5
Saint Gall	4	3	—	—	—	—	5
Schwyz	2	2	—	1	—	—	2
Solothurn	4	2	—	—	—	1	6
Thurgau	—	—	1	—	—	—	1
Valais	—	2	1	1	—	—	3
Nidwalden	1	1	—	—	—	—	1
Zug	1	—	—	—	—	—	1
Zürich	1	1	2	—	3	2	8
Berne	9	7	6	1	1	2	17
Sub-total	29	19	17	4	6	7	57
Cantons where it is not in practice: *							
Basel-City	1	—	1	—	1	—	2
Basel-country	1	—	—	1	—	2	3
Fribourg	1	—	—	1	—	1	3
Geneva	2	—	—	2	1	—	4
Giarus	—	—	—	—	—	2	2
Lucerne	1	—	—	—	—	2	3
Ticino	1	—	—	1	—	—	1
Vaud	6	1	—	—	—	—	6
Sub-total	13	1	1	5	2	7	24
Total	42	20	18	9	8	14	81

*According to the information given in the questionnaire. No answers were received from Schaffhausen, Uri, Obwalden, or Appenzell-Interior Rhodes.

not so good in referenda which have been demanded by a petition, it should be noted that of the laws and decrees subject to an optional referendum, only about eight per cent have been so challenged.[17]

TABLE 2

Results of Federal Referenda and Initiatives 1848–1967

Type of Vote	1848–1920 Accepted	1848–1920 Rejected	1920–1967 Accepted	1920–1967 Rejected
Obligatory Referenda *	23	14	36	11
Provoked Referenda †	12	20	17	23
Initiatives	4	6	4	37
Counter Projects – Initiative Withdrawn	1	0	4	2
Counter Projects – Initiative Maintained	0	0	3	2

Sources: *Tableaux des votations fédérales depuis 1848*, Berne, Chancellerie fédérale, 1965. *Annuaire statistique de la Suisse*, 1967, pp. 540–1.

* Constitutional amendments submitted by the parliament.
† Laws challenged by 30,000 or more citizens. It is the law which is accepted or rejected.

Some cantons and communities have more difficulty than does the federal government, but 'rebellion' by the electorate is still less likely than popular ratification. On the other hand, the record might be much more dramatic if the eventual outcome of a referendum were not considered during the formulative stages of a given proposal. This is one of the important trump cards of conservative forces, who can use the threat of a referendum against reform efforts in the sensitive areas of taxation and economic policy. Such arguments, stated or implied, are not unusual in parliamentary discussions and are undoubtedly a consideration of the government when it prepares its programmes. The necessity or possibility of a referendum is generally believed to be an important source of the tendency to establish broadly-based compromises in Swiss politics. That the influence of this factor is not hypothetical may be seen from the following inquiry:

[17] Jean Meynaud and Adelbert Korff, *Les organisations professionnelles en Suisse*, Lausanne, 1963, p. 305.

Does the threat of a referendum or an initiative remain a factor in parliamentary discussions?

	Yes	No	No Opinion
Members of Federal Parliament	23	3	0
Other socialist leaders	46	3	2
Total	69	6	2

Several respondents commented that this was principally true of a referendum, less so of an initiative. The leaders who answered negatively may feel that the record of popular votes in their cantons is such that the eventuality of being disavowed by the people is not significant enough to play a role in the discussions.

While speculation on the reactions of the citizenry is a natural means by which conservatives can encourage prudence on the part of the public authorities, it is not the preserve of these forces alone. It has already been seen that the obligatory finance referendum can be of use to the socialists in some circumstances. The left may also find a referendum useful in the case of fiscal reforms. A tax increase can sometimes appear inevitable to all but the most extreme groups, as mounting government costs are admitted by everyone. In 1966, the Federal Department of Finance issued a report warning of approaching heavy deficits in the federal budget. A hastily prepared request for an across-the-board rise in direct and indirect taxes was submitted to parliament, but required a referendum since it involved a constitutional change. The Socialist Party took a cool attitude towards the project in the early debates, introducing amendments designed to increase the progressivity of direct taxes, and suggesting that they might not be able 'to defend before the people' the original proposal.[18] When even the most moderate of suggested compromises failed to obtain grace from the other parties, the Socialist Central Committee, sensing a breeze of revolt blowing in the party, voted to oppose the measure in the referendum campaign.[19]

It is not true that the opposition of one major party to a

[18] The speech of Pierre Graber, socialist leader in parliament, is reprinted in *Le Peuple-La Sentinelle*, 28, 29, 30 December 1966.

[19] *Ibid.*, 20 February 1967.

fiscal project is sufficient to cause its defeat – that of 1958 passed despite the active opposition of the socialists.[20] But in 1967 the move was successful. The radicals, arguing that the socialist attitude had condemned the project, voted it down in final debate.[21] The socialists were thus able to approach any new discussions of fiscal reform from a position of greater strength. They were still handicapped, of course, by the fact that theirs is the party most interested in securing additional revenue. But the incident suggests that the referendum is a knife which in some circumstances can cut both ways.

THE INITIATIVE – LIMITS ON ITS UTILITY

As can be seen in Table 2, it is difficult to induce the electorate to accept a popular initiative. Since 1935, twenty-six initiatives to alter the federal constitution have been voted upon; only one, a proposal to suppress certain wartime restrictions on the use of the referendum, was accepted – by a hairline majority.[22] The popular reflex against an expansion of governmental activity, upon which the sponsors of a referendum count for core support, is a current against which the usual kind of initiative must swim. The initiative is not therefore an equitable balancing institution to the right of the referendum, since the likelihood of success for its employers is significantly less.

In federal affairs, and especially from the point of view of the Socialist Party, the obstacles to successful use of the initiative are greater because of the requirement that the proposal be accepted by a majority of the cantons as well as of the people. In many of the rural cantons, the arguments of the socialists do not carry much weight, and may even be considered as representing the urban viewpoint as opposed to that of the countryside. Hence in 1955, a socialist initiative aimed at providing increased protection for tenants received a popular majority, but since this was derived from only seven

[20] *Rapport de gestion du Parti socialiste suisse*, Berne, Secrétariat du P.S.S., 1957–8, pp. 40–3, 60. (Administrative report of the Socialist Party – hereafter cited as *Rapport de gestion*, year, . . .)

[21] *Le Peuple-La Sentinelle*, 16 March 1967.

[22] *Annuaire statistique de la Suisse*, 1949–67 *passim*. (Section: *Votations fédérales*).

cantons, the initiative was defeated.[23] This double handicap means that the prospects for an initiative launched by the Swiss Socialist Party are less encouraging than for its member parties in cantonal politics. The only socialist initiative ever approved at the national level was that introducing proportional representation in 1919, largely conceded by the other parties in the wake of a general strike. But judging from the record in the canton of Vaud, the left's prospects for successful use of the initiative at the cantonal level are also thin.[24]

In light of the problematical outcome of a campaign in favour of an initiative, it is not surprising that the cost factor takes on a notable importance. According to François Masnata, the expenses incurred in support of such a campaign can mount to over $200,000.[25] Compared to the resources at the disposal of the SPS, this is a redoubtable sum. It means among other things that the party considers it almost a prerequisite to enlist the support of the Swiss Trade Union Federation before embarking on the road to a plebiscite. Moreover, the party can hardly afford to engage in more than one such battle at a time and must attempt to space its initiatives in accordance with its financial possibilities. The socialists began to consider an initiative against land speculation as early as 1955, but despite pressure from within the party, it was postponed until 1963, partly because of financial limitations.[26] The necessary prudence with which the socialists must use the means of direct democracy involves a risk that other groups will seize issues upon which the party intends to act when it can, and start initiatives of their own. The lack of co-ordination and co-operation among elements of the centre and left in these matters is a source of suspicion and tension.

A final drawback to the use of the initiative by the Socialist

[23] *Ibid.*, 1955, p. 528. The cantons accepting were Zürich, Berene, Vaud, Geneva, Neuchatel, Ticino, and the two half-cantons of Basel. This was, however, one of only two cases of such a defeat of an initiative.

[24] Meynaud *et al.*, *Études politiques vaudoises*, pp. 85–6, 92. The only successful initiative from the left in the period studied (1938–62) was the approval of three weeks of legal vacation in 1960.

[25] François Masnata, *Le parti socialiste et la tradition démocratique en Suisse*, Neuchatel, 1963, p. 217.

[26] *Protokoll über die Verhandlungen des Parteitages der S.P.S.*, Berne, Sekretariat der S.P.S., 1961, p. 104. (Record of debates at Socialist Congresses – hereafter cited as *Protokoll*, year . . .)

Party is the absence of a right of legislative initiative in federal
politics. While in nearly all cantons the public can propose a
simple law or revision of a law, at the federal level an initiative
must concern a change in the constitution. This situation often
obliges groups desiring change to follow detours to their goal
and to give an impression of equivocation. A simple legislative
action would often suffice to achieve the desired result, but
since the sponsors cannot address themselves to the question in
the most direct manner, their initiative may lack clarity and
hence appeal. Because some of the specific measures favoured
by the Socialist Party undoubtedly have a following which is
greater than that of the party itself in elections (about 25 per
cent nationally) the socialists would seemingly benefit from
the possibility of using a legislative initiative. Moreover, such
a measure would presumably be placed on the same basis as
the legislative referendum – that is it would not require the
double majority of the people and the cantons.

The Socialist Party in fact favours the introduction of such
a practice and in 1958 decided to start an initiative to this end.
Former Federal Councillor Max Weber remarked in his report
to the party congress, '... the legislative initiative will be a
worthwhile means for the struggle of a minority'.[27] At the
time, it was meant to be presented especially as an instrument
which would facilitate the improvement of social security
benefits. Before the project came to a vote in 1961, however,
the socialist, H.-P. Tschudi, had taken charge of the Department of the Interior and had begun to give the necessary
stimulation to the revision of the social security laws. The
socialists were weakened in the campaign by the refusal of
the trade unions to participate, although they did benefit from
the co-operation of another party, the *Landesring*. The
initiative was defeated by an overwhelming majority, with all
cantons voting against it.[28]

Considering the obstacles mentioned above, however, one
might wonder whether the introduction of the legislative initiative would actually make a difference for the Socialist Party's
effectiveness. Hence the following question was posed to
socialist leaders:

[27] *Protokoll*, 1958, p. 101.
[28] *Rapport de gestion*, 1961–62, pp. 61–3.

Would the introduction of the legislative initiative in federal politics have a practical usefulness to the Socialist party?

	Yes	No	No Opinion
Members of Federal Parliament	24	0	2
Other socialist leaders	44	8	2
Total	68	8	4

If one makes the reasonable assumption that few such initiatives would be accepted by the people, as has been true in the cantons, it is necessary to look beyond the simple result of public votes and examine the more subtle influence of the right of initiative.

THE INITIATIVE AS CATALYST

If the likelihood of popular acceptance of an initiative is slim, it is not an eventuality to be discounted altogether. Should it materialize, the governing majority would find imposed upon it a text of which it had not controlled the composition. To avoid this unpleasant possibility, the parliament may be willing to produce a counter-project which would be reasonably satisfactory to the sponsors of the initiative. For the latter, this solution has the advantage of adding the sanction of the government and parliament to the text which will be voted upon, and of frequently reducing the cost which would be involved in campaigning for the original text against the will of the parliamentary majority. Although this does sometimes happen, the different parliaments are not often prepared to present actual counter-projects. From 1935 to 1967, the Federal Parliament submitted only eight to the people, five of which were accepted.[29] Jean Meynaud points out that the government of Vaud seldom makes gestures designed to induce the withdrawal of an initiative.[30] Still the provocation of a counter-project remains one of the objectives of most groups who engage in the collection of signatures for an initiative.[31]

Even in the absence of a counter-project, the supporters of

[29] *Annuaire statistique de la Suisse*, 1949–67 *passim*. (Section: *Votations fédérales*).

[30] Meynaud *et al.*, *Études politiques vaudoises*, p. 76.

[31] Petitions frequently contain an authorization of the sponsors to withdraw the initiative in case of a suitable reaction from the authorities.

an initiative may prefer to withdraw their proposal if the parliament takes legislative action or even if the government indicates its intention to act. A number of initiatives aimed at extending social security benefits have been withdrawn following revisions of the system by the Federal Council and Assembly. By the same token, the socialist initiative for a federal disability insurance was withdrawn in 1959 after the passage of a law setting up such a programme.[32] François Masnata points out that the Socialist Party is normally satisfied if some promises of action are made and it does not have to persevere with an initiative.[33] This is not automatically the case, however, as the party maintained its initiative on land speculation in 1967 despite acknowledgements by the Federal Council and numerous other political figures that action in the realm of land-use planning would have to be taken.

Not the least of the effects of an initiative can be its capacity to provoke a public debate over a given issue. As Professor Dusan Sidjanski has pointed out, an initiative obliges the various groups to take concrete positions on a matter which may have remained vaguely in the air for some time. As a result, the executive authority may be able to use the occasion to elaborate a project susceptible of bringing the various interests together in a compromise. He used the example of the *Landesring*'s initiative for anti-cartel legislation, which brought action after a long series of fruitless proposals in the Assembly.[34] However, this strategy runs the risk of having the ensuing debate become confused and distorted by the adversaries of action. This is a particular danger in the case of constitutional initiatives in federal affairs. Since the text of the initiative may be heavy with legal terminology, and since a constitutional amendment may not in fact be the most appropriate approach to a problem, the idea may be vulnerable to a multitude of criticisms which tend to discredit it unfairly before the public. In such a case, support for reform could be reduced through the placement of a specific proposition in the public forum.

[32] *Rapport de gestion*, 1959–60, p. 52.
[33] Masnata, *op. cit.*, p. 218.
[34] Dusan Sidjanski, 'Les partis politiques et le processus de décision en Suisse'. Paper presented to the annual meeting of the Swiss Political Science Association at Lucerne, 9 March 1968. See also Meynaud and Korff, *Les organisations professionnelles en Suisse*, pp. 177–8.

Another risk which the would-be sponsors of an initiative must consider is the effect of an eventual defeat in a popular vote. As suggested by Federal Councillor Tschudi: 'A reversal in a popular vote can remain an obstacle for decades.'[35] This threat of repudiation may explain the preference of the Socialist Party for composed texts rather than initiatives of principle, a tactic which some socialists have criticized.[36] The rejection of a specific text can be attributed to disagreements over detail, whereas the defeat of a general request for action could be interpreted by the party's adversaries as a popular disavowal of the principle itself. But even the clear defeat of an initiative may not be a complete setback. If the vote reveals that a definable sector of the population is found among the minority, the authorities may take this into consideration in determining their future course. Thus in the case of the Socialist Party's initiative regarding atomic weapons, its approval by the four purely non-German cantons was considered a warning to the government that any decision to proceed in this direction might disturb the federal equilibrium of the country.

The issue of land speculation and land-use planning provided the most notable occasion for the use of the federal constitutional initiative by the Socialist Party in recent years. The affair was a long time in preparation. An initiative had in fact been started during the 1940s by a few agricultural groups but had not stirred up much interest. In 1955, after a report by Central Secretary Mascha Oettli, the Socialist Congress resolved to resort to an initiative if its parliamentary efforts remained without success.[37] Despite the mounting cost of urban land prices and the ensuing pressures on rent costs, seven years passed without action by parliament. In 1962, with the hint of a move from other quarters in the air, the party congress voted to collect signatures for an amendment which would empower the public authorities to engage in land-use planning and to exercise a right of pre-emption, or first refusal, in the sale of real estate.[38] The trade unions, while reserving the right to approve the final text, promised their support.[39]

[35] *Protokoll*, 1961, p. 101.
[36] Notably the editors of *Domaine public*, an independent socialist bi-weekly published at Lausanne, no. 61, 7 November 1966, p. 3.
[37] *Protokoll*, 1955, p. 173.
[38] *Ibid.*, 1962, pp. 5, 53.   [39] *Ibid.*, 1962, pp. 74–5.

Again time passed as the Federal Council and the various interest groups reflected over the socialist initiative. Two expert committees were set up to study the matter.[40] In the meantime, credit restrictions passed in the face of a too rapid economic expansion had the side effect of dampening land speculation. Still, most people seemed to believe that the problem of land-use planning had to be dealt with.[41] Finally in 1966, the Federal Council recommended the rejection of the socialist initiative without proposing a counter-project. Parliament duly followed, only the left supporting the initiative.[42] Needless to say, the socialists were not pleased, and the scheduling of the vote during the summer vacation period did not help. The campaign was a bitter affair. The socialist proposal was represented as nothing less than an attempt to nationalize the soil. It was simultaneously attacked as a serious menace to private property and an ineffective gesture. Posters representing the map of Switzerland in red appeared at every corner. At the same time, grave promises to resolve the problem of land-use planning were made by the adversaries of the initiative; just before the vote there was talk of a forthcoming government project of constitutional revision. The initiative was defeated by a two-to-one majority, the socialists proving unable to mobilize even their normal electorate. On the other hand, the five principal cities of Switzerland along with Bienne and La Chaux-de-Fonds produced majorities in favour of the initiative, demonstrating the pressure of the housing situation in the urban areas.[43]

Shortly after the popular vote, the Federal Council did in fact publish its proposed constitutional articles, which the Swiss Trade Union Federation greeted as acceptable and substantially close to the text proposed by the left.[44] The new project was discussed by the two chambers of parliament in the winter of 1967–8. Despite attempts to weaken it in the federal chambers, it appeared in the spring of 1968 that a text reason-

[40] For a résumé of the tortuous debate over the initiative, see Peter Gilg and François-L. Reymond, 'Année politique suisse 1965', *Annuaire suisse de science politique*, VI, 1966, pp. 186–9.

[41] The terms in German and French are *Landesplanung* and *aménagement du territoire*, respectively.

[42] *Le Peuple-La Sentinelle*, 29 September and 1 December 1966.

[43] *Annuaire statistique de la Suisse*, 1967, p. 544.

[44] *Le Peuple-La Sentinelle*, 4 September 1967.

ably satisfactory to the left would be approved by the parliament and submitted to the people late in 1968.[45] For an idea of
the opinions of socialists on their experience with this initiative, one may examine the results of the enquiry shown in
Table 3, made after the Federal Council had presented its proposals but before their consideration by parliament.

TABLE 3

Socialist Leaders' Views of their Experience with an Initiative

After the popular vote of last 2 July, do you consider that:

A. It is regrettable that the Federal Council did not present
   a counter-project before the consultation?
B. The engagements undertaken by the authorities and certain
   bourgeois circles would not have been obtained without
   the initiative?
C. These engagements will probably be kept?
D. The Socialist Party must reconsider the utility of constitutional initiatives?
E. Other.

French and Italian Switzerland	A	B	C	D	E	Received
Members of Federal Parliament	5	8	1	3	0	8
Members of Central Committee	3	4	1	1	1	6
Other cantonal leaders	9	7	2	4	0	9
Sub-total	17	19	4	8	1	23
Germanic Switzerland						
Members of Federal Parliament	17	17	4	3	0	19 *
Members of Central Committee	21	22	0	5	0	23
Other cantonal leaders	15	16	6	5	0	16
Sub-total	53	55	10	13	0	58
Total	70	74	14	21	1	81

* Includes one 'No Opinion'.

Several propositions seem to be reasonably verified by these
figures. A comfortable majority of socialist leaders continue to
believe that the constitutional initiative is a useful weapon
for their party, despite repeated defeats before the people. It is
true that a minority is sceptical in this respect, proportionally
more so in French Switzerland than in German Switzerland.
The enquiry also confirms that party leaders had hoped that

[45] *Ibid.*, 20 December 1967 and 7 March 1968. *Tagwacht* (Berne socialist
daily), 30 January and 8 March 1968.

the actual vote could have taken place on the basis of a counter-project presented by the Federal Council.[46] This would have made success probable and avoided the necessity for the sponsors of the initiative to undertake a costly campaign in a losing cause. A few respondents remarked, however, that a counter-project might not have been as acceptable as the projects presented after the vote. This is in fact the most interesting aspect of the enquiry – the conviction of party leaders that their initiative had obtained the commitment of the Federal Council and their adversaries to act finally on the problem of land-use planning. Certainly only a few are confident that the matter will be effectively pursued, while 35 respondents answered point (C) with a question mark. But it is clear that socialists view with guarded optimism the results of their initiative, which appears to have served as a meaningful stimulus to action.

CONCLUSION

It can be seen from this brief discussion that the referendum and the initiative are an integral part of Swiss political life and have an undeniable effect on the behaviour of the Socialist Party. There is a tendency among observers to attribute to the influence of these institutions some of the other characteristics of Swiss politics. Compromises and attempts to obtain the acquiescence of the different elements involved in a debate are encouraged by the possibility that one of them may resort to a referendum if it is too unsatisfied. Naturally, the tradition of federalism and the presence of important national minorities have also played a role in this regard. By the same token, it is probable that the practice of direct democracy has affected the relative position of the political parties and the interest groups in Switzerland. Just as the minority in parliament may attempt to overcome the majority by appealing to the people, interest groups can short-circuit the parliament and parties in the same way. When they do, they frequently dispose of more important financial resources than do the parties. Using the threat of this weapon, these groups can present themselves for

[46] The party offered twice in 1965 to withdraw its initiative if suggested counter-projects were approved. Gilg and Reymond, 'Année politique suisse 1965', p. 188.

negotiation directly with the executive at the stage of preparation of legislation. The formulation of governmental proposals
in consultation with the various interest groups is virtually an
institution in Switzerland, one which has reduced the discretion of the political parties in parliament.

The influence given to interest groups by direct democracy
would seem to be enhanced by the low levels of voting participation common in referenda. The most serious problem in this
respect is in French Switzerland, where 20 per cent participation is not uncommon. But German Switzerland shows only a
relatively better record. In the 1968 vote on women suffrage
in the canton of Berne, a subject which normally should have
attracted a high turnout, only 45 per cent of the electorate
went to the polls.[47] Of course, the frequency of such votes must
be considered to be partly responsible for this apathy. Judged
by the levels of voting participation, the composition of the
various parliaments could be said to be more representative of
the popular will than the outcome of a given consultation of
the 'sovereign'. Moreover, the apathy of the general populace
permits the minority which is actively concerned with a given
question to magnify its importance. This might appear at first
glance to be an advantage to the left, but socialists generally
believe that it is more difficult for them to mobilize their
clientèle than for middle-class groups to do so. To the extent
that interest groups are more capable of demonstrating to their
members the significance of a given vote than are the political
parties, the influence of the former is reinforced by the
diminishing interest of the general public in the exercise of its
authority.[48]

Another question which is raised by the practice of direct
democracy in Switzerland is the capacity of democratic institutions to respond to the challenges of modern society. The
efficiency of parliaments and their ability to carry on a meaningful dialogue with the executive is a problem which faces
many democratic countries. In Switzerland, it is aggravated by

[47] *Tagwacht*, 19 February 1968.
[48] Referring to the effects of referenda, Christopher Hughes has written,
'Swiss democracy is geared to pressure groups: it is a form of government
calculated to call such groups into existence and give them power. The
system could conceivably continue for a time without parties, but without
pressure groups it would not work at all.' Christopher Hughes, *The Parliament of Switzerland*, London, 1962, p. 34.

the displacement of authority from parliament to the electorate. But the executive is not necessarily strengthened by this
situation. Unquestionably, its role as arbiter and frequently
initiator is enhanced – it becomes the focus of the political
scene to a very great degree. On the other hand, in so far as
modern government requires planning and co-ordinated programmes, the Swiss executive may be in a weaker position than
in other countries because of the necessity to be able to justify
each of its measures before the citizenry at large. Such a task
frequently requires a demonstration of the gravity of a problem and the urgency for action. Hence measures designed to
have a beneficial effect only in the long run or to meet problems expected to develop in the future are likely to be more
difficult to enact than in a purely parliamentary system. Of
course, one need not agree that planning and co-ordinated
policies are desirable even given the complexities of the modern world. But the need for such policies has been acclaimed
from all sides in Switzerland in recent years.[49] Their absence
has been frequently blamed on the heterogeneous make-up of
the Federal Council. But as Federal Councillor Willy Spühler
has remarked, much of the difficulty is attributable to the constitutional structure of the country itself.[50]

The problems posed to parliaments by the increasingly technical nature of political decisions and the need for efficiency
are thus even more acute in a system of referendum and initiative. One might reason that the maintenance of close contact
between public authorities and the citizenry is itself a form
of efficiency – that the mutual interaction which results would
tend to avoid a breach between the actions of the one and the
reactions and needs of the other. Certainly many communities
make a remarkable effort to inform their citizens about the
matters upon which they must decide. But in fact the gap between government and citizen (and between government and
press) has been another source of discontent in Switzerland.
One may take the simple matter of the payment of taxes, for
example. Faced with widespread evasion, the government has

[49] In September, 1967, the National Council adopted a motion of the
Catholic deputy Leo Schürmann demanding that the Federal Council present
a four-year governmental programme to parliament. For an exposition of
Schürmann's views, see his article, 'Probleme der Allparteienregierung',
Annuaire suisse de science politique, VII, 1967, pp. 83–94.

[50] *Tagwacht*, 16 December 1967.

had to resort to a fiscal amnesty three times in less than thirty years. While one could not blame this breach on the system of direct democracy, it seems clear that those institutions have not greatly helped to heal it.

The effects of the rights of referendum and initiative on the Swiss political system are thus varied and not altogether what might be expected. The subject has been only partially explored in this article; little mention was made, for example, of their relevance to Swiss federalism. For the Socialist Party, the existence of these institutions entails several handicaps. The negative impact of the referendum and the premium awarded to groups of substantial financial means may outweigh the impulsion which can be given to reform through the use of the initiative. But these rights are embedded in the political culture of the country. It should not be expected that their existence will be put in question, by the socialists any more than by anyone else.

J. E. Spence

The Origins of Extra-Parliamentary Opposition in South Africa*

'THERE IS CAUSE FOR GRAVE CONCERN THAT SOUTH AFRICA HAS thus far been unable to develop any significant party, aggressively committed to a liberal solution of the racial problems.'[1] These words, written in 1956, by a distinguished South African historian, imply an important truth about South African politics, namely the extent to which the crucial issues of race relations have become, over five decades, interlocked with disputes between the two white language groups and partly submerged in the process.

These disputes have been ventilated in the context of a parliamentary system which since its inception in 1910 has remained the exclusive preserve of a white minority, determined to resist any challenge by the non-white majority for representation in the process of decision-making. This determination is partly a function of numbers and partly one of belief. As the largest white community on the continent, comprising three million out of a total population of fifteen million, its members, unlike their counterparts elsewhere in Africa, possess a degree of cohesion which finds expression in their self-identification as an indigenous group entitled to claim, on historical grounds, a role and a destiny as an African people.

This study will attempt to explain why this sense of peculiarity and its articulation in ideological terms has proved impervious to demands by liberal critics for wider participation of the non-white majority in the political process. This has occurred principally because the Afrikaner nationalist has so entrenched his party in power that it has proved impossible for

[1] C. W. de Kiewiet, *The Anatomy of South African Misery*, London, 1956, pp. 30–1.

* Vol. 1, no. 1, October 1965.

opponents, whether liberal or not, to dislodge it by the normal processes of constitutional change. Thus, paradoxically, a system which in the limited area of white politics was initially flexible enough to permit the gradual capture of power by an Afrikaner Nationalist party, has since become an abnormally rigid one, totally excluding a further extension of its boundaries to include the non-white majority.

This concentration of power in Afrikaner hands has proved disastrous to the liberal cause in South Africa. The bulk of its support has traditionally come from those who are excluded from a political system, the legitimacy of which extends only to the white electorate. Nor traditionally has the non-white majority been able to focus its aspirations on a parliamentary opposition which depends for its continued existence as an opposition on a white electorate and which, by definition, is forced to play the parliamentary game with a government which has not been averse to changing the rules from time to time. And since 1948, the non-white majority have become increasingly disillusioned with the efforts of white liberal spokesmen to improve their political and economic lot. Conversely, this loss of confidence has been paralleled by a heightened sense of African national self-consciousness, which has from time to time clashed openly with its white counterpart. In these circumstances, the liberal has inevitably found himself caught between two extremes, with each of the protagonists openly hostile to his plea for a gradual evolution to a more democratic society.

I propose to examine here the role of the United and Progressive opposition parties and at the same time, to stress the central dilemma facing the white liberal opponent of the South African government and the events which have forced on him a choice between parliamentary impotence or alignment with those non-white movements which have adopted extra-parliamentary positions, with all the dangers and moral dilemmas that opposition on this level inevitably entails.

THE TWO WHITE GROUPS

The ideological weakness of the English-speaking group helps to explain the significance of de Kiewiet's allusion to the absence of forthright and broadly based liberal opposition to the

policies of Afrikaner Nationalism, and in particular its refusal
to consider African claims for advancement. However divided
English and Afrikaner may have been about the status question, however concerned the former may have been about the
need to preserve the English language, the symbols of the
British connection, and the structure of English education, the
fact remains that they shared the assumptions of the Afrikaner
about the importance of maintaining the white man's dominant position in the political and economic life of the country.
They were often less articulate than their Afrikaner counterparts in defining precisely how this was to be done; absorbed
in business and professional interests, and enjoying a higher
standard of living, they were comparatively insulated from the
threat of competition from below – unlike 'poor white' Afrikaners whose demands for protection against the alleged indignities of manual labour, or 'kaffir' work, lent credence to the
Nationalist claim that the English-speaking community would
not scruple to ally itself with the non-white majority to further
its own interests.[2]

Yet this argument implied a degree of political sophistica-
tion on the part of the English-speaking South African which
simply did not exist, and which however attractive in principle, would have been ruled out by the unwillingness of the
group to accept the long-term political implications of such an
alliance.[3] Nevertheless the myth of this 'unholy alliance' has
persisted in Nationalist thinking and its convenience as a
political weapon in their struggle to gain maximum Afrikaner
support is obvious.

The electoral victory of the Nationalist Party in 1948 and
the consolidation and extension of its rule since that date have

[2] Cf. the Nationalist argument that the policy of accepting non-white
students followed until 1960 by the open English-speaking universities, was
designed to produce 'black Englishmen'. Since that date a number of 'tribal'
colleges have come into being, ostensibly to cater for the educational aspirations of the non-white on an ethnic basis.

[3] It is true that the English-speaking business class would benefit from the
relaxation of the industrial colour bar; the entry of non-white workers into
skilled and semi-skilled occupations would involve an increase in their
propensity to consume and open up the prospect of a large and hitherto
untapped market for the products of South Africa's manufacturing industry.
There are signs that this is already happening as the expansion of the
economy imposes intolerable strains on the government's policy of job reservation, and many industrialists have unilaterally raised non-white wages in
recent years.

placed the English-speaking minority in an unenviable position. Because of their attachment to the *status quo* towards the non-white majority, benefiting their position as members of a white minority – and despite the fact that the price of these benefits has meant accepting the leadership of the Afrikaners whether moderate or Nationalist – they have been unable to offer any parliamentary alternative and more liberal solution to South Africa's problems as a counter to the Apartheid policy. An alliance with the non-white communities, and an attempt to promote radical political change, appears to involve infinitely more dangerous possibilities than a *status quo* in which their security as whites seems to be guaranteed by a government determined to resist any internal or external threat to political stability and economic growth.

Traditionally, English-speaking South Africans have resented the exclusive nature of Afrikaner nationalism, especially its insistence that white unity is only possible on the assumption that non-Afrikaners accept the values of Afrikanerdom and recognize its special claim to embody the 'Volkswil'. For the Afrikaner Nationalist, the English-speaking group has been regarded as having a 'special relationship' with Britain, conflicting with any loyalty its members owe to the South African state. Their traditional attachment to the symbols of this relationship – the crown and the Union Jack – their loyalty to the Commonwealth ideal and their cultural and educational links with Britain, all suggested to the Afrikaner that his English-speaking counterpart was divided in his allegiance. This attitude was reinforced by conviction that this group constituted a British 'presence' in South Africa, acting as a constant reminder of the role that British imperialism has played in the Afrikaner's history.

Thus the politics of the first forty years of the Union were dominated by a struggle for power between the two white minorities, and one in which the Afrikaner Nationalist enjoyed an inestimable advantage over his English adversary. For the former, the conflict could be interpreted in terms of an ideology which emphasized two related themes: his struggle to achieve national self-determination (in practical terms this meant the breaking of the British connection and the establishment of a Nationalist Republic), and secondly, the positive and peculiar contribution which Afrikaners alleged that they

H

alone could make to the solution of the 'native problem'. The
achievement of the second aspiration was dependent on the
first, for only when a Nationalist Party was firmly established
as the government of South Africa, could the necessary
measures be taken to safeguard the Afrikaner heritage against
the challenges posed by a large and restless non-white majority.
Self-determination would, by itself, constitute a barren and
short-lived victory, if nothing substantial was done to halt the
insidious process of racial integration which had followed
South Africa's industrial expansion in the decades before and
after union in 1910.

Thus, precisely because Nationalist policy was ideological in
content, its protagonists appeared to have a comprehensive
answer for South Africa's problems, appropriate not only for
the relatively narrow issue of English–Afrikaner relations but
also in the wider context of the white determination to with-
stand any threat to its position of dominance from non-white
sources of pressure. Afrikaner resentment against the English-
speaking community's lack of sympathy was not mollified by
the tendency of the latter to accept the leadership of 'moderate'
Afrikaners like J. C. Smuts and J. H. Hofmeyr, branded by
extreme Nationalists as deserters from the Nationalist cause.
They were condemned as prepared to sacrifice 'real' Afrikaner
interests on the altar of a spurious South African nationhood,
ostensibly designed to unite both white groups but in practice
nothing more than a cunning ideological device to keep political power by deceiving enough Afrikaners into giving their
support to what was in reality the English-speaking interest.[4]

For many Nationalists, there was an obvious danger in the
laissez-faire attitude of the predominantly English business
community, who welcomed labour migration from the African
reserves to the towns and cities of the Union – regardless of
the long-term political implications of this development. Their
worst fears were confirmed in the depression years of the
1930s as hundreds of rural Afrikaners found themselves forced
off the land into the cities and into competition with African
labour, particularly in the semi- and unskilled employment

[4] Cf. the following contrasting statements: 'All South African politics is a
quarrel between Afrikaners on what attitude they shall take to the English'
(General J. C. Smuts, speaking in the 1930s). 'All politics is to bring together
those who belong together' (Dr D. F. Malan, leader of the Nationalist Party
1934–54).

categories. It is in this period that Afrikaner intellectuals like Dr H. F. Verwoerd and Dr W. W. M. Eiselen (both of the University of Stellenbosch) began to grope tentatively towards an uncompromising solution designed to protect Afrikaner interests, reverse as far as possible the mounting tide of economic and social integration, and at the same time divert African nationalist feeling into ethnic channels as a basis for the establishment of separate Bantu homelands. Between 1933 and 1948 the opposition Nationalist Party, led by Dr D. F. Malan, represented itself as the guardian of ideological purity, devoting its energies to formulating policies which it believed in time would weaken Afrikaner support for Smuts and ensure electoral success.[5]

Not surprisingly English-speaking South Africans, in their opposition to Afrikaner Nationalism, found it difficult to match the latter's ideological fervour. Pragmatic in outlook, they recognized intuitively that only in association with Afrikaners who rejected Nationalist appeals could they hope to exert political influence.[6] They rallied to Smuts who offered them the vision of a united white South Africa in which national origins would be increasingly irrelevant. With the coming of fusion in 1934, this goal seemed at last in sight. But this apparent reconciliation between Boer and Briton depended upon a degree of compromise which was anathema to Nationalist politicians who knew that their political strength lay in the schools and universities of Afrikaner South Africa. From these there emerged a generation of young men and women imbued with ideals which sharply contrasted with the liberal ethos of English universities like Johannesburg and Capetown. The history they learnt lent itself easily to an in-

[5] In 1933 J. B. Hertzog, Prime Minister and Leader of the Nationalist Party (in power since 1924), formed a coalition with Smuts's South Africa Party. A year later the two parties fused to become the United Party. A small rump of Nationalists remained in opposition as the Gesuiwerde Nasionale Party (the purified Nationalist Party) until their defeat of the United Party in 1948.

[6] This group was severely handicapped numerically for Afrikaners have always formed a majority in the electorate. In 1936, for example, the number of Afrikaner adults was 15 per cent higher than the figure for English-speaking South Africans. Under the age of seven, the ratio was 215 to 100 in favour of Afrikaner children; similarly, in the age group 7–20 the ratio was 180.2 to 100 again in favour of the Afrikaner. (I am grateful to Mr S. Trapido, of the Institute of Commonwealth Studies, for permission to make use of these figures which appear in an unpublished paper read at an Institute seminar on *The South African Party System.*)

terpretation which emphasized the injustices meted out to
their people by British imperialism. Nor did the process of
national identification stop in the schoolrooms and the lecture
theatres. Throughout the 1930s, Afrikaner Nationalism manifested itself in a host of separatist cultural and commercial
organizations, designed to give the embryonic nationalist that
crucial sense of self-awareness essential for the realization of his
political destiny.[7]

The Nationalist confidence in the electoral success of their
cause was buttressed by the knowledge that the Afrikaner
birth-rate was higher than that of their English-speaking
counterpart; electoral strategy was therefore shrewdly directed
at winning the maximum support in the less sparsely popu-
lated 'platteland' constituencies (the rural areas) where Afrikaners were in a clear majority and which were allowed a 15
per cent advantage over urban constituencies in delimiting
their size. In time, so Nationalist Party managers argued, Afrikaners in these vital constituencies would answer the call to
close ranks against the twin threats of continued English dominance in the country's domestic and external affairs and the
more fundamental challenge of African political aspirations.[8]

THE UNITED PARTY

The United Party has always been a coalition of diverse interests. It embraced at its right wing those Afrikaners for whom
the ideals of Botha and Smuts and their emphasis on a common
South African patriotism uniting English and Afrikaners have
represented the best hopes for progress. In the centre could be
found the vast majority of English-speaking South Africans
whose support for the party has traditionally been based on a
fear of domination by an exclusive Afrikaner Nationalism and
who, during Smut's lifetime, accepted the latter because of
his attachment to the Commonwealth and his willingness to

[7] These range from business and commercial associations (Chambers of
Commerce, Trade Unions, etc.) to cultural movements, Women's Organizations, and the Afrikaner equivalent of the Scout and Guide movement.

[8] The effect of this electoral loading has been supplemented by the fact that
the urban constituencies, traditionally the strongholds of the opposition
parties, have often produced large majorities for successful candidates, and
many of the votes are therefore wasted. Thus the Nationalist Party won the
1948 election with 40 per cent of the votes cast, and in 1961 51 per cent was
sufficient to give them 103 of the 156 seats at stake.

defend their interests against Nationalist encroachment. On the left, the liberal wing of the party, often associated with the leadership of Jan Hofmeyr, until his death in 1948, has never been numerically powerful and the difficulties of coexistence with the majority on racial issues have imposed stresses on party unity which have never been satisfactorily resolved. (Many left the party in 1959 to form the Progressive Party, the role of which is discussed below.) This lack of cohesion of the United Party has militated against it adopting an ideological programme attractive enough to counter Nationalist policies based on the emotional appeals to Republican sentiment and fear of black domination. Its leaders have always fought shy of committing the party to a liberal platform involving a promise of political rights to the voteless majority on the grounds that this would be tantamount to inviting self-destruction at the hands of an electorate which, despite revealing disagreement on a wide range of issues, is essentially conservative on questions affecting African political advancement.

The dilemmas facing a party of this kind are amply illustrated by its historical response to the crucial issue of non-white representation in South Africa's political institutions. In 1936 Hertzog and Smuts obtained the two-thirds majority of both Houses sitting together, required by the Constitution, for the removal of the small minority of Cape Africans (about 11,000), with the necessary qualifications, from the common voters' roll. In terms of the Representation of Natives Bill, passed in that year, these were placed on a separate roll and their representation was confined to three whites in the House of Assembly, while Africans throughout the country were allowed to elect by an indirect process four whites to the Senate. At the same time legislation was passed extending the size of the African reserve areas, but removing the right to purchase land outside these areas.[9] Hofmeyr, the Minister of the Interior at the time, and the avowed spokesman for liberal ideals in the Cabinet and the party as a whole, voted with ten others against this legislation, basing his opposition on the grounds that the Cape Africans were being deprived of a

[9] In addition a Natives Representative Council was established consisting of twelve elected African representatives, five white officials and the Secretary for Native Affairs as Chairman.

vested right and being given, instead, a 'qualified, an inferior citizenship'.

His speech on that April day in 1936 deserves analysis if only because it demonstrates the strength and weakness of the liberal position both at that time and in the later post-war period. Hofmeyr and his successors have always stressed the dangers of following a policy based on the assumption that there is a fundamental divergence of interests between white and non-white. This explains his objection to communal representation, particularly in its application to the educated African, and he correctly foresaw the emergence of a disillusioned African élite, no longer willing to place their faith in the so-called trusteeship policy of their white rulers.

His words deserve quotation at greater length: 'By this Bill we are sowing the seeds of a far greater potential conflict than has been done by anything in existence today. Let me explain. To my mind, as I have always felt, the crux of the position is in regard to the educated Natives. Many of them have attained to, and many more of them are advancing towards European standards. They have been trained on European lines, they have been taught to think and act as Europeans, we may not like it, but those are the plain facts. Now what is the political future for these people? This Bill says that even the most educated Native shall never have political equality with even the least educated and the least cultured White or Coloured man. This Bill says to these educated Natives: "There is no room for you, you must be driven back upon your own people." But we drive them back in hostility and disgruntlement, and do not let us forget this, that all that this Bill is doing for those educated Natives is to make them the leaders of their own people, in disaffection and revolt.'[10]

But the liberalism[11] of men like Hofmeyr was essentially defensive in orientation, and, as such, as two Afrikaner writers have pointed out: 'the Liberals were decisively defeated in 1936, while the northern point of view achieved its greatest

[10]Alan Paton, *Hofmeyr*, OUP, Cape Town, 1964, pp. 227–8.

[11] Professor W. M. Macmillan has described the Great Trek (the migration of Boer farmers from the Cape in the 1830s and 1840s) as a 'substantial defeat of the enlightened liberalism that triumphed in the Cape in the emancipation of the Hottentots in 1828, and of the slaves in 1838 ...' *Bantu, Boer and Briton*, London, 1936, p. 167.

victory'.[12] This was hardly surprising, given the ideological terms in which Hertzog defined the issue of white self-preservation in introducing the Bill: 'It is a sacred principle, a Christian principle just the same as any other principle, and it stands equally high – I place that principle still higher, it is the only principle, that of self-preservation, that of self-defence, by which humanity itself and Christianity itself will ever be able to protect itself.'[13] Against claims of this sort liberal arguments could make little headway. English and Afrikaner could unite to support Hertzog on an issue which fundamentally affected their interests as whites and forget for a moment the narrower grievances dividing them. And for Smuts, as Deputy Prime Minister in Hertzog's United Party government, support for Hofmeyr's stand would have meant the danger of splitting his party at a time when tensions in the outside world made it imperative that white South Africans of both national groups unite to face their consequences.[14]

While the United Party's attitude on the question of the political future of South Africa's non-white majority continued to be ambivalent, its Nationalist opponents were, by 1948, in the fortunate position of being able to offer a simple and easily comprehensible formula as a solution for South Africa's problems. The Apartheid policy, and all that it promised those who were disturbed by the apparently limitless process of economic integration between black and white, was given added relevance by the disturbing and, for Smuts, quite unexpected criticism levelled at South Africa's policies at the United Nations and elsewhere. In this situation the United Party was hopelessly vulnerable to attacks on its liberal wing as represented by Hofmeyr. Nationalist propaganda offered the electorate a straightforward choice between 'equality and a coffee-coloured race' – the inevitable consequence of returning Smuts and his heir-apparent Hofmeyr to power – or Apartheid which, as Eric Walker has defined it, meant 'the permanent physical,

[12] N. J. Rhoodie and H. J. Venter, *Apartheid*, HAUM, Cape Town, 1960, p. 140.

[13] Paton, *op. cit.*, p. 224.

[14] Smuts's decision to support Hertzog's legislation is well-expressed in the following quotation from the speech he made in the debate in the House of Assembly: 'Of course, I could have died in the last ditch so to say, I could have said, I fight to the bitter end for the Cape Native Franchise, but what would have been the result? It would not have been I who died, but the natives, metaphorically speaking.' *Ibid.*, pp. 224–5.

mental and, as far as might be, spiritual separation of the four
great racial groups in the Union, each from the other, partly to
preserve the racial purity of each, partly to do away with the
friction that arose from intermingling and partly to give each
the chance of developing along its own lines in its own appointed place'.[15] Nationalistic tactics were triumphantly vindi-
cated by the result of the election of 1948: United Party
strength in the House of Assembly was reduced by 32 seats, the
vast majority of which were situated in the Afrikaner-domi-
nated rural areas.

The choice for the defeated party seemed clear: outdo the
Nationalists at their own game, offering the electorate a more
sophisticated version of 'baaskap' or cut its losses on the
platteland and adopt a vigorous liberal policy, trusting to the
good sense of the white electorate to exercise in the fullness of
time a degree of rational self-interest, recognizing that power
would have to be shared with their non-white fellow-South
Africans. In the end the United Party did neither. Hofmeyr
survived pressure from the right wing of the Party to force his
resignation, but his death shortly afterwards ended speculation
that he might in time resign and with his closest supporters
form a Liberal Party committed to joining the racial issue
squarely with the Nationalists.

For the next eleven years his party contrived to maintain
a state of uneasy coexistence between left- and right-wing
elements.[16] At times it has given the impression of hoping to
profit from Nationalist mistakes rather than formulate any
clearly defined alternative policy to that of Apartheid, in the
belief that this will provoke a split within its opponents' ranks
and make possible a return to the golden era of fusion.[17] The
United Party's emphasis on 'White leadership as the vehicle
of Western civilization in South Africa in the interests of both

[15] Eric Walker, *A History of Southern Africa*, London, 1962, p. 769.

[16] In 1954 a small number of right-wing conservative United Party MPs
formed the National Conservative Party. This party had a short life: its
members either joined the Nationalist Party or lost their seats at the next
General Election.

[17] In this context it is worth pointing out that rumours of a right-wing revolt
in Nationalist ranks appear spasmodically in the English-speaking press. Supporters of this mythical revolt are alleged to be in favour of a return to a
policy of straightforward white supremacy, and object to the Bantustan
doctrines as being too 'liberal'.

white and non-white'[18] was rarely spelt out in detail in the electoral context of the 1950s and its ambivalence on the crucial question of non-white political rights hardly commended itself to the electorate. Moreover, the fundamental ambiguities of United Party policy in the long years of opposition were a source of political capital to its opponents. The tension between the two wings of the United Party in the years before 1959 and the resulting ambivalence on the crucial issue of recognition of non-white political claims forced the party into an unenviable position in the competition for power: the relatively liberal attitudes of the left wing of the party could be attacked with impunity by Nationalists who fully understood the hostility of most white South Africans to egalitarian doctrines, deemed to have no relevance (except perhaps as an incitement to discontent among non-whites) to the peculiar problems of South Africa. The right wing and predominantly Afrikaner supporters of the United Party could be exposed as pale and inadequate imitations of their Nationalist counterparts, unwilling to recognize that their true political allegiance lay with the Nationalist Party and divided from it because of irrational grievances which no longer had any substance in reality. This two-pronged attack on the United Party has in fact paid substantial dividends, for Afrikaner support for the party has steadily decreased since 1948. The vast majority of those who have reached voting age since that date, and for whom the old controversies between Smuts and Hertzog are matters of history rather than personal experience, support the Nationalist Party, particularly as government service has always been a major source of Afrikaner employment.[19] Continued success at the polls has had a cumulative effect on the party's standing among Afrikaners in general. Nor has the United Party's position been helped by the changes made by the Nationalist government in the franchise arrangements laid down in the 1909 Constitution. The removal of the Cape Coloured voters from the common roll in 1956 was justified by its supporters as a logical step in the implementation of Apartheid 'in all the

[18] *Handbook for Better Race Relations*, issued by the United Party, August 1963.

[19] For confirmation of this point, see S. Trapido, 'Political Institutions and Afrikaner Social Structures in the Republic of South Africa', *American Political Science Review*, no. 1, March 1963, pp. 75–87.

spheres of living', including the parliamentary area. But even if this ideological element was present in the decision to establish a separate roll for Coloured voters, there can be no doubt that the Nationalist Party had at the same time strengthened its position as the ruling group. Its tacticians had calculated, just as their predecessors in the 1920s and 1930s had done in the controversy over the removal of Cape Africans from the common roll, that the elimination of the Coloured voter would give them control in those constituencies where previously it had held the balance in the competition between the parties.[20] The discouragement of immigration for many years after 1948 and, more important, the creation of six new seats for South-West Africa, all of which returned Nationalist candidates, together with the lowering of the voting age to eighteen, must be seen in the same context.

THE NEW OPPOSITION, INSIDE AND OUTSIDE PARLIAMENT

A number of other factors have also contributed to the United Party's difficulties as a vehicle of opposition. Perhaps the most important is the fact that from time to time dissatisfaction with the quality of the party's role in opposition has led to the formation of (a) organizations outside the parliamentary arena dedicated to fighting the Nationalist Party on *specific* issues which in their view have been soft-pedalled by the official opposition; and (b) political parties such as the Liberal and Federal Parties (both established in 1953) and the Progressive Party (established in 1959) which emerged because of radical disagreement within the United Party on ideological grounds.

Examples of the former were the Torch Commando, a body of ex-servicemen formed in the early 1950s; the Black Sash, a women's organization, the Defenders of the Constitution, the Anti-Republican League – all of whose membership was predominantly English-speaking and concerned specifically to act as organs of radical protest against what they construed to be Nationalist attempts to manipulate the constitution in the

[20] 'In 1927, General Hertzog calculated that 12 seats would fall to the Nationalists if African voters were removed from the roll. Similarly, in 1948, the Nationalist Party made no effort to hide the fact that they hoped to win 8 seats by removing coloured voters from the roll.' S. Trapido, unpublished paper, *op. cit.*

interests of Afrikanerdom and its permanent entrenchment in power. But few if any of these groups were prepared to advocate a fundamental recasting of the structure of South African politics, and as such found themselves supporting a return to the *status quo ante* – a weak position from which to assault a government which made no secret of its claim that only forceful measures could ensure the security of a white minority in a continent increasingly hostile to its very existence.

Three political parties emerged in the 1950s and attempted to challenge the United Party's monopoly of opposition to the Nationalist government. The Federal Party, which drew the bulk of its support from the predominantly English-speaking province of Natal (where many of the organizations mentioned earlier derived a large measure of their support), acknowledged the long-term desirability of allowing specially qualified non-whites a place on the common voters roll.[21] Yet its major objective was the creation of a federal system in which the rights of an English-speaking province like Natal would be protected by a rigid constitution. It vehemently opposed the establishment of a Republic and regarded the United Party stand on this issue as thoroughly unsatisfactory.

The Liberal Party, which drew together on a multi-racial basis many of those for whom Apartheid was intrinsically immoral, offered in the six years before the emergence of the Progressive Party in 1959 a political refuge to those who thought that the United Party's leadership lacked the courage to challenge the government on the most fundamental issue of South African politics – the political destiny of the non-white majority. Its membership, though genuinely non-racial, was never large, drawn mainly from the ranks of South Africa's tiny intellectual minority. Many of its white supporters were Jewish (which for many of the Nationalists was enough to damn the party irretrievably), many were university teachers

[21] 'The present system of limited group representation of natives to be maintained, and an interim period of group representation of Indians on a system similar to that accorded to natives to be initiated. Subject always to due safeguards against disproportionate representation of any one section of the non-European population, the long-term policy to be taken in steps over a considerable period of years, is the ultimate placing of those non-Europeans who have passed suitable tests of a high standard, upon the common roll of voters.' From the programme of the Union Federal Party in D. W. Krüger, *South African Parties and Policies, 1910–1960*, Cape Town, 1960.

or students, or members of the professional middle-class who in the 1930s and 1940s had pinned their hopes on Hofmeyr as the one United Party leader capable of revolutionizing his party and forcing its policies in a liberal direction. Its non-white membership was concentrated among those Africans, Coloureds, and Indians who found the politics of the Congress Alliance[22] too extreme, and in Natal where their numbers were largest, the majority could be found in the rural areas, particularly among those who owned property and were therefore vulnerable to government policies designed to eradicate 'black spots' in areas scheduled for exclusive white occupation.

Liberals, however, made little impact on a white society, many of whom were effectively insulated from contact with members of the educated non-white élite, and for whom even the modest qualified franchise proposals of the Liberal Party were too extreme. The party put up candidates at general elections, but these invariably did poorly, even in the allegedly 'liberal' English-speaking constituencies in Cape Town and North Johannesburg. Its membership was scattered and it lacked even the regional base that Natal to some extent provided for the Federal Party. It was essentially a party of protest and few of its members ever expected to win any substantial victory on the parliamentary front. Some of its most distinguished members, most notably Mrs Margaret Ballinger, Mr Walter Stanford, Senators Leslie Rubin and William Ballinger, did, however, win election to Parliament as Native Representatives and were a most articulate opposition to government policies.[23] In the later 1950s the party formally approved in principle the use of extra-parliamentary non-violent pressure against the government.[24] But appropriate

[22] This consisted of the African National Congress, the Natal Indian Congress, the Multi-Racial South African Congress of Trade Unions, and the white left-wing Congress of Democrats.

[23] This native representation was abolished in 1960, and the party lost its precarious foothold in the House of Assembly and the Senate. Their role had become increasingly difficult as the following comment by Professor Julius Lewin makes clear: 'By 1950, if not before, Africans had lost all confidence in white liberal leadership and in the restrained and moderate policies which it presented in the face of the formidable challenge of the Nationalists.' *Politics and Law in South Africa*, London, 1963, p. 45.

[24] See the following extract from a Liberal Party statement printed in 1960: 'As long as the political struggle in South Africa is confined to the Parliamentary field alone, the Nationalists have shown that they cannot lose. They have marked the pack and every deal gives them all the aces. It is in any case

techniques were never worked out in detail and perhaps in the nature of things could not be – especially in view of the failure of passive resistance movements early in the post-war period. Individual members identified themselves with the non-white cause in this particular struggle, but given the resources of the party, the small membership and other organizational difficulties, Liberals were rarely if ever in the position to mount an organized non-violent campaign against the government on a unilateral basis.

THE PROGRESSIVE PARTY

A more fundamental challenge to the United Party was the emergence of the Progressive Party in 1959. This consisted initially of twelve MPs belonging to the liberal wing of the United Party, who had long been in conflict with more conservative elements. Their influence on the United Party was implicitly condemned at the 1959 Annual Congress as the following resolution makes clear: 'In view of the liberalistic principles attributed to our party, we ask Congress to reaffirm our policy on matters of race relations ... that the United Party must be conservative in approach to South African problems and avoid at all times the Liberal view so prevalent in the Party's debates in Parliament.'[25]

The party's programme, adopted at an inaugural Congress in November 1959, advocated a non-racial qualified franchise, a reform of the constitution, involving the establishment of safeguards for the protection of minorities and the inclusion of a Bill of Rights. Its twelve representatives in Parliament, together with the three Native Representatives, were vigorous in their opposition to Nationalist legislation, and for the first time since the death of Hofmeyr in 1948 the underlying issue of South African politics was forced into the context of

impossible for four-fifths of our people, and the majority of members of the Liberal Party, to do anything at all through Parliament. They are excluded from it completely. Extra-Parliamentary pressure is therefore quite justified in South Africa and the Liberal Party is committed to its use so long as it is non-violent.' 'Symposium on Racial Policies of South Africa's Main Political Parties', *Race Relations Journal*, Johannesburg, vol. XXVII, no. 4, October/December 1960, p. 141.

[25] The reference to the 'liberal view so prevalent ... in Parliament' may be seen as a grudging admission of the liberals' greater articulation and energy in the debate with the Nationalist government.

electoral debate by a party representing white voters. In effect
the electorate were at last being given a clear choice between
Apartheid and the creation of six or seven Bantustans (where
the African majority would, so Nationalists claimed, have the
right to political and economic self-determination on a separate
but equal basis) and Progressive policy which asked white
South Africa to recognize that the country was a multi-racial
society requiring a political structure which took this crucial
factor into account.

Since the formation of the Progressive Party, the United
Party was forced to fight the electoral battle on two fronts,
resorting to accusations that Progressive candidates would
inevitably split the vote of the anti-Nationalist opposition in
any future election. Progressive strategy was tacitly directed
not so much at defeating the government at the polls (a long-
term aspiration), but at supplanting the United Party as the
official and legitimate opposition, in the eyes of the white
public. This was the only alternative, given the fact that the
Nationalist Party was electorally secure so long as it was backed
by the great majority of Afrikaners dominating the rural constituencies, many of which the United Party had lost irretrievably in the years since 1948.[26] But these hopes received a severe
setback in the 1961 election when the party lost all but one of
its 12 seats in the House of Assembly and it is significant that
the government went to the country two years before this was
constitutionally necessary, suggesting a determination to
eliminate Progressive strength in Parliament and reduce their
effectiveness as an opposition challenging the government's
policy on a root and branch basis.[27] Clearly the Nationalists
prefer a situation in which formal opposition is confined to a
party which appears to share many of its assumptions about
the importance of maintaining white rule, and which can be
exposed to the taunt that it has no clear alternative policy for
meeting the political aspirations of the non-white majority.

Another result of the emergence of the Progressives was to

[26] In the 1961 election the United Party conceded one-third of the total
number of seats to the Nationalist Party – a move which hardly enhanced
their claim to be an alternative government.
[27] See the remarks of Mr B. J. Vorster, the present Minister of Justice: 'They
[the Progressives] were a dangerous Party, undermining the foundations of
our existence.' *Rand Daily Mail*, September 1961, quoted by S. Trapido, unpublished paper, *op. cit.*

induce a reconsideration of the United Party native policy. Its platform for the 1961 election promised legal and political equality to the Cape Coloured population, an undertaking to negotiate with the Indian community on their future status and finally a Race Federation as an alternative to the creation of independent Bantustans. The concept of the Race Federation envisaged a federal legislature in which groups rather than geographical units would be represented and responsible for central finance, defence, foreign policy, trade, commerce, and inter-race relations. In addition each racial group would be entitled to the 'widest possible measure of communal government, especially in such matters as education, cultural affairs, local government, and certain matters of public health'.[28] Africans would be entitled to eight white MPs elected on a separate roll, although in time direct African representation would be considered, but the party's preoccupation with the notion of 'white leadership' as the dominant feature of any new constitutional pattern remained strikingly evident, as does its insistence on the necessity of retaining 'wise conventions like social and residential separation without these being symbols of oppression to any race'. It is significant too that the long-term proposal for direct African representation was not given wide prominence during the electoral campaign of 1961. What is perhaps new, and here the influence of Progressive thinking is discernible, is the emphasis on 'standards of civilization' as the qualification for group representation in the central Parliament.[29]

Clearly the policy is being presented as a compromise between what are conceived to be the doctrinaire extremes of Nationalist Bantustan theory and Progressive multi-racialism. And as a compromise it suffers from all the defects of a policy lacking a firm ideological foundation. Bantustans are rejected because their establishment as viable states appears economically impossible and politically dangerous in so far as they contribute to the fragmentation of the State's territorial integrity. By the same token, a qualified non-racial franchise

[28] *Handbook for Better Race Relations*, United Party publication, August 1963.
[29] '. . . Each race is represented in the Central Parliament in accordance with that state of civilisation it has reached, so that the most advanced groups will retain political power, although sharing it with the less advanced.' (Mr Marais Steyn, a prominent United Party leader.) *Ibid.*

for individual voters on a common role is regarded as committing the country to black majority rule and by implication the collapse of any attempt to retain power in the hands of civilized responsible elements. Instead each racial group is offered a *'predetermined* [author's italics] share in the government of the country' – a proposal which in effect tries to knit together the Progressive emphasis on non-white participation in government with Nationalist determination to maintain power in white hands.[30]

THE LIMITATIONS OF PARLIAMENTARY OPPOSITION

It seems fair to conclude from this analysis of Parliamentary opposition in South Africa, that neither the United Party nor the Progressives are capable of projecting themselves as an alternative government. Neither party can hope to make inroads into the solid phalanx of Afrikanerdom which is becoming increasingly monolithic in character. Nor is it clear that the United Party can count on automatic support from English-speaking voters, some of whom appear to be shifting their allegiance to the Nationalist camp, if the recent provincial elections are any guide in this context.[31] If the outlook is bleak for a conservative United Party, it is even more depressing for the future of the Progressives whose task is complicated by the fact that for the majority of the electorate (including many English-speaking South Africans), Nationalist policies appear to have guaranteed not only security but an extraordinarily high standard of living as well. Progressives are thus handicapped by the fact that their criticism of the government relates to the possible long-term effects of its policies and cannot therefore be easily identified with a *status quo* which appears stable and prosperous. Progressives are in effect asking the electorate to give up the benefits of the present dispensation on the grounds that these are illusory and short-term, in the expectation that a redistribution of power between black and white can and will operate peacefully, remain subject to con-

[30] '. . . The Party gives the electorate a guarantee that it will not extend non-white political rights beyond those specifically defined above without first seeking the approval of a decisive majority of the electorate.' *Ibid.*

[31] The United Party lost 10 seats in these elections, most of which were in English-speaking areas.

trol by constitutional formulae, and induce a measure of long-term political and economic stability. Thus Progressive strategy rests on the assumption that a majority of white South Africans can in time be induced to make 'rational' long-term calculations about their future prospects under continued Nationalist rule, based on an enlightened estimate of their own self-interest in survival. They are following the prescription of a distinguished South African constitutional lawyer who has argued the need 'to break fear with counter-fear and to make the counter-fear felt'.[32]

But to be effective the party requires a substantial base in the House of Assembly and this of necessity has involved them in a competition with the United Party for recognition as the only real opposition to the Nationalist government. Underlying this short-term aspiration is the assumption that the status of being the most important opposition party will enable it to challenge the government directly and force it into a genuine debate on the merits of their rival and opposed solutions for the Republic's problems. This, however, is to place too much faith in the alleged advantages to be gained from a situation in which government and opposition take extreme positions. Even if we assume (and this is highly unlikely) the virtual elimination of the United Party and its replacement by an articulate and ideologically coherent Progressive opposition, it is not clear that the government's hold on power would be seriously jeopardized. Progressive gains on this scale would be largely confined to English-speaking centres of influence and confirm the Afrikaner Nationalist in his traditional distrust of his white opponents as supporters of African advance to the detriment of Afrikaner interests. Then again the real difficulty with the Progressive long-term aspiration to be recognized as an alternative government with a substantial claim on the potential allegiance of a majority of the electorate, is that it assumes an electoral model in which the electorate is relatively homogeneous, whose aspirations can be satisfied by a party

[32] 'Indeed it might be accepted almost as an axiom that there is no prospect for the lasting success of any alternative to apartheid, and in particular no hope of bringing about a *peaceful* change in current trends of policy, unless it is possible to convince the white man that the dangers implicit in apartheid are very much greater than the risks involved in a common society organised on a democratic and non-racial basis.' D. V. Cowen, *The Foundations of Freedom*, OUP, Cape Town, 1961, p. 73.

structure in which ideological loyalties are weak or non-existent, and portions of which can be persuaded to detach their support from a government which has neglected particular group interests in a tangible way.

The Nationalist Party, however, is not lightly deserted by its supporters who see it as more than just an agency for providing benefits to sectional interests such as the farming community or the skilled urban workers. The party has combined a conventional appeal based on promises to protect the material interests of Afrikaners with a charismatic invocation to remain united against the forces that threaten the national identity. The party strength depends therefore on cultural factors which impose a pattern of conformist behaviour on its supporters. This makes a Nationalist government less responsive to the demands of pressure groups, whether Afrikaner or English-speaking, and in the last analysis the former can always be relied upon for electoral support however much their short-term interests may be damaged by the government. Rarely, if ever, will such groups question the legitimacy of the Nationalist claim to defend their fundamental long-term interests as members of a white Afrikaner minority. Thus so long as the present government continues to persuade Afrikaners to vote as Afrikaners, Progressives cannot hope to oust it from power even if we assume their substitution for the United Party as the major opposition group. Thus whatever advantages Progressives may hope to win by their role as a militant, ideologically orientated opposition, will be nullified by their inability to offer themselves as an alternative government in an electoral context unable to provide for the possibility of a rational conversion of their opponents.

One conclusion that does appear to follow from this analysis is the fact that the traditional functions of an opposition – both to oppose and project itself as an alternative government – have not been easily reconciled in the South African context. It has been argued that a party which finds itself committed to a long spell in the political wilderness is bound to find its electoral prospects dimmed if it persists in the attempt to fulfil the second of these traditional conceptions of the role of an opposition.[33] In the period before 1959 the United Party, be-

---

[33] Bernard Crick, 'Two Theories of Opposition', *New Statesman*, 18 June 1960, pp. 882–3.

cause of its internal dissensions and its crucial ambivalence on native policy, could fulfil neither of these functions: it was unable to project itself as diametrically opposed to Nationalist ideology, nor by the same token convince the electorate that it was capable of governing the country more efficiently than its rival. For it to adopt a policy based simply on the thesis of opposition for opposition's sake, assumed a move to the left by the party as a whole and the victory of the liberal wing over the conservative elements. The defection of the Progressives, however, with their policy different in every important respect from that of the government, represented a victory for the right-wing whose members comforted themselves with the illusory assurance that the electorate would in time recognize the party's claim to be an alternative government and, wearying of Nationalist mistakes, return them to office. It was essential, therefore, so party strategists calculated, to emphasize that their leaders, like their Nationalist counterparts, stood for the maintenance of power in white hands, confining disagreement with the government to the issue of the best means of achieving this objective. But for reasons which have been made explicit earlier this strategy has proved unsuccessful.

Conversely, the Progressive Party, since its defeat by the United Party on the Parliamentary front, has been in no position to offer itself as an alternative government; on the other hand, despite the fact that its policies are fundamentally opposed to those of the Nationalists, it has to avoid appearing 'irresponsible', suffering the fate of the Liberal Party and being condemned by the electorate as a party of cranks and idealists, lacking any appreciation of the realities of South African politics. The government has effectively capitalized on these dilemmas facing the opposition. It has been able to offer itself as a party with a carefully devised programme to meet the aspirations of both black and white in the Republic. Whenever it is challenged on the ideological merits of this programme, it need do no more than point to the failure of the United Party to suggest a viable alternative, and confirm the electorate in its assumption that a United Party government would do little to alter the *status quo* and be less successful than the Nationalists in maintaining it. On the other hand, Progressive attacks can be ignored if only because the government is secure in the knowledge that the vast majority of voters find its policies totally irrelevant to South Africa's problems and positively dangerous in so far as they contribute to the encouragement of African nationalist aspirations.

EXTERNAL AND ECONOMIC SIDE-LIGHTS

Two other factors remain to be considered in analysing the reasons for Nationalist success at the polls and the corresponding decline in the effectiveness of opposition to them. One is the effect of external hostility to the Apartheid policy on the political attitudes of the white electorate. The attacks on South Africa by the African states at the United Nations and elsewhere, the possibility of intervention posed by the sanctions threat, the successful attempts to expel the Republic from a number of international organizations, have all contributed to a hardening of white opinion in the face of demands from the outside for a reversal of current policies and the institution of a more liberal regime.[34]

This antagonism to South Africa has clearly strengthened the government's position. The large propaganda machine at its disposal has spared no effort to draw a parallel between the attacks of 'alien liberalistic' forces and the efforts of those within the Republic to discredit Nationalist policies. The latter's motives are held to be at best misguided and naïve, and at worst suspect and designed to subvert the security of the state and the welfare of its inhabitants. The equation of liberalism with communism is not uncommon and the following quotation from a speech by the Minister of Justice, Mr B. J. Vorster, is a striking example of the government's manipulation of an external threat in the context of domestic politics: 'It is obvious to my mind that the people in South Africa who are not only primarily the victims of communism, but who, particularly because we have declared communism to be unlawful and do not give it an opportunity to show its true colours, are easily, wittingly or unwittingly, the prime promoters of communism, are liberalists. I do not want to say for one moment that all liberals are communists. I have said

[34] For a fuller discussion on this point, see J. E. Spence, *Republic Under Pressure, a Study of South African Foreign Policy*, OUP for Chatham House, 1965, especially pp. 11–34.

repeatedly that this is not necessarily the case, but I do not know of one single Communist who has not at the same time pretended to be a Liberal.'[35]

Nor is this assessment of the external dangers threatening the Republic confined to Afrikaners. English-speaking South Africans are proving to be as sensitive as their Afrikaner counterparts to outside criticism and resent in particular attempts by the Republic's opponents to promote radical change through boycotts and other pressures.[36] Increasingly the issues that divided Boer and Briton are being submerged by a common belief that their survival as a white minority is at stake, and that this would still be the case even if the Nationalist government were ousted by a 'moderate' United Party.

Thus for many among the English-speaking minority the possibility of African majority rule is more profoundly disturbing than any inroads made by their traditional opponents into the structure of civil liberties. Their passive acceptance of Republican status since the departure from the Commonwealth in 1961 presents the most striking evidence of this shift in English-speaking attitudes while the country's high rate of recovery since the dark months following Sharpeville in 1960 has convinced them of the government's ability to maintain a prosperity of which they are the chief beneficiaries. In these circumstances it is not surprising that the government's attacks on liberalism have become increasingly acceptable to an electorate seeking for a single-cause explanation of their country's internal and external difficulties.

Equally important has been Nationalist success in dealing with internal threats to the *status quo*. The elaboration of effective techniques of social control – banning orders, house arrest, 90-day detention – appears to have successfully intimi-

[35] House of Assembly Debates, 6 March 1964, col. 2632.

[36] See, for instance, the work of the South Africa Foundation, a private propaganda organization established in 1959, consisting predominantly of businessmen and industrialists and concentrating its efforts in those countries which have important trading links with South Africa. An important feature of its propaganda is the stress laid on the material advantages enjoyed by non-whites in South Africa as compared with the inhabitants of newly independent black African States. Note also the argument in a recent leading article in the Johannesburg *Sunday Chronicle*: 'It is a pity there is no way of testing the validity of the often repeated claim by the sanctions minded that Africans in the Republic are overwhelmingly for a world boycott in South Africa. In the absence of such a sounding, do those who will not even miss a meal have the right to decide for those who will unquestionably starve?'

dated the use of violence by non-white opponents on any large
scale and these measures have received bi-partisan support.[37]
This bi-partisan approach to the problems posed by internal
and external threats has given Dr Verwoerd a useful weapon
in the domestic arena. Appeals for white unity can be
addressed to an English-speaking audience disillusioned by
seventeen years in opposition and prepared to concede, however grudgingly, that their economic interests have not
suffered unduly under Nationalist rule, and more positively,
aware of its vulnerability as part of a white minority. Entering
the Nationalist 'laager' would appear to guarantee their
security in the short term at least; by contrast, rallying to the
Progressive ranks involves a readjustment in attitudes and
expectation too painful to contemplate seriously. Nor would
there be any guarantee in the latter instance that the outside
world would be satisfied with the promise of slow, orderly
evolution in the direction of a multi-racial society, integrated
at every level of economic and political activity.

This consensus on the importance of keeping the outside
world at bay not only materially benefits the Nationalist grip
on power but complicates the task of the two opposition parties
in their efforts to find alternative formulations of domestic
policy. Neither the United Party nor the Progressives can
afford to risk offering the electorate choices which suggest that
their leaders are bending over-much to the pressures of the
outside world. To do this is to risk identification with what are
considered to be 'extremist' elements in the coalition ranged
against the Republic, thus laying themselves open to the
accusation that they wish to damage the government's position
for purely self-interested reasons of electoral strategy. The
failure of the Progressives to capture a single seat (with the
exception of two in the Cape Peninsula representing Cape
Coloured voters on the separate roll) is perhaps evidence of
the extent to which this interpretation has been laid on their

[37] See an important speech by Sir de Villiers Graaff in Durban in April
1964, in which he accepted the government's assumption that 'Over all hangs
the shadow of Communism and the cold war' and asked for a joint standing
committee of parliament to keep national defence problems on a non-party
basis (*Rand Daily Mail*, April 1964). It is also significant that the government's
1964 White Paper on defence was accepted by the House of Assembly with only
minor criticisms, indicating a high degree of bi-partisanship on the importance
of defending South Africa from external attack.

policies by many among the white electorate. In this context it is significant that Dr Verwoerd attacked the Progressives' attempt to win Coloured support as 'meddling in non-white politics', and has indicated his intention of passing legislation which will make it difficult if not impossible for Progressive candidates to be nominated in these particular constituencies.

Another factor is the possible effect of economic developments. Many Progressive and United Party supporters tend to place their faith in the erosion of Apartheid by the pressure of economic forces alone. They point to the growing shortage of skilled labour in the Republic's booming economy, and the sheer impossibility of reversing the increasing drift of Africans from the rural areas to the urban, highly-industrialized regions. In time, they argue, the official policy of reserving jobs in a wide variety of occupations for white workers will crumble as the demand for skilled workers, regardless of racial group, becomes impossible to resist.[38] In these circumstances the government would be unable to prevent the emergence of an African middle and lower-middle class, permanently domiciled in the large cities of South Africa and with whom a political settlement of some kind would ultimately have to be made. Both the United Party and the Progressives opposed for example the Bantu Laws Amendment Act of 1964 on the grounds that this legislation in effect denied any claim on the part of the urban African worker to a settled existence in these areas with all the property and personal rights this would imply.[39]

Underlying this opposition to government policy is the assumption that the emergence of an African middle class will act as a buffer between the white minority and a dissatisfied African majority. Moreover as industrial expansion increased, more and more non-whites would be absorbed into this group, the majority of whom would have a vested interest in peaceful,

[38] Cf. a letter to the *Spectator* (21 August 1964) from Jan Botha, National Public Relations Secretary of the Progressive Party: 'Continued prosperity in the Republic with the added momentum of economic integration and closer economic ties with the Republic will do more to break down the artificial barriers of Apartheid than all the talk of sanctions will ever do.'

[39] 'The Urban Bantu will be given a stake in the maintenance of law and order by . . . the United Party policy of actively fostering the emergence of a responsible middle class as a bulwark against agitators . . .' *Handbook for Better Race Relations.*

orderly constitutional change. From this group would come
those non-whites which the United Party believe deserve
representation in terms of its Race Federation policy, and by
the same token Progressives would argue for their enfran-
chisement on a common roll, provided certain well-defined
educational, financial, and property qualifications could be
met by prospective voters. Thus, apart from electoral considerations, both parties resent external pressure, because its
exponents seek to do quickly and without regard to the long-
term interests of all racial groups, what economic forces alone
can do – that is, alter the *status quo* peacefully and without
the destructive element involved in any attempt to change it
by violence. In effect both parties, in endorsing this particular
view of the future, are asking for a respite from the chorus of
attacks levelled at South Africa by the outside world. Given
enough time and a relaxation of the tension at present
surrounding South Africa, the iron laws of economic necessity
would, they claim, surreptitiously change the political climate
and make possible an orderly advance to constitutional stability.

THE NON-WHITE AND EXTRA-PARLIAMENTARY OPPOSITION

This theory rests on several crucial and by no means self-
evident assumptions and their analysis is essential for an
understanding of the attitudes of non-white political movements, particularly in the period of Nationalist rule. For
much of the Union's history in the period before 1948, African
demands for recognition were based on the assumption that
the government and the white electorate could be persuaded
to institute reforms as the result of rational argument. These
demands were largely connected with the disabilities imposed
by the operation of the colour bar, and included a call for
direct Parliamentary representation on a modest scale. The
approach to the government throughout this period
was moderate in tone and cautious and 'responsible' in action.
Deputations, meetings and petitions were the chosen techniques of the African National Congress (established in 1912)
the principal organization representing African aspirations,
although its more radical membership advocated a more
militant confrontation with the government. Their influence

became increasingly important in the period after 1936 (the year in which Africans from the Cape were removed from the common roll), although even as late as 1947 ANC representatives on the Natives Representative Council were still content to press for the extension of the principle of the Cape communal franchise to the Northern provinces. By 1949, however, the militants were in control of the organization and the 'programme of action' issued in that year was couched in language which reflected the growing nationalist sentiment of the urban African worker, and the need for new and more dynamic techniques for inducing a radical improvement in their lot. Henceforth passive resistance, boycotts, strikes, and anti-pass campaigns were the weapons chosen in the struggle to end Apartheid and support was welcomed from Indian and Coloured organizations with similar aspirations.

Nevertheless an examination of their objectives reveals little with which an English or American liberal would quarrel. The emphasis throughout has been on the attainment of political and legal equality and by implication the right to seek work free of hindrances such as the 'pass' system and the right to live and own property in any area of the country.[40] Indeed it was not until 1955 that the African National Congress pressed for universal franchise and in the same year, with the adoption of the Freedom Charter, with its emphasis on the public ownership of 'the mineral wealth, the banks and monopoly industry', the movement became committed to a more radical opposition to the government. Yet it would be a mistake to see the ANC as a racist body dedicated to substituting black supremacy for white. It remained committed to the achievement of a multi-racial society and however illusory this particular goal may seem to the political realist, it remains

---

[40] Indeed, as Professor Lewin has pointed out, these are essentially 'bourgeois' demands. See his remarks on the African middle class from which the great majority of ANC leaders have emerged: 'The African élite in the Union represent less a rising economic interest than an emotional and intellectual revolt against restrictive laws and personal indignities resulting from the colour bar. The equality they would prefer is that which prevails in a free competitive society based on capitalism, not that in a classless society based on socialism. But because this is only an embryonic middle class, and because it has been denied all opportunities of advancement as a group distinguishable from the mass of black labourers, it has in effect been forced to throw in its lot with the working class and to make common cause with it against the disabilities imposed on all Africans as such.' Lewin, *op. cit.*, p. 53.

true that the bulk of the ANC leadership genuinely aspired to this objective.[41]

It would be equally fallacious to see the ANC as communist dominated, and this is a myth which dies hard in South Africa. It is true that some of its more articulate supporters were also members of the South African Communist Party (banned in 1950) but the movement was basically nationalist in orientation and indeed was criticized by the Communist Party because of its tendency to think in bourgeois rather than socialist terms. The party, especially in the 1930s, was the only multi-racial political organization in existence. It certainly exerted an influence on the ANC in so far as it advocated a more militant programme for African advancement. As Professor Lewin points out, it was instrumental in persuading Africans 'to distrust moderate liberal effort on their behalf and to demand, in their own right and in a militant temper, nothing less than full racial equality in every sphere of South African life'.[42] But the distinction between nationalism and communism has always been difficult to grasp for the majority of white South Africans, and the government's use of the Suppression of Communism Act against African nationalist opponents has strengthened their predisposition to equate the two as different but related aspects of a single threat to their existence as a white group.

Why then did the movement fail? It is true that throughout its history it was hampered by poor organization (partly the result of the system of migratory labour) and lack of funds. It is true that its active membership probably never exceeded 100,000 and these were primarily concentrated in the urban areas.[43] But even if all these difficulties had been overcome,

[41] 'All people, irrespective of the national groups which they may belong to and regardless of the colour of their skin, who have made South Africa their home and who believe in the principles of democracy, are South Africans. All South Africans are entitled to live a full and free life on the basis of the fullest equality. ... The struggle which the national organizations of the non-European people are conducting is not directed against any race or national group. It is against the unjust laws which keep in perpetual subjection and misery vast sections of the population. It is for the transformation of conditions which will restore human dignity, equality and freedom to every South African.' Joint Declaration of the African National Congress, July 1951.

[42] Lewin, op. cit., pp. 51–2.

[43] 'The ANC ... can best be described as a movement with a strong élite leadership, with mass goodwill, considerable prestige and influence, but little

the fact remains that its campaigns against Nationalist policy, however dramatic in scope and technique, were bound to fail when employed against a government prepared to use force to suppress any resistance, however passive and restrained it might be. The Defiance Campaign of 1952, in which large numbers of non-whites courted arrest and imprisonment by ignoring Apartheid barriers in post offices, railway stations, and other public places, can plausibly be interpreted as an attempt to emulate the success of M. K. Gandhi in India.[44] But while the British government could be embarrassed by *Satyagraha*, and compelled for a variety of reasons to display restraint in their handling of passive resistance situations, the Nationalists were never handicapped by inhibitions of this type. Stage by stage the present government has erected a massive barrier of repressive legislation which had made the task of open and organized opposition by non-white political organizations virtually impossible. Not surprisingly, non-white resentment has mounted as individuals find themselves at the mercy of arbitrary power, conferred on the government by the Suppression of Communism Act and other legislation, and exemplified by the rapid growth of discretionary powers at the disposal of those Ministers responsible for non-white affairs. On the other hand, the existence of non-white political movements with a coherent programme certainly influenced the establishment of the Liberal Party, and later the Progressive Party.

The emergence of the Pan-African Congress in March 1959, under the leadership of Robert Sobukwe, was symptomatic not only of bitter dissatisfaction with the trend of government policy, but also an impatience with the liberal multi-racial approach of the Congress Alliance. This group made no secret of its hostility to what it regarded as Communist domination of the Congress Alliance, and in particular the activities of the white Congress of Democrats. Sobukwe insisted that Africans can and must work out their own political salvation, refusing the assistance and co-operation of non-African

effective organization. It always had many more adherents than actual members.' C. and M. Legum, *South Africa – Crisis for the West*, London, 1965, p. 175.

[44] And indeed his limited success in South Africa in the years before the First World War.

political organizations in the struggle against Apartheid.[45] For many in the Congress movement and elsewhere PAC ideology was overtly racialistic in its appeal and in the remaining months before ANC and PAC were banned (in April 1960), there was evidence of a bitter competition for the allegiance of the uncommitted African.

This brief exploration of the pattern of non-white opposition parties in South Africa illustrates the poverty of the thesis that economic forces together with the emergence of a bulwark against violent change in the form of an African middle class, will provide a long-term solution to the country's problems. It may well have had relevance in the period before non-white attitudes had hardened into a complete rejection of piecemeal concessions by the ruling white minority. The periodic outbreaks of violence which have characterized South Africa's non-white opposition during the last two years suggest that it may be too late for any policy based on long-term economic trends to succeed. Nor can the danger of infiltration and subversion from independent Africa be ignored, however weak and haphazard efforts in this direction have appeared to date. In any case the notion of a conservative African middle class prepared to wait on the slow operation of economic laws ignores the possibility that social tension may well be maximized precisely at the moment when a degree of affluence becomes a possibility. Supporters of this theory sometimes draw elaborate comparisons with the experience of industrial societies undergoing rapid economic and social change. The example of 19th-century Britain and more particularly the gradual extension of the franchise between 1832 and 1921, is seen as especially relevant. What these comparisons ignore is the fact that South Africa is racked by a conflict of nationalisms, different in kind and degree from the tension between classes in European societies in the 18th and 19th centuries.

To expect African nationalists, and by implication dissatisfaction with the burdens of Apartheid, to wither away because of the counter-attractions of an increasing prosperity,

---

[45] '. . . We reject Apartheid and multi-racialism as pandering to white interests, arrogance, and as a method of safeguarding white interests.' P. N. Raboreko, 'Congress and the Africanists, The Africanist Cause', *Africa South*, vol. IV, no. 3, April–June 1960.

is to ignore the fact that the gap between white and non-white achievements in the economic sphere would still be present and probably in an accentuated form. And however affluent the clerk, the schoolteacher, and the skilled worker may become, they can hardly be expected to remain unaware of the fact that the white man's superior economic position is largely the result of his political supremacy. Thus even if we assume a lessening in international pressure, and an indefinite continuation of the Republic's industrial expansion, the élite thrown up by this process may present the South African government (and the opposition parties) with their most fundamental challenge. In these circumstances – the most favourable South Africa can legitimately expect – the choice will still lie between yet more authoritarian methods of control and a widening of the area of participation in the political process on terms distinctly more radical than those currently envisaged by the two major opposition parties in the Parliament based on the present electorate.

Dennis Austin

Opposition in Ghana: 1947–67*

HOW SIMPLE THE GHANA PICTURE NOW SEEMS! FIRST, THE opposition of nationalistic demands to colonial rule; later, the opposition of local movements to the national government, then the internal opposition of sectional groups within the single party until the military intervened to turn everything awry. The story has a familiar ring to it. Anti-colonialism, one can argue, was mistaken for nationalism; but as soon as it became clear that the British were preparing to withdraw, politics became a destructive conflict between the would-be nationalist movement and tribal interests. In terms of this argument the overthrow of the Nkrumah regime has to be seen as simply one more example of the weakness of the structure of control in the newly-independent states. Frailty, thy name is African nationalism! The African colonies became self-governing before it was clear that a single 'self' existed; they are states before they are nations, and lack that 'self-aware unity' which is needed as the basis for a stable political system. Ghanaian history under Nkrumah (one concludes) is the history of every African ex-colony, the only difference being that the rise and fall of first the opposition and then the Convention People's Party in Accra occurred a little earlier in time than comparable events in other capitals.

There is a journalistic simplicity about such arguments that should make one hesitate about accepting them at face value. There are (I am sure) universal truths about political behaviour in the newly-independent countries, if only one could grasp them: but if one examines closely the situation in a particular country one is likely to end as a nominalist. I should certainly argue that the pattern of Ghanaian politics

* Vol. 2, no. 4, Winter 1967.

between 1947 and 1967 was *sui generis*: the similarities with neighbouring and distant states were there on the surface, but the differences were fundamental, and bear directly on the question of an 'opposition'.

THE DISTINCTIVE FEATURES OF GHANAIAN POLITICS

Firstly – and Ghana is certainly in a special though not unique category in this respect – it is an easy state to govern in physical terms. There is a favourable ratio of land to people, no one starves, the annual income per head (£76) is relatively high, communications are good, and there is an impressive wealth of administrative talent, the dearth of which is a melancholy feature of most new states.

Secondly, and it must be by way of a long chain of argument – Ghana is not greatly troubled by 'tribalism'. It is true that local conflicts abound, Ghanaian society being very quarrelsome, but one should not equate (as Nkrumah was prone to do) the struggle between neighbouring villages, chiefdoms, districts, or regions with opposition to the authority of the state, although one side or the other in these local disputes was very likely to be opposed to the party in power.[1] Only among the Ewe-speaking people of the eastern Volta region has there been substantial opposition to the form of the new state and a refusal to accept the authority of the government as legitimate. (The Ewe spill across the frontier into the neighbouring state of Togo where the government, being primarily from the Ewe-speaking people of southern Togo, constitutes a rival, attractive force to the government in Accra.) But one cannot explain the whole of Ghanaian politics in comparable terms. The picture one must have of the country is of a central core of peoples who share a common 'Akan' language (divided into dialect groups – Fanti, Twi Asante, or Brong-speaking). They share not only a common culture, including the interesting traditional structure of an elective chieftaincy and a confused pattern of Christian and Akan beliefs, but a basically similar economic life – peasant

---

[1] As Nkrumah complained in 1962; 'Here and there a chief's stool becomes vacant. Two party comrades contest for enstoolment; one succeeds. Immediately the loser turns against the Party and the Government.'

small-holders and traders who have entered fully into a cash-crop, wage economy. Grouped around this central bloc are the 'peripheral peoples' – of the Dagomba, Gonja, Mamprusi, and smaller chiefdoms of northern Ghana, the sophisticated Gà-speaking inhabitants of the capital city, other minor groups in the south-west, 'sub-dominant peoples' (often of pre-Akan origin) scattered throughout the country, and the Ewe. But even these 'peripheral peoples' should not be regarded as wholly distinct from the Akan. The Gonja are distant cousins of the Akan, sharing with them a common language structure and similar traditions of origin. Many of the social habits, religious beliefs, loan words, and songs of the Akan have been absorbed by their neighbours (e.g. the Gà) to the point where there are innumerable social ties, not only among the Akan but between the Akan and other groups.

The Akan could, I suppose, be regarded as a tribe, but one cannot understand Ghanaian politics on that assumption. A distinguishing feature of local history – and of Ghanaian politics – has been the rivalry between the various divisions of the Akan: Ashanti versus the Brong, Ashanti versus the Fanti, the power of Kumasi versus the power of the outlying Ashanti chiefdoms, the rivalry of one Fanti state against another. Similarly, although there is some evidence of Gà hostility to non-Gà groups, there is equal evidence of the rivalry between different sections of the Gà community. The point needs to be made as clearly as possible, namely: that demands based on local interests cannot be seen simply in terms of tribal conflict, nor as evidence of a major threat to the stability of the state. The multiplicity of conflicts may make the life of the central government complicated: it must manoeuvre endlessly among local groups, and distribute its prizes so as not to offend too many interests. But the competition that it has to control is for favours within the general framework of the powers of the central government; it is not a fundamental conflict between the need to enforce and the passionate wish to reject the power of the state.

How might such a system work in practice? Nkrumah manoeuvred very successfully within it for a time. Consider, for example, the so-called Ashanti-Southern conflict in the 1950s. At first sight, it might be thought to have been a tribal struggle: the Ashanti (represented by the National Liberation Movement) versus the South (predominantly CPP), and it did have *something* of that character – except that both the Ashanti and the southern Fanti chiefdoms belong to the same 'tribal group'. On closer inspection the picture became more complicated, for it was also a Kumasi-based NLM versus a western Brong-based CPP, the traditional rivalry between Ashanti and the Brongs reappearing in party form. On a narrower view still, it was *inter-alia* a struggle among the Brong – between, for example, the Dormaa state and its allies on one side (CPP), and a rival group based on the Wenchi chiefdom (NLM). Similarly, there was a struggle in Ashanti between Kumasi (NLM) and the neighbouring Kumawu state (CPP). And (to look yet more closely) the CPP–NLM conflict included a myriad local disputes like that within the Dormaa state itself, between the paramount chief (CPP) and his local subordinate chief at Wamfie (NLM), and within the Wenchi state between the paramount chief (NLM) and candidates to the stool from the rival royal family (CPP).

The nature of these territorial–chiefdom conflicts often appeared to be based on the Middle-East formula: 'My neighbour is my enemy and my neighbour's neighbour is my friend': but it was never quite as simple as that. Minor skirmishes constantly upset the main battle-lines, between rival Muslim groups, between Catholics and Protestants, between competing lineages of an Akan stool or a northern 'Skin', and between families whose ancient feuds were enlarged and recast in party form until the political scene was a bewildering whirling pattern of alliances and counter-alliances which the national leaders constantly had to try and maintain in some sort of working order. The rival parties reached into local disputes in their search for allies. Local individuals (e.g. the Queen Mother of Kumawu who supported the NLM when its chief supported the CPP) looked to the parties for support. The party leaders (e.g. Krobo Edusei, CPP, from Kumawu; e.g. Kofi Busia, NLM, from Wenchi) tried to weave constituency support out of these quarrels. Such is the nature of national and local politics in Ghana, the two being closely interwoven, and it is quite absurd in these circumstances to suppose that there is 'no room for opposition'. It is there all the time in the clash of local interests over the powers of the chief's court, the distribution of traditional and modern offices,

I

the grant of government funds for development, the siting
of a new secondary school, etc.: a multiplicity of demands,
some old, some new, which it is beyond the power of any
government in Accra to satisfy.

How was it, then, that the CPP won the general elections
of 1951, 1954, and 1956, a presidential election in 1960, a
referendum in 1964, and a general election the following year?
Was it merely because of the party's skill in manipulating
these local quarrels? One must first discount the party's later
successes: the 1960 election was crooked, the referendum a
farce, the 1965 election an absurd charade – 198 candidates
selected by the CPP central committee and then declared to
be elected unopposed in 198 constituencies. It was simply a
non-election. But in 1951, 1954, and 1956? To begin with, one
must also note that neither in 1954 nor 1956 did the CPP win
the support of the majority of the adult population, nor even
of those who took the trouble to register, but only of those who
actually got to the polls: even then, it won less than 60 per
cent of the votes. Still, it did win both elections, defeating the
array of local interests against it, and holding together as a
composite political organization. How did it do it? The explanation is really very simple. Having been elected to office
in 1951 on what was then an irresistible programme of 'self-
government now', it was able to use its powers as a government
to underpin its appeal as a party. Thereafter, it could reward
those who supported it and threaten its enemies with the
withdrawal of government favour. The message was clear:
'The King's wrath is as a roaring lion but his favour is as dew
upon the grass.' By such means the party cemented together
the aggregation of interests which constituted its rank and
file, and attracted to its side a wider support than its opponents,
to such an extent indeed that it was often a matter of surprise
that non-CPP candidates were able to do so well against those
of the nationalist party in power.

How did the opposition hold together as a motley alliance of
local and individual interests? It, too, could manoeuvre and
enlist support from among the infinite number of local disputes up and down the country. It also tried to counter the
nationalism of the CPP with its own appeal to an Ashanti and
Northern sentiment – although only with limited success precisely because of the intensity of local rivalries within each

region. But where was the leadership (and the Leader) to come from which could lift these particularist movements to a national level of opposition to the CPP and Nkrumah?

Here we must turn to the third distinctive feature of Ghanaian politics. One has to use terms, like 'the intelligentsia', which are misleading historically, or descriptive categories like 'class' which suggest more than is warranted in a Ghanaian context. Yet the fact remains that between 1946 and 1951 Ghana began to experience a measure of social revolution in which power was seized by new leaders drawn from a section of society hitherto unknown in national politics. To understand the significance of the end of colonial rule in what was once the Gold Coast, one needs to trace not only the successful demand for self-government – a revolution by ballot – but the shift in power which took place within Ghanaian society itself. It was led by a People's Party which appealed to the population as a whole but built its organization very largely on the growing number of elementary school leavers who had begun to look for employment in the towns and villages during the 1940s. And it was opposed by the wealthier, better-educated minority which placed its talents at the disposal of the local opponents of the CPP. I used to think that the 'distinctive feature' of Ghanaian politics in the 1950s was the great flood of elementary school leavers who gave their support to a homespun People's Party which they saw as a commoners' movement with an emotional appeal for self-government. Now I am not so sure. The elementary school leaver has probably been the mainstay of most would-be nationalist movements in Africa: but the small 'intelligentsia' group in Ghana (as its leaders once styled themselves) has few parallels in the continent. It has its origins in that small band of lawyers, doctors, and businessmen who were formerly an established part of the political landscape; they constituted then – and now – a *bourgeoisie manquée,* too small in number to be regarded as a distinct class, but forming an able, energetic group of leaders in the southern coastal towns of Accra, Cape Coast, and Sekondi-Takoradi. They ran the local newspapers which were the main weapons of political action; they were reformists rather than revolutionaries, and, under leaders like J. E. Casely Hayford in the 1920s (an interesting writer on African customary law as well as an able lawyer), they wanted an end to particular abuses rather than the end of colonial rule. But they, too, were carried forward by the post-war movement against colonialism, and in 1947 a new party was formed by Grant, a wealthy Sekondi timber merchant, and J. B. Danquah, a lawyer, writer, historian, and politician. They called it the United Gold Coast Convention, and gave it a programme that was clear but cautious: 'self-government in the shortest possible time'.

THE CPP–INTELLIGENTSIA CONFLICT

The UGCC could claim to be the first post-war nationalist movement, and it tried to act like one. It set up a working committee, hired a full-time general secretary – Kwame Nkrumah – opened local branches, and began to recruit members on payment of a modest annual subscription. In true orthodox fashion, its leaders then went to prison, six of the working committee being detained by the colonial government on grounds of their complicity in the 1948 February riots. A little unfortunately for them, perhaps, they were released after a brief period to give evidence before the commission of enquiry which arrived from London, and thereafter they were immersed in the very enjoyable business of working out a new constitution as members of the all-African Coussey Committee.

It was their undoing. For they were now outflanked by their general secretary and deserted by their rank and file. On 12 June 1949, a break-away party was inaugurated by Nkrumah: the Convention *People's Party*. Its programme was couched in more national terms than that of the UGCC since it demanded 'self-government now', and its appeal was to 'the commoners' or 'young men', as distinct from the 'aristocrats' and chiefs on the Coussey Committee. Throughout 1949 and 1950 the new party spread its appeal through the southern half of the country, like fire through the dry African bush. It brought together the multitude of local complaints against the colonial government – the high price of imported goods, the compulsory cutting out of swollen-shoot diseased cocoa trees, the slow rate of Africanization of the public service. And, as the sovereign remedy for all these ills, it held out the prospect of independence under a new leader whose return from London at the end of 1947 as a somewhat elderly student (he was then

38) was portrayed in Messianic terms. Before such an on-
slaught, the UGCC crumpled and died. And when the CPP
carried everything before it in the first general election in
February 1951, it looked as if *both* revolutions were virtually
over: nationalism had won its first victory in British Africa,
and the young men of the elementary schools were in office,
having defeated the triple ruling élite of British officials,
indirect-rule chiefs, and the intelligentsia. But although the
colonial officials accepted what had happened with true British
phlegm, followed by many of the chiefs who hastened to come
to terms with the party in power, the intelligentsia held out.
They fashioned new parties which faded almost as quickly as
they were formed, quarrelled among themselves, turned to
Dr Busia rather than to Dr Danquah, and continued to criticize Nkrumah as a would-be dictator and the CPP as an un-
educated party of incompetents. They also looked round for
allies, and found them among the innumerable local disputes
which divide Ghanaian society. In their bitter dislike of
Nkrumah, they hastened to place their talents at the disposal
of the Northern People's Party which was formed in April
1954, the Ashanti National Liberation Movement in September the same year, the Moslem Association Party, the Wassaw
Youth Organization, the Bekwai State Improvement Society,
the *Krontihene* in Dormaa, the *Queen Mother* in Kumawa,
the Ahmadiyya movement in the northern Muslim area around
Wa, the Ewe separatists, the Gà protest movement in Accra,
etc. etc. etc. They talked in terms of the need to devise constitutional checks and balances; they quoted from Burke and
Montesquieu rather than from Rousseau or Marx. And they
gave a national focus to innumerable local protest movements
which, in turn, provided the intelligentsia with solid local
backing in the constituencies. Thus it was that the small group
of wealthy, educated leaders succeeded in July 1956 in winning
43 per cent of the vote against the CPP, in the last general
election before independence.

One talks of 'wealthy, educated leaders' in much the same
way as the CPP spoke of those who opposed them as being
'feudal aristocrats' or 'traditional illiterates' – that is to say,
unthinkingly. But one must be careful. Within a brief period
of independence the CPP leaders had accumulated wealth to a
degree unknown in colonial times. And although the intelli-

gentsia, by definition, were the products of the very good local
secondary schools and universities, they also included northern
leaders (like S. D. Dombo and B. K. Adama) who were neither
rich nor very well educated: they simply disliked the autocratic
ways of Nkrumah and his followers. The opposition was also
reinforced in the 1950s by former CPP leaders – Joe Appiah
and R. R. Amponsah in Ashanti, Kwesi Lamptey, T. K.
Mercer and Kurankyi Taylor from Cape Coast: they had been
an intellectual minority in the CPP and left the party out of
distaste for its exaltation of Nkrumah and the corruption
which was spreading among its leaders. Nor could one align
the opposition with the chiefs in pejorative terms as a 'conservatism of the right', for there was absolutely nothing to
choose (in the north) between the Yabumwura, paramount
chief of the Gonja, who for reasons of local advantage sided
with the CPP, and the Wa-Na paramount chief of the Wala
who backed the NPP; or, in Ashanti, between the Kumawu-
hene (CPP) and the Essumejahene (opposition). A fair description of many of the chiefs would be that they were in the
difficult position of a Vicar of Bray, having to adjust not only
to frequent changes of regime but also to popular favour: too
persistent a defiance of the government might lead to reprisals,
too persistent a disregard of local opinion might lead to 'de-
stoolment changes'. There was no basis in these uncertainties
for a permanent 'right-wing' opposition.

By 1966, therefore, one might have thought that the day of
the intelligentsia was over. Danquah had died behind bars,
Busia was in exile, others were still in prison under the cruel
operation of a Preventive Detention Act. Nor was it sure
whether their influence had left any permanent impress. The
public service, police and army were would-be neutral sectors
of the state, although subject to pressure from the single party
to conform to its beliefs (or what its leaders purported to believe); a number of senior civil servants had left the country
to work with the United Nations rather than submit to the
absurdities of the Nkrumah régime. But it was impossible to
say whether they, or the army and police officers who were
similarly dismayed by what was happening, saw their future as
being bound up in any way with this small opposition group
of unsuccessful politicians.

Today, a little over twelve months after the coup, the picture is clearer. Fortune's wheel has turned almost full circle. The National Liberation Council of police and army officers has turned for help, not only to its civil servants, but to those who were defeated by Nkrumah and the CPP: men like Dr Busia, Akufo Addo (a lawyer and member of the UGCC), Victor Owusu (a leading member of the Ashanti National Liberation Movement and now Attorney General), and others who may very loosely be described as belonging to the 'intelligentsia' – educated leaders, many of whom have had some professional training, and whose educational background puts them in a very different category from the members of the now banned People's Party. So the opposition is apparently within sight of power, and its opponents are in prison, or recently released from prison. The social revolution has been turned back (or arrested?). And such is the nature of Ghanaian politics that the effect of the downfall of the CPP has been felt up and down the country, for not everyone can have welcomed the overthrow of Nkrumah: certainly not the Brongs, and others who drew support in their local affairs from the power of the CPP in Accra. When the great wheel runs downhill, it drags down many with it, and throughout the country, chiefs have been destooled or enstooled, chiefdoms upgraded or downgraded, local offices have changed hands, and new appointments have been made. Those who once joined in the chorus of praise for the Osagyefo are now cautiously changing tune as they try to change their allegiance; but not all can succeed, if only because their local opponents are determined not to let them succeed.

ARGUMENTS AGAINST AN OPPOSITION

Such is the political history of the past two decades in Ghana. What does it tell one about the nature of 'opposition' in the country? Its eclipse at national level was not the result of a withering away of support for Busia's United Party since it could always find some lodgement in the country at large by sponsoring local grievances; it happened because those in power were determined to see it blighted. It would seem reasonable, therefore, to look for the implication of the disappearance of the opposition, in political terms, as being the direct result of a number of decisions taken by Nkrumah and his followers, and then to go on to ask why these decisions were taken. So simple an explanation? Is there nothing to be said for those ingenious arguments which sought to explain – and to gloss the unpleasantries of – the Nkrumah régime in terms of an African tradition, or political sociology? For my own part, I do not think there is, if only because of the uncertainty with which first one and then another line of justification was defended. An 'opposition' was not possible (it was said) because of the absence of a class situation, or because of the tradition of 'consensus' in Ghanaian political life, or because of the legacy of colonial rule, or because of the sense of national emergency after independence, or because its virtues could be preserved by the free play of criticism within the single party in power – an extraordinary mumbo-jumbo recital of differing explanations.

Each can be dismissed very quickly. The assumption that Ghana is a 'conflict-less' society because of the absence of class divisions is absurd. The primary question has been whether such conflicts as existed should be crammed within a single party or allowed to become the raw material for competing organizations. The history of the years between 1947 and 1957 shows how local quarrels can put on national dress, given the sharp and abiding quarrel between the intelligentsia and the CPP. That such a conflict might produce not the alternation of government and opposition but government by a dominant party and the opposition of minority factions opens a new line of argument: but it has nothing to do with the nonsense of a monopolistic single party and its origins in a classless or pre-class society. How far Ghana is, or is not, divided along class lines, one simply does not know. Very little economic analysis has been done to provide the data on which to judge. There are rich, poor, and 'middle income' cocoa farmers, but do they see themselves as being divided in terms of status or political objectives? Miss Polly Hill has shown how closely related are landowner and farmer, farmer and share-cropper, creditor and debtor. The labourers who pluck the cocoa might be thought to be among the radical dispossessed, but they are largely migrant workers from outside the country, whose fortunes are closely tied to those of the farmer who employs them. On the other hand, there is growing urban unemployment as the elementary school leavers continue to crowd into the towns, and the beginnings perhaps of *a lumpenproletariat* in the large cities, although kinship ties are still an important social bond among the majority of town-dwellers. I would argue that the differences between the CPP and the opposition at independence in 1957, when they had 72 and 32 seats in parliament, were primarily in terms of 'class' in respect of the small intelligentsia group of UP leaders and the CPP; and primarily 'territorial' in the rural and urban constituencies: but only 'primarily', for the CPP had *some* appeal as the 'party of the common man' throughout the southern half of the country, and the UP was always able to enlist some support for its attacks on the corruption and incompetence of the ruling party.

The argument from tradition was, at best, obscure, at worst a calculated pretence. One might as plausibly have argued in favour of a two-party system because of the rivalry of opposing royal houses within an Akan chiefdom as try and justify single-party rule in terms of the supposed communalism of traditional society. All one could say was that Akan society was neither hierarchically ordered, in the sense of there being permanent superiors and inferiors, nor loosely-articulated like the segmentary, lineage societies of the far north. Its structure was such as to sustain the operation of a centralized government without losing the advantages of political competition between the centre and its outlying subordinate chiefdoms, and between candidates from rival royal families whose power, when elected to the stool, rested on the consent of a finely-spun web of lesser chiefs and advisers. Even the generality of commoners were held to have political rights, particularly as heads of families, but also because they were members of an Akan clan; even slavery was a servitude 'qualified by rights'. It was when the colonial government transformed the Native Authority into administrative agents, and extended the powers of the chief beyond customary bounds, that the commoners began to be restive, and to talk in exaggerated terms of a golden age 'before the white man came'. Thus, there were undoubtedly traditional restraints on the power of the chief, and observers of the Akan states in early, or pre-colonial, times gave the same stress to the competitive nature of its government as to its corporate qualities. But how could one translate the traditional values of an Akan chiefdom – politically decentralized,

economically primitive – into an apparatus of control to check
the power of a president, even supposing that a president like
Nkrumah was prepared to accept such limitations? The CPP
was actually shaped by those who were struggling to free themselves from the limitations imposed on them within the former
Native Authorities, and they had no fear – at first – of concentrating power in the hands of the central government. Both
the leaders and the rank and file welcomed the destruction of
the opposition, in gross ignorance of the danger that they were
sharpening a knife which might later be held against their
own throats.

The equation of single-party rule with colonial government
was particularly absurd. Throughout the colonial period there
were open struggles between rival candidates and parties in
the southern municipalities (admittedly on a restricted franchise); there were sharp clashes between the intelligentsia and
the chiefs within the provincial councils; there was a lively
press which thought it was gagged by the colonial government
– until it learned after independence what gagging, to the
point where it was choked to death, could really involve. A
more accurate criticism of colonial government might be that
it tends to rob those it governs of the power of taking decisions,
creating a source of dependence on external help which
inhibits an energetic approach to local problems: but it is not
at all easy to see Ghanaians in those terms.

The justification of the harshness with which the United
Party was treated after independence in terms of national
urgency had a spurious plausibility when one looked at the
troubled scene in Africa from 1960 onwards, the outbreaks of
terrorist attacks in Ghana, including two attempts to assassinate Nkrumah, and the economic hardship imposed by the fall
in the world price for cocoa. But one must be careful not to
confuse the chronology. Which came first: the clear intention
of the CPP government to destroy the opposition, or the decision by some of the United Party leaders to adopt extra-
constitutional, violent measures to overthrow Nkrumah? I
would argue that these two disastrous decisions were taken at
about the same time, in 1957–8, and that neither can be explained in terms of the other, as cause and effect. The fall in
the cocoa price was certainly a great misfortune, but the crisis
years did not come until after the opposition had been elimi-

nated. The price per ton was £358 in 1957 compared with £285 in 1951, and it was not until 1961–2 that it began to tumble sharply to catch the government unawares at a time when it was already over-committed on development expenditure. Public hardship was then made worse by party corruption. And although a great deal was said by Nkrumah about the evil of private wealth and the need for a new 'Socialist Man', virtually nothing was done to curb the venality of the party leaders. Politics in Ghana must necessarily be the politics of scarcity: but Nkrumah's warnings of the need for unity against the dangers of neo-colonialism must have sounded very hollow to those who were denied a share of the spoils.

Finally, there was the naïve argument that the single party could reproduce within its own ranks the benefits to be derived from the existence of a separate opposition. But the refutation was plainly there in the actual history of single party government after 1960, when Nkrumah became president: deprived of a formal enemy, the CPP turned in on itself. It was then that Nkrumah, having used the 1958 Preventive Detention Act to cripple the United Party, began to detain his own supporters – Quaidoo, Gbedemah, Tawai-Adamafio, Ako-Adjei, etc. Far from achieving greater security, the legalization of the single-party state bred further insecurity. Nor was anything done to try and institutionalize, or even encourage, competition within the CPP, either at the centre or in the constituencies. It is easy to be over-impressed by the Tanzanian device of an enforced contest between rival TANU candidates, but at least the virtue of public competition is recognized in Dar-es-Salaam. No such recognition was made in Nkrumah's Ghana. Instead, there was the mockery of the 1965 election, and a furtive manoeuvring for advantage between different sections of the CPP and its auxiliaries which Nkrumah – far from welcoming as an augury of the freedom of expression and dissent which the single party was said to encourage – condemned as untimely and unacceptable.[2]

2 See, for example, his condemnation of the party's ancillary organizations and the national assembly members in April 1961: 'While I was away certain matters arose concerning the Trades' Union Congress, the National Assembly, the Co-operative Movement and the United Ghana Farmers' Council. These matters created misunderstanding. . . . Some Parliamentarians criticised the Trades' Union Congress and the other wing organisations of the Convention People's Party. The officials of these organisations objected to the criticism

So one is driven back to asking a number of simple questions. Why did the CPP eliminate its opponents? Why did the opposition leaders give every excuse to the CPP to adopt such a policy? And what are the obstacles to an openly competitive system within which there is room for government and opposition, policy decisions and criticism, authority and freedom?

I am still not very sure. And I am concerned for the moment, looking at the two decades of party conflict between 1947 and 1967, to argue primarily that it was always possible to draw together an 'aggregation of interests' in the country which was distinct from that which sustained the CPP. The proof was there in the clash between the elementary school leavers of the People's Party plus local interests, and the intelligentsia plus *their* allies. I would argue further that the rivalry between these opposed groups (though sharp and occasionally turning to local violence) did not constitute a threat to the stability of the political system as a whole, and that Akan society was strong enough to contain these conflicts both at constituency and national level. I absolutely agree with Donald MacRae when he says – one of the few generalizations which seem to me to say something pertinent – that in the West African states we are 'dealing with societies unusual in being ultimately stronger than their states'.[3] Nor should one see the lines of division between the CPP and its opponents as uncrossable. Admittedly, an irreconcilable element existed on

---

and made counter-criticisms against certain Parliamentarians and this started a vicious circle of criminations and recriminations. . . .

'This is not the time for unbridled militant trade unionism in our country. . . . At this stage I wish to take the opportunity to refer to an internal matter of the Trades' Union Congress. It has come to my notice that dues of 4s. per month are being paid by some unions, whereas others pay 2s. . . . I have therefore instructed . . . that Union dues shall remain at 2s. per month.

'Coming to the integral organisations of the Party I consider it essential to emphasise once more that the Trades' Union Congress, the United Ghana Farmers' Council, the National Co-operative Council and the National Council of Ghana Women are integral parts of the Convention People's Party, and in order to correct certain existing anomalies the Central Committee has decided that separate membership cards of the integral organisations shall be abolished. In all Regional Headquarters, provision will be made for the Central Party and these integral organisations to be housed in the same building. . . . Also the separate flags used by these organisations will be abolished and replaced by the flag of the Convention People's Party. . . ,'

[3] *Government and Opposition*, vol. 1, 4, pp. 544–5.

both sides, grouped around Nkrumah and Busia, but the main body of electoral support, and even the rank and file of each party, were quite capable of shifting their allegiance. The United Party, like the CPP, was a loose bundle of interests which, amoeba-like, extended or contracted its scale of operation to take in or disgorge this or that area of support as local issues formed and disappeared. It is true that the opposition leaders were obliged, in order to add weight to their cause, to encourage local interests to assert themselves; but that was not a bad thing in a country like Ghana, where the horizon of ordinary people's interests is very narrow. And if one asks what 'cause' was it that the intelligentsia in Ghana wanted to promote, the answer is clear, and not at all sinister: they wished to replace the CPP with themselves, and to reverse certain trends that they professed to dislike.

There is one last point to make. It is fashionable at the present time in any argument about the 'politics of new states' to begin by dismissing the 'Westminster model' as unsuitable for those unhappy countries which were forced by the ex-colonial power to adopt it. A world of argument is contained in such phrases. But a remark by Giovanni Sartori remains lodged in my mind when (in a somewhat different context) he says of his students: 'They were eager to discover something new, but they knew nothing about what had already been discovered.' It might be said of the CPP and their attitude to the framework of parliamentary government which both Nkrumah and Busia welcomed at independence. It may be that society in many African states is either too heterogeneous or structured in ways hostile to the recognition of opposed groups, and therefore unable to support the open competition engendered by a free suffrage and a party-divided parliament. But, for the reasons given earlier – namely, Ghana being surprisingly homogeneous, and there being nothing in Akan political traditions which was counter to the notion of political competition – other explanations must be sought for the early demolition of the Westminster model, the collapse of the opposition, and the overthrow of the CPP. Perhaps the answer is so obvious that it is overlooked. When they can, men pursue advantage, and in the long run the advantage lies with the man with the gun: the CPP took a mercantilist view of politics, believing that their security lay in the elimination of the opposition, and in

February 1966 the soldiers came to the same conclusion *vis-à-vis* the CPP.

But why? Why – for example – does Dr Olivier not try to eliminate Mr Mintoff's Labour Party by breaking the rules of the parliamentary game in those little Maltese islands where a Westminster two-party system flourishes despite all the strains of independence? Why did the Indian Congress Party not try and move in the direction of a single-party monolith from its position of dominance after 1947? I would not like even to venture an explanation of a vast and difficult field of argument: but one can perhaps begin to measure the problem in Ghana by noting a particular feature of the situation which may account for the difficulties which the opposition had to face during these twenty years.

THE INSTABILITY OF SUCCESS

The CPP was a successful party which came to power very early – within two years of its formation. The effect of its rapid accession to office might have been much less had the party been no more than a re-grouping of an established élite. It was not: it was the political expression of a new social group – the elementary school leavers. Again, the degree of social revolution which this implied might not have been so traumatic an experience but for other aspects of the Ghanaian scene – the existence of the third distinctive feature discussed earlier, the intelligentsia. Consider the position of Nkrumah and the CPP in, say, 1953 when all seemed plain sailing – no reefs in sight, fair weather, and a contented crew. Nkrumah expressed his confidence:

There is no conflict that I can see between our claims and the professed policy of all parties and governments of the United Kingdom. We have here in our country a stable society. Our economy is healthy, as good as any for a country our size. In many respects, we are much better off than many sovereign states. And our potentialities are large. Our people are fundamentally homogeneous, nor are we plagued with religious and tribal problems. . . .

Then the intelligentsia rallied; local interests began to stir; the two joined together to challenge the CPP and Nkrumah was thrown off balance – an undignified position for a nationalist leader with a taste for theorizing in Marxist terms. There was an obvious gap now between theory and practice. The CPP was a nationalist movement which claimed to embody a whole nation; it also laid claim to being a commoners' party which sought to represent 'the masses'. What was it to do? It might have abandoned theory for practice and settled down as a 'dominant party', reasonably tolerant of dissent. And, had it done so, my guess is that it would still be there now. But neither Nkrumah nor the CPP would have found such a role easy to perform. Nkrumah liked to take a unique view of himself and his place in history; the other CPP leaders and the rank and file, though more sensible, were a new and not very well-educated élite which lacked the ease and confidence of power which the representatives of a long-established social order might have possessed. They had no experience of conflict, even within their own party organization, before they took office; and they knew nothing of the laborious, inadequate years of apprenticeship which the chiefs and intelligentsia had been obliged to accept as members of the early legislative councils. They were also faced with an opposition whose leaders, being more articulate, were generally, though often mistakenly, believed to possess superior ability. For their part, the UP leaders in 1957–8 ignored the dangers of straying beyond the strict constitutional field of opposition. Out of a fierce distrust of Nkrumah, and of the party which had snatched power from their grasp, they began to talk in terms of revolution and, thereby, gave the CPP good grounds for opposing them on extra-constitutional grounds. Amidst these uncertainties, made worse by the novelty of independence in 1957, the CPP leaders clung to their mythology; they were very ready to label any opposition to themselves as unpatriotic, reactionary, tribal, and/or non-existent. But they could combat the persistence of the intelligentsia opposition, and the multiplicity of local conflicts, only by employing harsh, extra-constitutional measures of a totalitarian kind. This they did – and extended their power over the country until they offended the one group which had the power to resist.

What the future may hold would require another article. The soldiers and police are now publicly committed to a process of disengagement not unlike that which faced the colonial officials in 1947. The interesting question is whether the 'intelligentsia' – if, indeed, they come to power sitting on the bayonets of those who put them there – can cope with the social revolution which the CPP, weakened by the instability of its own success, failed to consolidate.

A. Jeyaratnam Wilson

Oppositional Politics in Ceylon: 1947–68[*]

INTER-PARTY RIVALRY BASED LARGELY ON SOCIO-ECONOMIC
lines took institutional shape in Ceylon, for the first time, with
the approach of general elections in August–September 1947,
under the newly inaugurated Soulbury Constitution.[1] The
issues at the general election of 1947 were simple and straightforward. It was accepted that the United National Party
(UNP) would form the government with its leader, D. S.
Senanayake, as the man who would lead the country to independence. The party had the backing of almost the entire
press. It enjoyed ample financial resources and commanded
the support of the 'big families', the landed interests, the
mudalalis (shop-owners), and government officials, particularly
the village headmen.[2] The choice posed to the electors was between a policy of progressive social reforms and stable government advocated by the UNP as against the revolutionary
changes that the three left-wing parties envisaged – the
Trotskyist *Lanka Sama Samaja* Party (LSSP) and its splinter,
the Bolshevik Leninist Party which later changed its name to
the Bolshevik *Samasamaja* Party (BSP), and the Moscow-

---

[1] The Soulbury Constitution came into operation in October 1947 and
lasted till 4 February 1948 when Ceylon obtained independence. It provided
for a large measure of internal self-government and for a cabinet of ministers
who would be collectively responsible to parliament. It derived its name from
the Chairman of the Commission on Constitutional Reform which visited
Ceylon on 22 December 1944, Viscount Soulbury.

[2] The latest census figures (1963) gives the distribution of population as
follows: Low Country Sinhalese, 4,473,000 (42·2 per cent), Kandyan Sinhalese,
3,047,000 (28·8 per cent), Ceylon Tamils, 1,170,000 (11 per cent), Indian
Tamils, 1,121,000 (10·6 per cent), Ceylon Moors, 662,000 (6·3 per cent), Indian
Moors, 27,000 (0·3 per cent), Burghers and Eurasians, 46,000 (0·4 per cent),
and others 20,000 (0·2 per cent). Of the Indian Tamils, 121,135 have obtained
citizenship under the Ceylon citizenship legislation of 1948 and 1949, thus
leaving approximately one million Indians in the category of 'stateless'.

[*] Vol. 4, no. 1, Winter 1969.

oriented Communist Party (CP). These left-wing groups were
ideologically in conflict with each other. They fielded only 51
candidates in the 95 constituencies and even in some of these
the CP and LSSP clashed. The UNP on the other hand contested 76 constituencies. There was no prospect at any time of
a united left front or an alternative left government. One of
the left-wing parties, the Communists, on the contrary were
ambivalent about their attitude to the UNP. The Left's sympathy for the Indian Tamil workers was exploited by the UNP
in the Kandyan areas, for here the Indians posed an economic
threat to the Kandyan Sinhalese. In addition UNP propa-
gandists presented Marxist materialism as a threat to the traditional religious values of the people and posters displaying
temples, mosques, and churches going under the samasamaja
fire were given wide publicity.

Since the Left did not consider presenting itself as an alternative to the UNP, it did the next best thing in concentrating
on ousting the UNP in a number of key constituencies. In this
it achieved a surprising measure of success – the UNP securing
only 42 of the 76 seats it contested. The Left succeeded in
organizing an alternative village leadership comprising sections of the rural intelligentsia against the privileged middle
class represented by the UNP. This leadership had the support of a fairly large number of workers and lower-rank government officials who were 'victimized' after the massive strikes
launched by left-wing parties in 1946 and 1947. The strike
as a political weapon, it might be noted here, has from time
to time been used by left-wing parties to embarrass governments which they disapprove of.

When the overall results of the general election indicated
that the UNP, though in the lead, was nevertheless, in a
minority situation, feverish attempts were made by groups
and independent members of Parliament opposed to it, to form
a united front which could offer itself as an alternative government.[3] These bore no fruit because the LSSP declined to
participate in such a government. Its parliamentary leader,
N. M. Perera, explained that they were a 'revolutionary party'
and would therefore not serve in a 'capitalist government'.

[3] The UNP secured 42 seats, the LSSP 10, the All Ceylon Tamil Congress 7,
the Ceylon Indian Congress 6, the Bolshevik Leninist Party 5, the CP 3, and
Independents accounted for the remaining 21.

They were willing, however, to assist those who might take office in an alternative 'progressive government'.[4]

DISUNITED OPPOSITION

Not only was the LSSP not willing to participate in such a venture, but all three left-wing parties, owing to differences among them, could not for nearly three years agree on a leader of the opposition. The LSSP being the largest party in opposition was very much in favour of the recognition of the office; but its splinter, the BSP, opposed this[5] and the CP denounced it as a 'reactionary British convention'.[6] It was only after the BSP and LSSP united in June 1950, almost three years after Parliament's first meeting, that the opposition groups met and elected the LSSP leader, N. M. Perera as their leader. The CP, however, refused to co-operate, its general secretary declaring that the idea of a leader of the opposition was 'based on the convenient theory for the ruling class that the opposition should be part and parcel of the Government, fundamentally accepting the continuance of the existing social order but only disagreeing about the best method of continuing it'.[7]

The Left's unwillingness to accept parliament as the ultimate arbiter of the nation's destinies led the UNP to adopt an uncompromising attitude towards its parliamentary representatives. The UNP's view was succinctly put by one of its leaders, Sir John Kotelawala, on 9 June 1950: 'Our Opposition today is an Opposition which does not believe in the democratic system. That is why the Government finds its task so difficult. We have to fight the Opposition not as an Oppo sition but as enemies of the State.' And, he added, '... once they got in they would not get out. There is no guarantee you would ever have a chance to go to the ballot again.'[8] The government therefore showed considerable reluctance to do business with the left-wing opposition. The needs of constituencies represented by the Left were ignored and there was very little consultation, in the early years, between the two

4 See *Ceylon Daily News*, 6 November 1947.
5 See *Ceylon Daily News*, 4 October 1947, *Ceylon Observer*, 7 October 1947, and *Times of Ceylon*, 11 October 1947.
6 See *Ceylon Daily News*, 13 October 1947.
7 See *Ceylon Daily News*, 22 June 1950.
8 See *Ceylon Daily News*, 12 June 1950.

sides, with regard to the transaction of parliamentary business. As a mark of protest the left-wing opposition resorted to boycotting parliament on important occasions. Its point of view was best expressed in the statement it issued on the decision to boycott the ceremony of 11 January 1949 in connection with the presentation of a mace and a chair by the British House of Commons. Among the reasons advanced was 'the consistent failure of the Government to consult the Opposition on all such matters on which by parliamentary tradition, it is the duty of the Government to consult the Opposition'.[9]

For the Left, the years from 1947 onwards were spent in trying to effect some measure of unity among themselves. The motivating factor for this was the hope of an alternative government to which the elections of 1947 had given rise. These efforts bore some result when the BSP and LSSP decided on 3 June 1950 to unite 'into one party which shall be called the LSSP'[10] but the advantage that was to be gained from this unification was to some extent minimized when a dissenting section in the LSSP led by Philip Gunawardene broke away in protest and formed a new organization which took the name of the *Viplavakari Lanka Sama Samaja* Party (VLSSP).[11] In a short time Philip Gunawardene formed a united front with the CP. There could however be no agreement between the CP and the LSSP. The deputy leader of the LSSP (Colvin R. de Silva) characterized, in May 1951, the CP's slogan of 'popular front' and an alternative government as 'a call for a capitalist alliance to form a capitalist government'.[12] Earlier in the year at its annual conference the LSSP resolved on a 'go it alone' policy. One of the resolutions adopted affirmed that the ultimate objective lay along that of 'a direct mass struggle alone and not through parliamentary devices and manoeuvres'.[13]

While left-wing parties were preoccupied with their ideological quarrels, the nucleus of a democratic alternative presented itself when S. W. R. D. Bandaranaike resigned his portfolio of health and local government on 12 July 1951 in D. S. Senanayake's UNP government and crossed over to the

9 See *Ceylon Daily News*, 12 January 1949.
10 See *Ceylon Daily News*, 5 June 1950.
11 This means the Revolutionary Ceylon Equal Society Party.
12 See *Ceylon Daily News*, 28 May 1951.
13 See *Ceylon Daily News*, 8 February 1951.

opposition. Bandaranaike claimed to represent broadly the middle layer of Ceylonese opinion comprising the national-minded and *swabasha*-educated intelligentsia.[14] His grievance against the Senanayake administration was that it did not adopt a bolder attitude towards the problems of religion, the national languages and social and economic development.[15] Bandaranaike's resignation helped to bring together a layer of opinion, hitherto neglected by both the UNP and left-wing parties. An organization to represent this interest, the *Sri Lanka* Freedom Party (SLFP) was inaugurated on 2 September 1951. The new party's middle of the road stance was expressed in the most unambiguous terms by Bandaranaike himself in a press release. He declared that it would be 'a middle party between the UNP on the extreme right and the marxists on the extreme left'. 'Religion,' his statement added 'is essential as a weapon against the completely material doctrines of marxism.'[16] The reason for this open disavowal of Marxism was that Bandaranaike's rivals in the UNP had already begun to say that the Left saw in him another Alexander Kerensky.

Anti-UNP opinion sensed the possibilities of an alternative government under the leadership of S. W. R. D. Bandaranaike. The Left especially was not slow to realise this. On 28 July 1951 the LSSP leader was reported to have declared at a public meeting that if Mr Bandaranaike could form a government of his own, his party would accept him as Prime Minister.[17]

The LSSP nevertheless was alive to the fact that the new party could eliminate the Left from the position it had hitherto held of being the only available electoral alternative. The problem for the party therefore was to keep the electorate continuously reminded of the fact that a left government could be within the realms of possibility. Thus the principal resolution adopted at the LSSP's annual conference in early

---

[14] *Swabasha* means 'one's own language'.

[15] Bandaranaike wanted (a) emphasis to be given to Buddhism, the religion of the majority of the people while at the same time the state should also provide assistance to other religions, (b) a switchover in the administration from English to Sinhalese and Tamil, and (c) more rapid economic development.

[16] See *Ceylon Daily News*, 16 July 1951.

[17] See *Ceylon Daily News*, August 1951.

1952 was that all the resources of the party should be directed towards forming a samasamaja government in the next parliament which need not 'necessarily mean a government of the party alone' but one pledged to implement the LSSP's fourteen-point programme.[18] The conference further resolved that a left united front should be formed with the CP, and efforts should also be made to come to a no-contest electoral pact with the SLFP. It was evident from all this that the LSSP was gradually getting attracted to the idea of utilizing parliament as the instrument to bring about the changes it envisaged.

In addition to the oppositional forces mentioned already, there was a hard core of Tamil communal elements which ranged itself against the UNP in defence of the rights of the groups it claimed to represent. A majority in the main organization of the Ceylon Tamils, the All Ceylon Tamil Congress, crossed over to the government in August 1948. Those who opposed this step stayed behind to form a new organization called the Federal Freedom Party of the Tamil speaking peoples of Ceylon (FP). This party was to play an important role in Ceylon politics from 1956. The other organization – the Ceylon Indian Congress – represented the Indian Tamil estate population.

THE 1952–6 PARLIAMENT

Ceylon's first parliament was dissolved on 14 April 1952 by the new Prime Minister, Dudley Senanayake, who had succeeded his father, D. S. Senanayake, on the latter's death on 22 March as a result of a fall from his horse. Elections were fixed for May.

From the commencement of the election campaign, the UNP was able to take the offensive against its rivals. It was able to capitalize on the mass emotional upsurge caused by the passing away of the 'Father of the Nation', the man who had won national independence. The party preferred to present its record of achievements to the election rather than raise new issues or enter into an auctioneering game on such issues with its principal rival, the SLFP. The party received wide support

[18] See official statement issued by Leslie Goonewardene, secretary of the LSSP in *Ceylon Daily News*, 3 January 1952.

from the rural areas as well as from the urban middle class. It used very effectively the 'Indian cry' against the left-wing parties.[19]

Bandaranaike's SLFP tried hard to exploit nationalist feeling on the issues of language and religion but these failed to create the necessary response among the electors. The SLFP's standing was somewhat weakened by contesting only 48 of the 95 constituencies. Bandaranaike found it difficult to answer the UNP's question as to how he could form a stable government even if the SLFP won all the 48 seats it was contesting. It was said that he would have in such an event to enter into a coalition with one or more of the Marxist parties thus exposing his government to infiltration by totalitarian elements. Further confusion was added by the SLFP clashing with left-wing parties in as many as 26 constituencies. In the end the SLFP only secured 9 seats.

On the Left there was just as much confusion. The CP–VLSSP combine campaigned for 'a progressive democratic government' which would comprise 'workers, peasants, the middle-classes, and those sections of the bourgeoisie which are anti-UNP and anti-Imperialist'. The LSSP on the other hand campaigned for an anti-capitalist samasamaja government. It was, however, quite clear that neither group was serious about forming a government.[20] After the elections, when the opposition had to choose its leader, the four CP–VLSSP members of parliament supported Bandaranaike. The LSSP leader would have secured the office had these four members voted for him.[21]

The emergence of the SLFP as a democratic alternative to the UNP government improved the situation considerably for the opposition, in Ceylon's second parliament. Further, the new Prime Minister (Dudley Senanayake) was known to have

---

[19] The Indian Tamil workers dwell mostly in the Kandyan Sinhalese areas, The UNP leaders accused the Left of caring more for the Indian Tamils than for their own countrymen, the Sinhalese. Earlier, in August 1948, the UNP Minister of Finance had characterized all three left-wing parties at the time (CP, BSP, LSSP) as 'Indian parties, financed by Indian money' and 'subject to the directives, control and the decisions of their party heads in India'. Cf. H.R. Deb., 19 August 1948, 1731.

[20] The CP–VLSSP united front contested 19 constituencies and won 4. It clashed with the LSSP in 7 of these constituencies. The LSSP put forward 39 candidates of whom 9 won.

[21] See Leslie Goonewardene, op. cit., p. 42.

liberal views. The leader of the opposition himself was able to remark in February 1953 that the Prime Minister was 'trying, at least in some way, to follow more closely democratic traditions than was the case in the past', but he added that there was a great deal that still remained to be done.[22]

Bandaranaike's concept of the role of a parliamentary opposition was altogether different from that of his Marxist associates.[23] Where the latter conceived of strikes, mass action, and extra-parliamentary struggles as forms of protest, Bandaranaike believed in organizing propaganda against the party in power and explaining issues to the electors. He had an advantage over the Marxists in that he was able to establish a link with the rural masses. His campaigns were more on the cultural plane, but he also tried to establish a relationship between economic want and the neglect of the national cultures. In time he was able to win the confidence of the rural intelligentsia – the Sinhalese schoolteachers, the Sinhalese native physicians, and the Buddhist clergy. These were the forces which gave him his victory in 1956.

The disillusionment which had overtaken the Left led them now to think in terms of extra-parliamentary agitation. In June 1953 the LSSP extended an invitation to all opposition parties to attend a joint conference to discuss 'what form of mass action could be taken to resist the measures that the present government has taken and is contemplating taking against the masses of this country in connection with the financial crisis facing the government'.[24] The opportunity for joint action came when Dudley Senanayake's government tried to solve its balance of payment difficulties by raising the price of rice (which at this time was issued at heavily subsidized prices to all consumers). The Left responded by organizing an island-wide *hartal* or boycott which resulted in disturbances, damage to property and some loss of lives.

[22] See *Ceylon Daily News*, Independence Supplement, 4 February 1953.

[23] 'The function of the Opposition ... is to point out ... their own views, in the national interest, on the proposals of the Government and how far, in their opinion, those proposals are likely to achieve even objects which the Government has in view. In a sense, the Opposition serves a purpose which the Government cannot serve, namely, that of forming as well as reflecting public opinion to a degree that is not possible for the Government.' (*H.R. Deb.*, 30 July 1952, 1756–7.)

[24] See the statement of the secretary of the LSSP in *Ceylon Daily News*, 13 June 1953.

Shortly after, in October 1953, the Prime Minister resigned.

The *hartal* brought out a significant fact. The people of Ceylon were still not sufficiently confident to think that they could oust a government they disapproved of by constitutional methods. They were prepared therefore to follow the lead given by the Marxist parties and register their protest in an extra-constitutional manner.

The SLFP played an ambivalent role in regard to the *hartal*. Apparently Bandaranaike did not wish to get involved with the Marxist parties and evaded participating in the protest.[25]

Dudley Senanayake's successor, Sir John Kotelawala was uncertain of his position throughout his tenure of the premiership and it was more for this reason than with the object of fostering democratic traditions that he was anxious to establish better relations with the opposition. There were occasions when the prime minister asked for the co-operation of the opposition on controversial issues.[26] It was at the Prime Minister's request that the leader of the opposition joined the official Ceylon delegation which went to New Delhi to negotiate a pact regarding the position of Indians in Ceylon.[27] On 4 August 1954 during a detailed discussion on foreign policy the Prime Minister acknowledged the fact that for the first time in the history of the House, the leader of the opposition provided advice on which his government could act.[28]

In the following year the opposition, in particular the SLFP directed its attack at the government's cultural and language policies. Bandaranaike criticized the government's interpretation of the language of the area clause in the Nehru-Kotelawala Pact of 1954 to mean Sinhalese and Tamil, not Sinhalese alone. This, it was pointed out, would be a danger to the

---

[25] The excuse, which was not convincing, given by the LSSP leader was that the SLFP could not participate as they had not been given sufficient time to prepare for the event. See *H.R. Deb.*, 1 September 1953, 2482–3.

[26] See *ibid.*, 27 November 1953, 996.

[27] *Ibid.*, 5 March 1954, 3267, note. Bandaranaike was wary about this request. It was his view that he held 'a certain crucial position' but it was the government's duty to solve the Indian question satisfactorily. If they could not, they should get out and let him solve it. The Prime Minister was evidently endeavouring to get Bandaranaike to commit himself to a solution acceptable to the oppostion so that he might not turn round later and criticize the government for having blundered in the negotiations. Bandaranaike was, however, astute enough not to let himself be roped in like this. See *ibid.*, 1136.

[28] *Ibid.*, 4 August 1954, 525.

Sinhalese of the Kandyan areas. Next the Prime Minister's promise to the Ceylon Tamils that he would amend the constitution to provide parity of status to the Sinhalese and Tamil languages exposed him to a full-scale attack from Sinhalese nationalist elements. In the end the Prime Minister could not keep his word to the Tamils. Instead he went so far as to get his party, in February 1956, to change to a policy of Sinhalese as the only state language. He thereby alienated the support of the Tamils, Indians as well as Ceylonese, and at the same time made himself suspect in the eyes of the Sinhalese. The Prime Minister was outmanoeuvred at every stage of the language debate in the country mainly because of the adroit handling of the issue by Bandaranaike, and the LSSP leader, N. M. Perera.

The controversy over whether both Sinhalese and Tamil should be state languages or only Sinhalese brought about a new alignment of political forces. The SLFP had earlier been in favour of both languages as the official languages of the country but in October 1955 Bandaranaike explained in the House of Representatives the reason for his party's decision to adopt Sinhalese as the only official language. He had come, he said, to appreciate the fears of the Sinhalese people which could not be brushed aside as 'completely frivolous'.[29] The Marxist group led by Philip Gunawardena (the VLSSP), a *Sinhala Bhasa Peramuna* (Sinhalese Language Front) led by W. Dahanayake, and a group of independent members of parliament led by I. M. R. A. Iriyagolle came out in support of Sinhalese as the only official language. These groups joined with the SLFP to form the *Mahajana Eksath Peramuna* (the People's United Front) on 21 February 1956 under Bandaranaike's leadership. It was this Front which defeated the UNP at the general election of March 1956. Two Marxist groups (the CP and the LSSP) stood by the principle of parity of status for both the Sinhalese and Tamil languages and as a result acquired a great deal of unpopularity in the Sinhalese areas. But both groups were anxious that the UNP should be defeated, and so on 24 September 1955 a no-contest agreement was reached between the SLFP and LSSP, and shortly thereafter a similar agreement was signed between the SLFP and the CP. Both these Marxist parties were content to contest a small num-

[29] *H.R. Deb.*, 10 October 1955, 684.

ber of seats. The LSSP was unwilling at this stage to accept Bandaranaike's invitation to agree on a common programme.

This new political formation, the MEP, received a further accession of strength with the presentation of the report of the unofficial Buddhist Commission of Inquiry on 4 February 1956. This report listed the grievances of the Buddhists in Ceylon and in particular drew attention to the 'ravages' that Buddhism suffered under the colonial powers, the Roman Catholic Church, western influences, and the Tamils.[30] A powerful organization of Buddhist monks – the *Eksath Bhikku Peramuna* (EBP)[31] – campaigned for the implementation of this report. It explained to the electors that only a national front like the MEP could be relied on to do justice to the Sinhalese Buddhists. In the context of this developing crisis for the UNP, Sir John Kotelawala dissolved parliament in February 1956. In the elections in April 1956 his party suffered a crushing defeat.

THE 1956 TURNING-POINT, AND AFTER

Language was the one dominant theme in the elections of 1956. There were other issues as well – the place to be given to Buddhism, the Indian question, economic problems, and foreign policy but the language issue from the beginning tended to overshadow all others. One other important issue was the choice of a Prime Minister. The question posed before the electors was not so much whether they would prefer a UNP or MEP government but whether the Sinhalese people would be safer with Bandaranaike or Kotelawala as Prime Minister. In the prevailing Sinhalese national resurgence there could be only one answer to this question.

In Ceylon's political development, 1956 proved a dividing line. For the first time in the history of any of the new states in Asia or Africa, an electorate replaced one government by another in a peaceful and constitutional manner. The defeated UNP and its leader accepted with good grace the verdict of the people and decided to act in opposition with a view to organizing propaganda against the new government. It sought

[30] See Buddhist Committee of Inquiry, *The Betrayal of Buddhism*, in English, abridged, Balangoda, 1956.
[31] In English the United Front of Buddhist monks.

to expose the inherent weaknesses of Bandaranaike's coalition of contradictory elements which was soon to split into a democratic socialist wing and a Marxist wing. The UNP realized that the MEP would find it hard to keep many of the extravagant promises it had made, and it therefore offered itself to the electors as the only democratic alternative in the country. In parliament, however, N. M. Perera, leader of the LSSP was elected leader of the opposition after a series of complicated manoeuvres.[32]

Though Bandaranaike's cabinet was nationally oriented, the majority of its members belonged to the English-educated élite. They were therefore not opposed to the parliamentary system. The differences between the two wings in the cabinet arose over policy rather than over the constitutional system.

The relations between the government and the main opposition group in parliament, the LSSP, during its first year in office remained friendly. In the debate on the first government speech from the throne, the LSSP offered its co-operation and its leader referred to 'the very unusual feature which will normally never appear in any amendment to the Address of welcoming certain proposals of the government'.[33] The opposition, however, was a heterogeneous group and the contradictions within it were manifested in the way the different groups voted on controversial bills.

The LSSP, however, was not going to give unconditional support to the MEP government. Differences soon arose on the communal and economic questions. The result was a spate of major strikes organized largely by LSSP trade unions both in the private and public sectors designed to embarrass the government.

Inside parliament, too, the LSSP opposition began to stiffen. Thus when the closure was moved during the second reading debate on the Public Security (Amendment) Bill, a bill which was aimed at curbing the activities of communal organizations as well as left-wing trade unions, on 12 February 1959, the

[32] The MEP won 51 of the 60 seats contested and polled 1,046,362 votes, the UNP won 8 of 76 seats contested, polling 738,551 votes, the LSSP won 14 of the 21 seats contested, polling 274,204 votes while the FP won 10 of the 14 seats contested and polled 142,036 votes. It was believed that a number of independent Tamil-speaking MPs could be persuaded to support the FP as against the LSSP.

[33] H.R. Deb., 4 May 1956, 416; for the LSSP amendment, see ibid., 290–1.

LSSP members of parliament dramatized their opposition by having themselves forcibly removed from the House by the serjeant-at-arms.[34]

Soon the LSSP developed sufficient self-confidence to regard itself as an alternative to the government. At its annual conference held in July 1959, it rejected the idea of a broad front of 'the so-called progressives', preferring to fight the next general election on its own. This feeling of confidence was to be accentuated with the rapid rise of N. M. Perera's prestige in the country. The LSSP leader was to show persistence and parliamentary skill in the efforts he made to bring to book those involved in the assassination of Bandaranaike in September 1959.[35] He also played the leading role in toppling Bandaranaike's successor, W. Dahanayake.

Bandaranaike's gravest problems, however, arose on the communal front. He had disturbed the harmony that had prevailed in the country by the virulent campaign he had conducted at the elections both against the UNP and the Tamils on the language question. When it came to fulfilling his pledge, he tried to minimize the hardships that would follow from the imposition of the official language on the Tamils. Opposition from extremist Sinhalese elements however prevented him from following this course. As a consequence he came into conflict with the Tamil Federal Party. The latter resorted to extra-parliamentary action to register its protest. The air was cleared, however, when the Prime Minister arrived at a compromise settlement with the Federalists on 27 July 1957.[36] But Bandaranaike's principal adversary, the UNP, seized on this pact to tell the Sinhalese people that they had been 'betrayed'.

The UNP did not seek to challenge the Prime Minister in parliament. Instead they placed greater hopes in campaigning in the country. They organized a 'pilgrimage' from Colombo to the Temple of the Sacred Tooth in Kandy with a

34 For the details of this incident, see ibid., 12 February 1959, 819–48.

35 See for details the debate on the no-confidence motion moved against Dahanayake's government by N. M. Perera in H.R. Deb., 30 October 1959, 950–1126 and the debate on the vote of censure moved by the opposition against Dahanayake's Minister of Justice in ibid., 27 November 1959, 1599–1764. Dahanayake held the premiership from 26 September 1959 to 20 March 1960.

36 See Ceylon Faces Crisis, Federal Party Pamphlet, Colombo, 1957 for details of this pact.

view to forcing the Prime Minister to repudiate his pact by
rousing the feelings of the Sinhalese people. Though the
'pilgrimage' ended in a fiasco, the UNP did not relax its efforts.
Many of its sympathizers in the public service aided the party
by obstructing Bandaranaike's efforts to contain the situation.
The Prime Minister in the end was forced by a demonstration
of Buddhist monks, many of whom were suspected of being in
league with the UNP, to abrogate his pact with the Federalists
in May 1958. Widespread disturbances were followed by the
declaration of an island-wide state of emergency on 27 May
1958. Emergency rule as a method of dealing with extra-
parliamentary opposition has since become the practice of
governments in office.

On the political front, the UNP campaigned against the
inclusion of Marxists in the cabinet.[37] It pointed to the danger
of a seizure of power by them. The frequent public airing of
the differences between the two opposing factions in the
cabinet was utilized by the UNP to tell the public that there
was a complete collapse of the principles of collective
responsibility.

UNSETTLED PARLIAMENTARIANISM

The assassination of Bandaranaike on 26 September 1959
brought into existence an unstable and politically eccentric
government headed by W. Dahanayake. He found it difficult
to hold his cabinet together and dissolved parliament on 5
December 1959. Elections were fixed for 19 March 1960. The
election was of some significance for many reasons. All polling
was, for the first time, to take place on one day. Previously it
had been alleged that polling had been staggered so as to
ensure that the safe seats of UNP leaders would poll on the
first day, leaving them free thereby to campaign in other, not
so safe constituencies. Stringent election laws had been enacted
to prevent impersonation and prohibit the use of private
vehicles for the transport of voters. The display of posters,
flags, etc., on public highways was banned – provisions which
were obviously intended to curb the advantages hitherto
possessed by the UNP. There had also been a fresh delimita-

[37] There were two ministers with Trotskyist antecedents in the cabinet but
they could no longer be described as Marxists.

tion of constituencies; their number had been increased by nearly 50 per cent. The Kandyan Sinhalese areas had obtained additional weightage and this would have worked to the advantage of the SLFP. An additional number of constituencies had also been carved out in areas where the Left was considered strong. For the first time a left-wing party, the LSSP, contested the election with a view to forming a government.

The results of the election were inconclusive. The new Prime Minister, Dudley Senanayake, having failed to get the support of the Tamil Federal Party, dissolved parliament on 23 April 1960.

The main issues at the elections of July 1960 were the question of a state system of education, and the position of the Federal Party. The only contenders for power were the UNP and the SLFP. The UNP alleged that its rival had a secret pact with the Federalists, and in a large number of constituencies maps of Ceylon, indicating those parts of the country to be ceded to the Tamils under this agreement, were distributed. The electors, however, chose to repose their confidence in the SLFP which was led by Mrs Sirima Bandaranaike. The emotional wave created the assassination of Bandaranaike and his widow's pledge to continue his policies contributed in no small measure to the SLFP's victory.

In the fifth parliament the position of the opposition was almost the same as in the third when Bandaranaike had been Prime Minister. The main opposition group was the UNP. There were in addition the LSSP, the FP, the CP, and Philip Gunawardena's group which called itself the MEP.

The UNP exploited Mrs Bandaranaike's legislation against the Roman Catholics and the Tamils to its advantage.[38] The Roman Catholics occupied their schools and refused to hand them over to the state for several weeks until a settlement with the Church brought an end to the impasse. The Federal Party retaliated with a civil disobedience campaign and compelled

---

[38] (i) Under legislation enacted in late 1960 and early 1961 for the take-over of schools by the state, the Roman Catholic Church was one of those adversely affected; (ii) the Language of the Courts Act passed by Parliament in late 1960 providing for the use of Sinhalese in all courts throughout the island to the detriment of the Tamil language, and Mrs Bandaranaike's government's decision to enforce Sinhalese as the one official language throughout the island from 1 January 1961 alienated the Tamils.

the government to declare an emergency which lasted several
months.

Mrs Bandaranaike had also to face trouble from the trade
unions, especially those controlled by the LSSP. An unsuccessful attempt at a *coup d'état* by leaders in the armed
forces in January 1962 was warning enough that right-wing
elements, chafing at the chaotic situation in the country, would
organize themselves against a middle of the road government.[39]
A little more than a year later there were allegations of another
coup, this time organized by Sinhalese Buddhist officers in the
armed forces.[40] The UNP leaders alleged that Mrs Bandaranaike's government was seeking to establish a dictatorship.
Their fears were increased when she appointed three LSSP
men to her cabinet in June 1964. The government's attempt to
nationalize the press further aggravated the situation. The
Buddhist clergy, as well as public opinion, was mobilized by
the UNP to combat this move. A section of Mrs Bandaranaike's
parliamentary following led by her own deputy, C. P. de Silva
became increasingly apprehensive of the LSSP's presence in
the government, crossed over to the opposition on 3 December
1964, and brought down the government. Parliament was dissolved on 17 December. The UNP had played a crucial role
in this whole affair.

The general election which followed in March 1965 was
again inconclusive. The UNP's leader, Dudley Senanayake,
nevertheless, with the assistance of the Tamil Federal Party
and five other minor groupings was able to form a stable coalition. Early in 1968 the SLFP with a view to organizing a united
front of all anti-UNP forces in the country, entered into a
coalition with the two left-wing groups – the LSSP and the
CP. All three parties agreed on a common programme. This
coalition of opposing forces criticized the government on two
fronts – for its failure to bring down the rising cost of living,
and for its secret arrangements with the Ceylon Tamil and
Indian Tamil leaders. It achieved some success when its propaganda forced Senanayake in July 1968 to abandon the

[39] See statement on the abortive *coup d'état* of 27 January 1962 by F. R.
Dias Bandaranaike in *H.R. Deb.*, 13 February 1962, 1120–1143.
[40] See *ibid.*, 3 September 1962, 1380–92. There was yet another alleged *coup
d'état* by high-ranking Sinhalese Buddhist army officers, this time against
Dudley Senanayake's 'national government' in February 1966. See statement
by J. R. Jayawardene in *ibid.*, 9 March 1966, 221–4.

District Councils Bill which had formed part of his under-takings to the Federal Party, in exchange for their support of his government.

This study has shown that despite the fact that Ceylon lacks some of the more conventional attributes of the parliamentary system – such as a well-defined two-party situation – local adaptations have enabled it to function reasonably well. The habit of toleration, as well as a commitment to constitutional methods of agitation, a measure of agreement over a fairly wide range of fundamentals and the presence of two clearly identifiable coalitions, one with a UNP bias, and the other SLFP-inclined, are evidence that a Ceylonese version of the Westminster model has come to stay. Most of the controversial issues in Ceylon politics – the Sinhalese–Tamil problem, the Indian question, Buddhism, the Roman Catholic Church, non-alignment in foreign policy – have been settled on the bases of compromises to which the two major parties are more or less committed, though with differing emphases. The ques-tions of democracy, dictatorship, Marxism, the separatist ambitions of Tamil parties, the paths to economic develop-ment give rise to debate and rivalry between the parties, but the electors are discerning enough to realize which of these are most pertinent at any particular point of time. There have occasionally been retrogressive trends such as the intervention of the Roman Catholic Church and the Buddhist clergy in politics, and abortive attempts at *coups d'état* by men in the armed forces but these have not gone so far as to endanger or undermine the system. The most heartening development therefore in Ceylon since it gained independence has been the emergence of a virile and responsible opposition. The latter, it should be admitted, has at times acted for narrow partisan gain, but by and large it could be said that the opposition is as efficient as any in the politically more mature countries.

K

W. H. Morris-Jones

Dominance and Dissent[*]

Their interrelations in the Indian party system

WITH LAL BAHADUR SHASTRI'S SUDDEN DEATH IN TASHKENT in January of this year, India faced for the second time within eighteen months the problem of succession to leadership. The task may have been easier on the second occasion: for one thing, it was not a matter, as it had been in 1964, of finding a successor to a man revered for a full generation as a national leader; for another, there was to hand the experience of the first occasion. On the other hand, while Nehru's end had been for long foreseen and considered, and came as the culmination of a period of declining grip, that of Lal Bahadur occurred without warning. Moreover, for all the respect that Shastri had attracted, the atmosphere in which his replacement had to be sought was not that of the somewhat hushed apprehension in which he had been chosen. But while the second succession was thus accompanied by greater noise and bustle, and while the element of conflict and rivalry was now expressed in the taking of a vote to determine the issue, both operations went with every appearance of smoothness. India felt proud, and most of the world relieved, to find that there was a system that could take the strain. But what is that system?

Problems of succession, strictly understood, may be said to arise when leaders are removed by fate. For when they are removed by politics, the force and instruments of removal – either by elections or by assassination – are, at least for some time, capable of furnishing alternative leadership. (How long is another matter. The skills required to arrive in power are not the same as those needed for its maintenance and consolidation; this seems to hold true of any kind of political system, but the contrast is more vivid when the way to power is irregular. Military officers who are so well placed for effecting

[*] Vol. 1, no. 4, July–September 1966.

a *coup* find that they have subsequently to change style and
create new structures or else hand over.) When fate intervenes
one of three situations arises. There may be – as in the United
States but in few other cases – a firmly pre-determined
successor. There may instead be an organized body with
established procedures which has the responsibility and the
capacity to choose a replacement. Or it can happen that the
leader's removal creates a situation of real ambiguity in which
new forces, hitherto suppressed or dormant, come to life. The
difference between the second and third cases depends partly
on a difference between liberal democracies and autocracies:
the arbitrary, rule-less character of the latter extends beyond
their end to their succession. But it does not follow that an
authoritarian or totalitarian regime must descend into disorder when the leader goes. The third case occurs only when
personal power has either destroyed independent institutional
structures or so balanced them as to cause uncertainty not
simply about men but about methods and regimes. In the
second case, on the other hand, the disappearance of the
leader discloses supporting structures of established legitimacy: what he rested upon can be depended upon to fill his
place. Communist leadership may often come into this category, along with liberal-democratic leadership. What made
the case of Stalin's succession interesting was that it fell
between the second and third types. To ask the question 'after
Franco, Mao, Castro, Nasser, ... what?' is to ask how far a
leader is sustained by an organized and institutionalized body
which has life without him. Positive answers might safely be
supplied in respect of Mao and Nyerere as well as Wilson. In
respect of others – Franco, Sukarno, Nkrumah (if politics had
not won the race against fate) – negative answers are called for.

Succession crises in other words are the moments of truth in
a political system's life. They direct our attention to the heart
of the matter. In India's case, there was no ambiguity: eyes
had to be fixed on the Congress Party. This is no bad thing,
for here is not only the central area for the understanding of
Indian politics but at the same time an instructive and critical
case for the general theory of political parties and the politics
of developing areas. For it is fair to say that the task of escaping from a framework of ideas about parties based mainly on
European inter-war experience is still very incomplete.

DOMINANCE, ALTERNATION, OR COMPETITION?

It is fifteen years since Duverger first published his 'preliminary general theory of parties, vague, conjectural and of
necessity approximate' – in which Turkey received some attention, Latin America a glance, and Asia and Africa not a mention. It was of course an achievement to bring together the
experience of more than a generation of Western party
activity. And if there was already in 1951 much that could
have been said about the political organizations of the third
world, it was admittedly after 1951 that the experience in that
field proliferated. Moreover, there is this tribute to be paid to
the pioneer effort: if it has been necessary to go beyond, it is
difficult not to start the journey from it. This is as true of the
classificatory categories employed to handle party internal
structures as of those used with respect to party systems.

So far as the latter are concerned, it has for some time been
clear that the number of parties in a system tells us too little.
For all that distinguishes single-party regimes from others, this
category still contains bewildering variety. It was awkward
enough when it had quickly to be admitted that there were
important structural (as well as social and doctrinal)
differences between communist and fascist parties. It becomes
a good deal more serious when Ghana's CPP and Tanzania's
TANU have to be found a place in the same box. We are then
bound to look at inner party structures, at government-party
relations and at the place of the party in society. Similarly,
multi-party systems present a strange assortment, unmanage-
able for most purposes until we introduce distinction in terms
of the relations between the many parties. When this is done,
at once the concept of dominance emerges.

This term, as introduced by Duverger, came in from economics and its use demanded fine discretion. A dominant party
was not at all necessarily a majority party, though it would be
larger than any other; it was a party whose influence
dominated the political atmosphere. It was explicitly said not
to be a 'self-contained type of party development' but rather
'one mode that can be assumed by the other types', such as
alternation. But this term has undergone subsequent modifi-
cation. So far from being a feature which can coexist with alter-

nation, only slowing down the pendulum swings, it has come to be used in a sense perhaps closer to its economics source: an important departure from competitive politics. In that sense the term has been used of parties which were on their way to the establishment of single-party rule. More generally, the term came to indicate a broad group of newly independent states in which the anti-colonial movement had been able to take over power. Coleman, for instance, in the well-known conclusion to *The Politics of the Developing Areas* (1960) found dominant parties in a number of such states including India, Algeria, Nyasaland, Tanganyika, Ghana, Tunisia, Malaya, and Mali as well as in Turkey and Mexico.

What is the relation between dominance, alternation, and competition? It has perhaps been too readily assumed that since domination in the post-Duverger sense rules out alternation it must also be antithetical to competitive politics. But this would follow only if we were to mean by competitive politics some form of alternation of parties in power. This seems too narrow a use of 'competitive'. Admittedly, it is well to be careful here: in the most extreme forms of autocracy, there can be intense competitive rivalry, if only for the ear and favour of the autocrat. To widen the meaning of the term to cover the intrigue of the palace corridor and the party committee room would blunt the edge of the analytical tool. Between these unhelpful extremes would be the idea of competitive as indicating a measure of the presence in a political system of opportunities for open and effective dissent. On this meaning, alternation without competition is conceivable though unlikely, while competition without alternation is perfectly possible though requiring special conditions. Our interest is in exploring a striking case of dominance coexisting with competition but without trace of alternation.

This particular case must be understood as occupying one position on a matrix expressing several variables. On one side, the scale runs from single through dominant to alternating parties. On the other side are placed degrees of 'openness' both in the internal structure and texture of the party or parties as well as in their relations with each other. Obviously, some positions cannot be filled: in single-party systems, relations between parties do not apply. But there are a number of different kinds of combinations which can be regarded as

K2

yielding a politics of dissent. So far from this being a peculiarity of alternating parties in open party systems and with open party structures, it can also characterize peculiar single parties of open structure[1] and certainly dominant party systems of open interaction and open party structure – such as India possesses.

THE DOMINANT PARTY-SYSTEM

The Congress Party has over a period of just under two decades and through three general elections enjoyed unshared governmental power at the centre and in most of the states of the country. It is not likely to be disturbed in this power by the coming elections of 1967. Its legislature majorities have mainly been massive, its proportion of the votes cast seldom over 50 per cent. Its dominance of the political system fits the Duverger usage in that it has set the tone of the country's political life. Like a shopkeeper in an Indian bazaar, it squats with its large flabby shape in the middle of its wares, the heart of a political market-place in which bargaining and dissent are the language of discourse.

The system over which it presides[2] is characterized by 'openness' of three distinct kinds. First, the party itself is open: movement in and out of the organization is fairly free; competition for power and status within the party is vigorous and increasing; knowledge of these inner shifts and struggles is quite accessible to the public. Second, it is open to other parties to enter the competition for power: they may not find funds easy to obtain and the electoral system presents them with difficulties similar to those encountered by English Liberals, but they normally (the Left Communist Party in the recent 'emergency' is an important exception) suffer no legal disabilities and no serious contrived unfairness – as their collecting of 55 per cent of the vote testifies. Finally, there is a most important 'openness' in the relations between Congress and the other parties: not merely is there an absence of

[1] Tanzania may be an example. See the illuminating article by William Tordoff, 'The General Election in Tanzania' in *Journal of Commonwealth Political Studies*, IV, 1 (March 1966), pp. 47–64.

[2] A concise but fairly detailed account of the system is attempted in 'Political Forces' Chapter 5 of my *Government and Politics of India*, London, Hutchinson University Library, 1964.

barriers, there is positive communication and interaction between them. The opposition parties neither alternate with Congress in the exercise of power, nor do they share power in any coalition form; rather they operate by conversing with sections of Congress itself. They address themselves not so much to the policy-deaf electorate as to like-minded politician groups in the dominant party.[3]

It may be helpful to attempt a diagrammatic representation of this system:

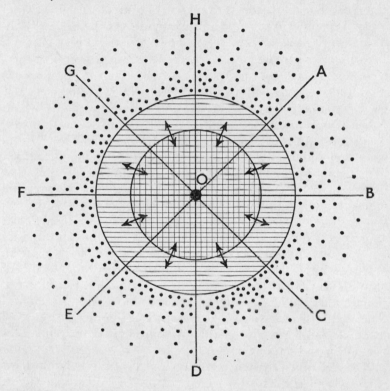

[3] The first clear analysis of this third aspect came from R. Kothari in 'Party System', one of a series of articles on 'Form and Substance in Indian Politics' published in *Economic Weekly* (Bombay), vol. XIII, no. 22 (3 June 1961), pp. 847–54. There he wrote:

The role of opposition parties in India is quite distinctive. Instead of providing an alternative to the Congress party, they function by influencing sections within the Congress. They oppose by making Congressmen oppose. Groups within the ruling party assume the role of opposition parties, often quite openly, reflecting the ideologies and interests of the other parties. The latter influence political decision-making at the margin. Criticism from the platform or in the legislature has often found response among Congressmen

The political leadership of the Congress Party is represented by the small solid circle at the centre, the Party itself by the area shaded with both horizontal and vertical lines. Outside that circle lie the other parties occupying the zone of horizontal shading. More precisely, they should be thought of not as covering the whole of this zone but rather as occupying non-contiguous patches within it. The opposition groups, that is, find for the most part that the distance (along the circumference) between themselves is greater than the distance (along the radii) between each of them and the adjacent part of Congress. The outer circle of diminishing dots is the people, politicized in varying degrees. (Note, however, that it is an expanding universe; it moves outwards as the political and social processes incorporate an increasing proportion of the population.) The lines HD, AE, and so on – which cut into Congress and even its leadership – represent the various ways in which political opinion is divided. Thus HD could separate 'right' from 'left', AE modernists from traditionalists, FB all-India from regional-oriented, GC communal from secular – and yet other lines would be needed to show cleavages such as that between liberal constitutional and authoritarian anti-regime views. The diagram manages to show that Congress is all these things, but it would be difficult to locate the other parties at all precisely for the reason that they too do not fall simply into any one of the sectors created by these lines of distinction. What is important, however, is that in any one sector of opinion, say HOA, in which right-wing, modernist, constitutional views are held, there are to be found Congressmen and others; the two-way arrows represent the interaction referred to above (and can also stand for some actual movement of persons in and out of Congress).

The continued existence of this particular kind of dominant party system is not to be accounted for by any single factor. History, social structure, and political style all have to be

and been echoed in the deliberations of the party. The political stature of an opposition leader and his personal relations with the high-ups in the Congress have often given him an influence with the Congress which has prevented frustration and bitterness which would otherwise result from his party being in a position of permanent minority.

See also his article 'The Congress System' in *Asian Survey*, IV, 2 (December 1964), pp. 1161–73.

called upon. It is a large fact of the recent past that Congress at independence was already sixty-two long years old. The earliest nationalist movement of the third world was left waiting longest, but its reward was correspondingly great: it could hold the power it got because it had built up political capital – in the forms of a legacy of loyalty and a reservoir of political skills. To have held Congress together over a period of changing political climates and in a country of deep cultural divisions required prodigious political ability. Every difficulty overcome before 1947 gave an added qualification for the years that followed. In different proportions at different times the whole array of political weapons from constitutional argument through the organization of dedicated cadres to the mobilization of mass agitation, had to be assembled and used. Above all, the skill of reconciliation and accommodation was needed as the movement spread out to encompass fresh social and regional sections. Nor were these skills wholly modernist in character. As Weiner has shown,[4] Congress leadership has been able to harness traditional roles and values of conciliation and consensus formation to the maintenance of the dominant government party system. The district politician is at one and the same time playing a part in a modern mass politics society and fulfilling a role traditionally expected of rural leadership.

To factors of history and political style are to be added considerations of social structure. Indian society is far from egalitarian but it is perhaps correct to describe it as not (so far) a sharply polarized society in terms of class. Large differences of income and marked contrasts of status there certainly are between top and bottom, but the intermediate stages are many and the slopes of the pyramid are gradual and even. The condition of the landless untouchables in village India is no doubt abject from almost every standpoint, but that of the low-caste tenant cultivator of an inadequate scrap of land is not all that much better. The casual unskilled labourer in the city has nothing but a rag and a piece of pavement but the slum-dwelling artisan or even the petty clerk is not so far away. Moreover, the indices of social rank do not wholly coincide;

[4] The outline is brilliantly given in his article, 'Traditional role performance and the development of modern political parties: the Indian case', *Journal of Politics*, vol. 26, no. 4 (November 1964), pp. 830–49, and the detail is spelt out in his forthcoming book, *Party-building in a New Nation: The Indian National Congress.*

high-caste status, weight of numbers and economic power do not go together; what a man or a group lacks under one heading he may to some extent be able to make up for under another. Further, education, transportation, urbanization, and political activity all introduce change and the prospect of change. Individuals and groups use whatever advantages they have to improve their position. Political influence is one instrument among many but not unimportant.

The social situation is not a sufficient condition for a dominant party but it facilitates the task of a capacious political organization. Even more important is the snowball effect of political power in a state like India. For here government is deeply accepted (as well as distrusted) and government is immensely influential. It is to government that all men and groups must look for assistance in the protection of what they have as well as for help in obtaining that more which they want. No group that enjoys some established position can afford to go it alone; every group that seeks new advantages and amelioration of its position must above all try to ensure that its voice is heard in the counsels of government. The level of government that is most relevant varies according to the kind of benefit that is sought: for a private commercial licence, it is the centre; for educational concessions for a caste bloc, it will be the state; for this or that development benefit for a cultivator, it will be, increasingly, the new indirectly elected local bodies such as the *Panchayat Samiti*. For these operations one must have friends who can influence people. Congress is such a body of organized friends.

It is true in this world of distributory politics as elsewhere that you can't please all the people all the time. Someone gets less than someone else and feels cheated. But more important than this are two considerations. First, a party that has collected over time the support of several sections at every level has the capacity to be sensitive and is trained to be so. It does not have to strain to catch the meaning of rumbling messages from beyond its walls; it has only to listen to the sounds from within. The chameleon-like ambiguity of its ideological colouring is an aid to this kind of sensitivity and flexibility. Second, the disappointed may in disgust and despair consider finding a new home. But how much there is to make them hesitate to move! Leave loyalty, habit, and even established connections aside, the simple fact is that elsewhere is relative wilderness. In any case, there can hardly be good ground for such despair: there are others in the same mood; make fresh factional alliances; get stronger from within; down need not be permanently out in this game. Of course, things do go wrong from time to time. The party in that district has become over-identified with and exclusively controlled by one powerful group. Rigidity sets in and the established leaders either do not notice or cannot adjust to a social change which is throwing up a new aspiring group. The latter then become alienated instead of accommodated. Or again, the disappointed ones are led away from the path of their own interests by their anger or their pride; they quit the party. They may hope to cultivate the wilderness; they may prefer to be big men in the desert than cogs in the city. After a little while they may seek readmission. If they are important enough the party will show forgiveness.

There is not one sole way of building political support within the Congress Party. Sometimes a local base of some 'natural' kind – economic influence, family status, political record – can be expanded through personal association until it becomes of a magnitude to be courted by higher echelons of the party. Sometimes the process may be from the opposite end: influence with a well-placed political leader will gain one such a reputation for being 'effective' that a local base can be won from men with lesser connections. More usually both processes are at work. Political support often tends to have some amount of social 'colour': blocs in state politics may be predominantly from a certain caste or group of districts in the state; party factions at district level may be associated with groups of villages or sets of families. But if social groupings are natural bricks for political builders to use, there are also inherent limits on such a policy of exclusiveness. For this makes enemies too. The social divisions are not often so unequal as to make this pay; even in places where there is a dominant caste, factions will run across that caste. The politician will strive above all to assemble a following [5] which is dependent on him,

[5] See F. G. Bailey, *Politics and Social Change*, London, Oxford University Press, 1964 which did so much to pioneer this field. Paul Brass, *Factional Politics in an Indian State*, Berkeley and Los Angeles, University of California Press, 1965, is a fine account of the linking of local factions to state Congress circles in Uttar Pradesh.

which he can 'serve' and which is held together by his services rather than by other kinds of ties.

This, then, is a world of snowballs, not pendulums – of dominance, not alternation. Yet it is an open political society in which dissent is freely expressed and in which a high degree of open competition between factions is a leading feature of the life of the main party. Nor is it the case that other institutions in the political system are rendered meaningless by the existence of this kind of dominant party. On the contrary, a very good case can be made out for holding that a party like Congress so far from making Parliament into a façade has saved its reality.[6]

THE FOUR PHASES OF THE CONGRESS

The key puzzle in all this nevertheless remains: does the role of accommodation and political integration (which we say the Congress Party so effectively performs) not conflict with its own integrity as an organization? If so, which yields and what are the trends? It is a vital question for if Congress falls apart, so will the whole party system; on that in turn depends the stability and character of India's political life. The threat to Congress' continuance comes not from the possibilities of opposition unity – which seem remote except in the shaky form of electoral 'deals' – but from its own lack of cohesion. So the puzzle can be put as a paradox: to dominate, Congress must accommodate; yet accommodation encourages incoherence which destroys the capacity to dominate.

Two rival images can indeed be seen to be competing for the party's soul. One, the 'open umbrella' version of the party, is that which has been stressed above and would be recognized as indicating well-known features of Congress. Seen thus, Congress is the party of generous shelter, mixed social base and very broad goals. Once upon a time it was the home for all who could agree that the important thing was the removal of alien rule and a transfer of power into the hands of Indian national leaders. Subsequently, as party in office, its hospitality has remained undiminished and it houses a great variety of persons, including certainly those who respect it for its past services to

[6] The arguments are indicated in my article 'Parliament and the Dominant Party', *Parliamentary Affairs*, XVII, 3 (Summer 1964), pp. 296–307.

the nation and those who recognize it as a source of future services to them. But it is a party, it has an organization, it entails
a structure of offices. Much is written and more is said in India
about the influx of men on the make, but Congress still contains its devotees. These are of two kinds. There are those for
whom, as just suggested, the party is the embodiment of certain
ideals of service in the cause of social justice. There are also
those who are, so to say, devotees from habit and experience,
men who have worked the organization and feel pride and an
absorbing interest in its functioning. From the devotees – the
term 'militants' scarcely fits Congressmen – comes continually
a rejection of the implications of the 'open umbrella'. For
them, Congress is a distinctive body with a life and style of its
own and its active members constitute a dedicated and purposeful national leadership. If Congress is an umbrella, it is on
this view one which is closed, has a point to it and is ready for
action. The context between these pictures of the party can be
examined by looking at two broadly distinguishable facets of
party life. First, there is the area of the Congress Party's constitution and internal organization. This comprises a number of
very detailed questions such as membership rules and qualifications, internal party elections to its controlling committees,
relations between the various organs of the party, matters of
training and discipline. These are not examined here.[7] Second,
attention has to be paid to the general relations of party and
government and to the balance between central and regional
or state power among the leaders.

The history of Congress since independence may for the
present purpose be divided into four phases. From 1947 to
1951 the party was left without effective leadership. A short,
sharp quarrel between Prime Minister Nehru and Congress
President Kripalani led at once to the latter's resignation and
emphasized that there was no independent power centre in
the party which could stand for a moment against the party's
leaders in the government, in particular Nehru and Patel.
Gandhi's attempt to transform the character of Congress into
a voluntary social service organization could, if successful, have
rallied one kind of party worker. But it seems unlikely that it
would have acted as more than a faint voice of conscience on

[7] A related paper, 'Dilemmas of Dominance', deals with these matters and
will be published shortly.

those in power. In any event, the Gandhian scheme was firmly rejected by the party's top men and Gandhi himself was soon removed by assassination. At the same time neither Nehru nor Patel had time to devote to party affairs.[8] With a government to take over, a new constitution to hammer out, refugee movements and other post-partition difficulties to handle and a communist uprising to subdue, they had preoccupations enough. Patel, who had a distinguished record as party organizer and might have been expected to do more than Nehru for the party, had the additional special responsibility for preserving and developing the national administration and bringing about the political and administrative integration of a multitude of princely states.

A second phase extends from 1951 to the late fifties. As the immediate crises were overcome, as competitive political life became possible and as the country's first adult-franchise general elections came in sight, activity and struggle within the party developed. With the aid of hindsight, one can say that these struggles were no doubt most complex and based upon a variety of different kinds of factions and groups at all levels. In each state the old guard of the party was splitting into rival blocs as regional and policy differences came to prominence, while at the same time newer, generally younger elements were pressing for advancement.[9] But the dominance of the Nehru–Patel 'duumvirate' and the contrasts of interests, temperaments and policies between the two men permitted the party's internal struggles to be presented in simplified form as a tension between secular socialism and communal conservatism. The election of Tandon as Congress President at the end of 1950 was taken as distasteful to Nehru; after a year of unpleasant conflict and after Patel's death, Nehru forced

[8] This way of putting it may beg an important question: why did the leaders not feel the need to use the party to help to overcome some of the problems which they were struggling with as members of the government? The answer is probably that they – Patel, in particular – had more confidence in the civil service than in a party machine which had grown rusty during the enforced inactivity of the war years (after 1942) and which had been by-passed during the frantic and tangled independence negotiations of 1946–7.

[9] Much of the story comes to light through recent studies of present patterns. The latter have their origins in the tussles of the late forties and early fifties. The evidence is given in the work of Brass on Uttar Pradesh (op. cit.), the district studies by Weiner in several states (op. cit.) and a Rajasthan study by L. Schrader (PhD thesis, 1965, University of California, Berkeley).

Tandon's resignation and was himself elected to the office of Congress President. While Nehru was by no means idle as party leader, much of his energy in this capacity was devoted to attempting to influence the party's selection of candidates for the 1952 elections to the legislatures and subsequently to drawing lines which, while nicely avoiding his own double position, would indicate the separate responsibilities of party organs and government. There is little sign that he applied his mind to matters of party organization. Nor is this surprising; apart from the range of his other duties, there is the fact that this area was one which he had been able largely to ignore. Social background and personal and family connections had in the twenties shot him into prominence at the top without the need for a painstaking climb up the rungs of the party ladder. If the repair of the machine was, therefore, hardly Nehru's subject, his own occupation of the party's presidency in a sense made the job less urgent; so much could be achieved by the leader's exhortations, and of these there was no lack. Nehru's own stature during these years obviated the need for radical re-examination of party organs. His own temperament too worked against such a course. Preferring on most matters to avoid nettle-grasping decisions and relying on his capacity to reconcile diverse positions, he discouraged the party from making too explicit the choices before it.

By 1955, Nehru, presumably satisfied that no threat to his leadership need now come from within the party, practised what he had preached to others – no state chief minister could be President of the Pradesh (State) Congress Committee – and relinquished the office of Congress President. A solid, capable, apparently unambitious, unexciting successor was found in Mr Dhebar. While, as expected, no great change took place immediately, Dhebar was freed from other duties – he had been Chief Minister of Saurashtra State – and able to devote himself entirely to the party. That, it seems, was enough. Gradually a revival of interest in party affairs becomes manifest and voices of complaint and dissatisfaction with the health of Congress are now joined by others proposing a variety of changes.[10] By the early sixties, talk of the need for 'purification',

[10] See my 'Dilemmas of Dominance' for the evidence.

'renunciation of office', and better discipline in the party was loud and monotonous. Even if still no dramatically effective reforms were achieved, it seemed that something was stirring inside the party and that awkward decisions were in future not easily to be swept away under the carpet. In this situation three events took place within nine months: in August 1963 the 'Kamaraj Plan' was accepted and implemented, unseating six Cabinet Ministers of the Central Government and six Chief Ministers of States, releasing them for the honourable task of reviving the vigour of the party; in January 1964 Kamaraj himself became President of Congress; in May of that year Nehru died. The current phase of Congress history had begun.

CONVERSATION AND DISSENT

The Congress Party thus not only survived years of organizational neglect but had started to show signs of rejuvenation – just before its leaders were called upon to deal with the succession crises. But how far does this rejuvenation imply an assault on the amorphous, 'open umbrella' style of party? The connection is admittedly indirect – at best: some restoration of importance and status to party organs and offices might be expected to work to the advantage of the devotees' image of the more defined and purposeful party.

The emergence in 1964 of Kamaraj as national party leader – and his re-election in 1966 for a further two years – at once reflected and heavily reinforced the restored significance of the Congress organization as such. The role of the Congress President as king-maker in the succession crises – he was expressly charged with the task on the first occasion – seemed not unnatural, but this was a tribute to the man and the change he embodied; it would have looked less natural under some of the past presidents. The change could also be seen in what appears to have been greater liveliness in the annual Congress mammoth sessions and in the meetings of the Congress 'parliament', the All-India Congress Committee. Government spokesmen have of course been prominent on the platform but the absence of a towering premier and the presence of a non-governmental party president have clearly shifted the balance somewhat towards the 'floor'. Demands that those in government should regard themselves as accountable to the party have not been evaded or rebuffed but accepted, and some machinery of party committees to give effect to this sentiment has been set up. It is also worth noting that the party's Working Committee has been, more clearly than before, the place where certain key decisions have been taken. This is true of the language policy worked out following the anti-Hindi riots in Madras in 1965 and the decision to make some concession to the Sikh demand for a re-drawing of the boundaries of Punjab State. The Working Committee under Nehru had no doubt always discussed large policy questions and passed resolutions; it is now evident that this is also an effective power centre.

It is also noticeable that Kamaraj in several speeches over the past two years has sought to stress and define the 'socialistic pattern of society' which Congress gave as its goal a decade earlier. He has done this in such a way as to acknowledge that there must be limits to the party's liberal accommodation policy, that there are those for whom Congress is not a suitable shelter. All this is tentative and a matter of emphasis and nuance, certainly no clear break of policy. But that it is nevertheless real is also suggested by Kamaraj's conduct of the party's campaign in the 'mid-term' election in Kerala in 1965. When the Kerala Congress organization split and many of its Nair and Christian elements — who were also its better-off and more conservative sections — set about forming a rival breakaway group, the party made little attempt to stop them. Instead, Kamaraj went out of his way rather to win to Congress numbers of poorer groups, especially the Ezhavas, who had previously backed the Communists. This was electorally dangerous but it seemed as if Congress was willing to think in terms of the longer run. It has in fact done much to break down Kerala's hitherto rigid community-party identifications. It may also have dealt a blow for party integrity; those who quit are no longer to be wooed back and those who stay must understand that a party has a discipline to impose.

It would, however, be grotesque to suggest that what was happening now was in some sense the domination of 'government' by 'party'. What can be reasonably suggested is that there has been growing concern about the integrity of the party. Along with this goes, oddly perhaps but not inconsis-

tently, less concern than heretofore about the precise boundaries of responsibility between party and government
institutions and also between centre and state leaders. Shastri
used a central Cabinet sub-committee to examine the conduct
of the Chief Minister of Orissa as a prelude to having him
resign. Kamaraj worked with a group of Chief Ministers of
States to organize support for Mrs Gandhi, once he saw that
she was the candidate likely to achieve the desired result of
defeating the persistent Mr Morarji Desai. The supposedly
powerful[11] group of leaders known as 'the syndicate' contains
holders of only party office as well as of government positions.
The central Cabinet, the Working Committee, the group of
Chief Ministers, the National Development and National
Defence Councils – in these key bodies many of the same men
wear different hats. The post-Nehru leadership is more
interested in who counts in terms of power or support than
in what office he holds. But all this is within Congress; it is
the party that holds them together and which they seek to
hold together. These are men whose road to power has lain
exclusively through and within the party. It is their political
home and they are familiar with its every room and corner.
They are politicians indeed, but they are also the greatest of
the 'devotees by experience' that the Congress possesses. They
would certainly deny that any choice has to be made between
power and 'purity', between the open and the closed um-
brellas. But their respect for, and interest in, party
organization could well lead them in the future to discovering
new ways of reconciling the two images.

To return to our starting-point: what has all this to do with
dissent? The party system sketched in the earlier part of the
article depends on the continuing coherence of Congress. This
coherence is no longer guaranteed by the presence of one
towering leader. It is guaranteed now by a group of party stal-
warts. They may well be less aware of other parties than was
Nehru, but they are not the stuff of which totalitarians are
made. They are bargainers and trimmers, but since they are
also men of the organization they are prepared to be ruthless
on its behalf; they will be willing to discipline some people
out of the party if that leaves the party stronger (and better

[11] Their role seems to have been less important in the second succession
crisis than in the first when they emerged to considerable prominence.

able to appeal to fresh sections entering the political arena). But they cannot make the party narrow or monolithic. So two things follow: the conversation between the segments of Congress and the parties outside it will go on; and competition and disagreement within Congress will remain.

Gerda Zellentin

Form and Function of the Opposition in the European Communities*

THE EXPERIENCE OF THE EUROPEAN COMMUNITIES CONFIRMS not only that, as the late Otto Kirchheimer put it, 'opposition is to be found under one form or another in every political community'; but also that a political community is to be found wherever opposition exists in one form or another. The purpose of this study is to investigate the manner in which opposition forces develop in the European Communities to block or to enhance integration.

THE EUROPEAN PARLIAMENT

The European Parliament is a mere torso of the nation-state type of parliament; hence it has either a consultative function only, or it is completely excluded from that part of the supranational decision-making process where 'power is produced by integration' (in the words of Talcott Parsons).

The European Parliament was established as the successor to the Common Assembly of the European Coal and Steel Community, (ECSC) for all the three European Communities – ECSC, Euratom, and the European Economic Community (EEC). The principles of its political form, of its range of activity, of its recruitment, and of its authority were developed during years of controversy between European federalists and functionalists which preceded the establishment of the supranational ECSC.

When it became impossible, largely because of the British veto on any form of supranationalism, to set up within the framework of the Council of Europe (established in 1949) a constituent assembly to draft a constitution for Europe, its

* Vol. 2, no. 3, April–July 1967.

members turned to economic functionalism. By a process of technical reorganization and fusion of some of the vital economic sectors, through supranational administration, integration was set in motion. Political authorities with limited but real powers were to be established. It was expected that the fusion of the economic and technical sectors would also have repercussions on the political realm. The original French proposal for an ECSC laid the emphasis of supranational action on the High Authority, which was in no case to be hampered by the particular interests represented by the national delegates to a European Assembly.[1] During the negotiations for the treaty, and under pressure from the other five delegations, above all from the small countries, which are always sensitive to questions of hegemony, a compromise was reached and the Schuman Plan was adjusted and modified so that a parliamentary assembly could be established. But at first the European Assembly was not to be directly elected, and it was to have only consultative status as far as legislation was concerned. It was not only the French delegation which had reservations about too wide a parliamentary competence. But it was French experience of the unstable governments of the Fourth Republic which proved decisive and was particularly influential in determining relations between the Parliament and the executive, and their respective functions.[2]

The European Parliament is extremely weak when compared to a parliament in a national federalist system. But it is much more developed, and presents a clearer image of a parliament in the making, when compared to the parliamentary assemblies in inter-governmental associations (Western European Union, NATO, and the Council of Europe). It is composed of 142 deputies (France, the German Federal Republic and Italy: 36 each; Belgium and the Netherlands: 14 each; Luxemburg: 6) which the national parliaments select at their own discretion. In principle there is no provision to prevent deputies being selected by direct election. A proposal was made in 1960 for a common electoral law, and was ratified by the European Parliament, but it has not yet been passed by the European Council of Ministers. It lays

---

[1] H. Schierwater, *Parlament und Hohe Behörde der Montanunion*, Heidelberg, 1961.
[2] Schierwater, *op. cit.*, p. 21.

down the principle of election by proportional representation.[3]
Finally, it should be remembered that the European Parliament itself has no direct influence on the criteria by which national parliaments select members of the European Parliament.

If one were to base an analysis of the European Parliament on a somewhat simplified form of Bagehot's classic definition of the functions of a parliament, one would find the following similarities and differences. The *elective* function (with regard to the executive) is lacking: the European Parliament is not an electoral chamber. The *expressive* function ('to express the mind of the ... people on all matters which come before it') would be more effective if there were direct elections. This is also true of the *teaching* function ('a great and open council of considerable men cannot be placed in the middle of a society without altering that society'). The *informing* function is zealously carried on by the European Parliament in order to familiarize the public with the administrative discussions and measures on integration. But it takes part in the *legislative* function only consultatively. As regards Bagehot's sixth function, namely the *financial* one, the European Parliament must be consulted during the preparation of the budget, but it is the Council, which is composed of the ministers of the six countries, which has the last word in this matter.[4] Finally, a seventh function should be added, *pace* Bagehot, which is most important for all developing parliaments of the continental type, namely the control of the executive. For this particular purpose, the motion of censure is in theory the strongest instrument in the European Parliament.[5] The two Commissions, representing the executives of the Common Market and Euratom, are alone accountable to the European Parliament. The Council of Ministers, as a Community organ, escapes democratic control. The fact that the ministers are responsible to their national parliaments is rendered ineffective by majority voting in the Council.[6] The range of activity

[3] See more particularly on this point F. A. Hermens, 'Europäische Wahlen und europäische Einigkeit' in *Festgabe für Alfred Müller-Armack*, Berlin, 1961.
[4] See my *Budgetpolitik und Integration*, Cologne, 1965 on the budgetary process.
[5] See below, p. 314.
[6] Resolution on the democratization of the European Community, doc. 93, session of 21 October 1964.

of the European Parliament is restricted by the objectives of the Treaty of Rome, and it does not have the universal competence of fully developed parliaments. Finally, when one comes to consider the integrative effects of a supranational parliament, one cannot but agree with E. B. Haas, that the modes of conduct evolved by the Assembly are probably of greater significance in tracing processes of political integration than the specific measures proposed by it'.[7] His view is substantiated by the activity of the European Parliament up to now. The actual impact it has had, in its consultative capacity, on the decision-making of the Council and the Commissions is hard to trace, whereas the efforts which it makes to strengthen the federalist democratic structure of the Communities are obvious.

An important phenomenon has been the appearance in the European Parliament of party groups. This is an event without precedent in any international assembly. The procedure for forming a supranational parliamentary party is described in the Standing Orders of the European Parliament, and three groups, the christian democrats, the socialists, and the liberals, were established as supranational parliamentary parties on 21 March 1958. A 'Group for the Democratic Unity of Europe', composed of Gaullists, was formed in November 1963 as an offshoot of the liberal group, but it does not constitute a supranational parliamentary party as defined by the Standing Orders. The following Table 1 shows the size and cohesion of political groups and national delegations in the European Parliament.

PROJECTION OF THE NATIONAL OPPOSITION ON THE INTERNATIONAL LEVEL

A national parliamentary decision-making organ influences the form and function of an opposition more strongly than a consultative representative assembly. Moreover, it should be remembered that the representation of political parties in the European Parliament is by delegation from the national parliaments according to an almost proportional representation of the government and moderate opposition parties. In the light of these two considerations it seems useful to inquire whether

[7] E. B. Haas, *The Uniting of Europe*, London, 1958, p. 390.

the attitude of the national opposition is projected on to the
international level. An examination of the national oppositions
to the ratification of the Treaties of Rome may serve to answer
this question.

TABLE 1 *

Delegations	% of seats in European Parliament	Cohesion Index average 1958–63	Cohesion Index average 1963–6
Germany	25·35	35·9	26·5
Italy	25·35	4·4	3·2
France	25·35	11·8	24·6
Belgium	9·85	30·8	19·8
Netherlands	9·85	6·0	9·1
Luxemburg	4·25	28·0	9·6
Average of national delegations		19·5	15·5
Parliamentary parties			
Christian democrats	43·7	15·2	14·9
Socialists	24·7	1·7	2·0
Liberals	18·3	13·7	17·6
UNR–UDT (UDE)	10·6	—	4·5
Average of the supranational groups		10·2	9·7

* The cohesion index is calculated from the percentage deviation of national
or ideological groups from unanimity in roll call votes. The higher the
percentage of deviation, the weaker the cohesion. (See P. H. Merkl, 'European
Assembly Parties and National Delegations' in *Journal of Conflict Resolution*,
March 1964, p. 58.)

This voting behaviour is not necessarily indicative of a
European opposition. Neither the ratification of the Rome
Treaties by a majority, nor the opposition votes can be explained in terms of a common attitude of like-minded parties,
cooperating across national frontiers, towards the idea of a
European commonweal. Whereas some support for the treaties
derived from the opportunistic thinking of several groups,
which each found some advantage in voting for them, conflicting motives such as nationalism, anti-supranationalism, or
free trade, for instance, were responsible for opposition to the
treaties. There seems to be a clear cleavage between those who

found something in the treaties which suited their positive economic and political expectations, and those who had only long- or short-range negative expectations, or apprehensions about, the project.

TABLE 2

Ratification of the Treaties of Rome by the National Parliaments
(1957)

Country	Lower Chamber For	Lower Chamber Abst.	Lower Chamber Ag.	Upper Chamber For	Upper Chamber Abst.	Upper Chamber Ag.	Negative Votes Parties
Germany *	Adopted by majority			Unanimously adopted			FDP; BHE
Italy *	Adopted by majority			Adopted by majority			Communists Nenni-socialists
France	342	5	239	222	—	70	Communists, Radical-socialists Gaullists, Poujadists
Belgium	174	2	4	123	2	2	Communists
Netherlands	194	—	12	46	—	5	Communists Liberals
Luxemburg	46	—	3	—	—	—	Communists

* No figures included in the minutes.

The basic opposition of national parties to the principle of supranationality can be clearly seen in Table 2. It became obvious that this initial dissent occasionally re-emerged in critical situations, as for instance in the formulation of a European power, cartel and transport policy etc.[8] But that in itself is not tantamount to an opposition of principle. For, apart from the communist parties, the German FDP, the Dutch liberals, the radical socialists, and the Gaullists allowed themselves to be elected to the European Parliament; but they did not engage individually or jointly in systematic opposition. Moreover, one should remember that the opposition was forced by the procedure laid down for ratification to accept or reject the treaties *in toto* – its members had been unable to influence the draft treaties since they were not negotiated through the parliaments.

[8] See the proposals on the merger of the executive, the political union, direct elections, etc.

L

This leads one to another aspect of the functioning of opposition in the European Parliament, notably the fact that some elements of the national oppositions have been eliminated from representation in it.

TABLE 3

	National Parliaments Seats %						European Parliament Seats % *
	G	I	F	B	N	L	Average of all countries	
Communists	—	26·4	8·5	2·8	2·7	8·9	10·97	—
Left-socialists	—	13·8	—	0·5	2·7	3·6	4·64	— †
Socialists	40·7	5·2	13·9	30·2	29·3	37·5	21·25	24·7
Liberals	9·9	6·2	21·2	22·6	10·9	10·7	12·25	18·3
Christian-democrats	49·4	41·2	8·1	36·4	51·7	39·3	35·64	43·7
Gaullists	—	—	48·3	—	—	—	11·52	10·6
Rightists a.o.	—	7·1	—	7·5	2·7	—	3·85	2·8

* Source: List of members of 27 June 1966 European Parliament Bulletin.
† Wanting: 4 seats (Italians).

According to article 138 of the EEC treaty, it is within the competence of the member states to lay down a procedure by which the parliaments nominate the number of representatives stipulated in the treaty. From a comparison of columns 1, 2 and 3 of Table 3, it can be noted that some of the political forces are not represented at all in the European Parliament, or they are not represented proportionately to their national strength. No delegates from the communist parties, or from the Italian Nenni-socialists, have yet been appointed.

When we compare the parties excluded from representation with those which voted against ratification, we find that of the opposition hostile to integration, the communists are excluded from representation in the Communities, whereas the liberals are over- and the anti-supranational Gaullists are slightly under-represented.

The exclusion of the left-wing extremists has been due not

merely to the consequences of the Cold War, or to the refusal of the communists to send representatives to organs of the 'state monopoly associations'.[9] It has been based on a concept of the role of a structural opposition in an integration plan.[10] The exclusion of part of the opposition from the West European integration plan was deliberately intended to further the development of consensus in the European Parliament (and in the other representative bodies of the Community).

The unusual, and indeed epoch-making, economic and social changes in the life of the European peoples brought about by integration demanded not only a strong initial consensus; it was necessary to ensure that this consensus should be continually reproduced while integration proceeded through its planned phases. The integration plan of the Rome Treaties is based upon predictable phases of successive economic and social innovation coupled with institutional reforms. In similar cases (e.g. the German *Zollverein*, the New Deal, or functional international organizations) the bureaucracy, interested parties, and economic groups co-operated to fulfil the plan. In a system composed of six governments, of which at least some, because of immobility or inherent constitutional weaknesses, were considered to be among the unstable democracies, it was understandable that non-dogmatic, co-operative, and pragmatic decision-making should be favoured at the expense of extreme forms of ideological party dogmatism. Those political forces which, because of their ideology or their position in the economic production or distribution process, were negatively disposed towards the project were denied a voice in it. A parliamentary, party-based working out of the integration plan might have placed it continually in jeopardy from sovereignty-oriented nationalistic considerations, and the demagogic claims of the parties which had been elbowed out. Acute parliamentary conflict was not needed in order to work out rational alternatives, at least not in the initial phase of integration.[11] It was for this reason that the political parties were

[9] This attitude was revised in 1956 by the Italian communists.

[10] The six governments agreed to exclude the communists prior to the establishment of the ECSC.

[11] Moreover it is doubtful whether acute political conflicts and clashing ideologies have a rationalizing effect. '... the historical record seems to offer little support for this view. For intense conflicts create their own irrationalities, particularly when conflict is fortified by ideology. It is a reasonable

given only a consultative capacity. The rival plans were ignored or eliminated[12] so that one integration plan could become the focus of the loyalties of political parties and interest
groups.

But the danger of manipulating the opposition in an incomplete democratic system, such as the European Community, is that the ending of the 'educational quarantine' of
those forces hostile to integration may be continually post-
poned. By excluding them from participation, even those
opposition forces which have been 'converted' to integration
may develop a new resentment against supranationalism.

ORGANIZATION AND FUNDAMENTAL
ATTITUDES OF THE OPPOSITION IN
THE EUROPEAN PARLIAMENT

The oppositional forces in the European Parliament fall into
four main categories according to the form of their organization: the non-organized, *ad hoc* opposition, according to
economic and social interests: the national delegations; organized groups of national representatives (e.g. the Gaullists);
and the supranational parliamentary parties. In turn, the degree of organization and the form of the opposition determines
to a certain extent the attitude of each force towards the principle of a supranational authority. An investigation of the
voting behaviour of the parties in the European Parliament
led to the following possible relationship between organization and fundamental attitudes towards supranationalism.[13]

---

hypothesis that the greater the discrepancy between the goals of the parties to a
conflict, the more that problem-solving and persuasion are likely to give way to
bargaining and coercion.' *Political Oppositions in Western Democracies*, ed.
R. A. Dahl, New Haven and London, 1966, p. 392.

[12] In the 19th century the concept of a Greater Germany under Austrian
leadership had to be discredited before the Little Germany solution under
Prussia could be realized. During the negotiations of the EEC Treaty, the project of a European Free Trade Zone (as an alternative to the Customs Union)
was coupled with the Community, and by this method temporarily divested of
its oppositional content. No common alternative plan was developed by the
communists in the six countries, though the Soviet Union tried to counter
the 'Spaak Report' in the framework of the Economic Commission for Europe
by working out a project for the Economic Co-operation of (All-)Europe.

[13] This is based on the results of a number of votes by roll call. Their
statistical value, because of the relatively short time that the European Communities have existed, is not particularly large; however, the use of a larger

The six national delegations have not been institutionalized, nor have they shown consistent voting behaviour (see Table 1). As can be seen from Table 4, the parliamentary parties cannot logically be opposed to supranationalism, because they were formed in order to support and influence the supra-national authority. The non-structured *ad hoc* opposition to certain measures put forward by the European Commission is issue- not authority-oriented. Only the Gaullists, who in

TABLE 4

Organization of oppositional forces	Dominance of supranational authority	Dominance of national sub-systems
National delegations	For or against	Against or for
Various groups of national representatives (e.g. Gaullists)	Against	For
Supranational parlia- mentary parties	For	Against

1963 broke away from the parliamentary group of the liberals, question the authority if the supranational institutions when they vote on political issues which touch upon the authority and the political structure of the Community. Otherwise they vote according to their economic interests. It can be deduced from this that in the European Community there is no con-sistent 'structural opposition' (in Dahl's terms) to this system.[14] One may also think that the *Europe des patries* is much too vague a conception for a programme of structural opposition to be based on it. The stability of a political system depends on whether it has a large or a small structural opposition. To judge by organized groups of opposition in the European Parlia-ment, opposition to the system is small. This is not so im-portant, since hostility to the system is shown by veto in the executive sector, not in the parliamentary sector. As the

---

quantity of statistical data raises the problem of the very different issues voted upon, with the result that the emergence of consistent behaviour patterns would not be easier to detect.

[14] See Strobel Report, doc. 110, 10 October 1966, *European Parliamentary Proceedings*.

Gaullists cannot be defeated in the Council, they can block
the supranational machinery when it is in their interest to do
so. None the less, if one were to distinguish the types of opposition conceivable within the European Community, and
provided that direct election were to include all the main
parties, a variety of sources of tension might arise (as indicated
in Table 5) which could only be counterbalanced by a strong
political authority.

Indications as to the organization and goals of the opposition
emerge from Tables 1 and 5. Their effect upon the integration
process can only be estimated when they are related to the data
concerning their size and cohesion, programme and consistency. Table 1 indicates that the socialists are not only the
largest minority, but that as a parliamentary group they consistently show the strongest cohesion.[15] Table 5 shows that the
socialists are actually the only force whose long-range dominant
goal is the establishment of an economic and political European community. By correlating Tables 1, 3, and 4 it becomes
clear that the other groups with relatively strong cohesion,
such as the UDE (UNR–UDT) and the Italian and Dutch
delegations, do not enter into consideration as a constructive
opposition, either because of insufficient size, or because of
lack of a constructive oppositional programme (such as the
socialists brought forward in 1963) or because of insufficient
ideological or organizational homogeneity (which the socialists had achieved through the International prior to the estab-
blishment of the European Communities). No other group
links its economic and social claims with the desire to
strengthen the supranational executive, while at the same time
bringing it under parliamentary control.

Thus, to use an expression of Kirchheimer's in a slightly
different context, the socialist opposition proves to be the

[15] Prior to any analysis of oppositional behaviour, it is necessary to consider
the advisory nature of the European Parliament and the fact that its representatives are not bound to vote the same way in their national assemblies as
they do in the European Parliament. This can lead them to profess an
insincere readiness to unite, which they have no intention of advocating at
home. This appears to afflict the European opposition as well, since otherwise
there would not have been an explicit appeal during the International
Congress of European Socialists (*Sorge um Europa*, 25–26 February 1964) to
make the votes of national representatives in the European Parliament
binding on their voting behaviour in their national parliaments.

'auxiliary engine' of the integration machinery.[16] Haas referred to it as a 'precursor opposition'. It opposes the entrenchment of the dominating national systems during the transitional phase, which might induce the supranational executive to move too timidly, and without sufficient continuity, towards greater autonomy. Indeed, the executive frequently allows its

TABLE 5

Opposition Patterns

By:		To:			
	Com- mission executive personnel	Individual measures of the Com- mission	Institu- tional structure	Economic/ Social structure	Supra- national structure
Interests: Short-term maximizing of welfare	No	Variable	No	No	Variable
Socialists: Supranational social reform	No	Variable	No	No	No
UNR: National political- structural reform	Yes	Variable	Yes	No	Yes
Communists: * Revolutionary inter- national transform- ation of state and society	Variable	Variable	Variable	Yes	Yes

* The behaviour of the communists can only be inferred from statements in the respective national parliaments. Their recent readiness to co-operate with the European Community could indicate that in contrast to previous years the communists show greater economic and political interest in the regulative and allocative competence of the supranational executive.

area of competence, as guaranteed by the treaties, to be curtailed, if only to facilitate some practical compromises with the national governmental authorities on more immediate issues. The socialist group first designated itself in 1955 as a 'supranational opposition'.[17] In their opinion the High Authority did not sufficiently exploit its autonomy. This criticism led the christian democrats and the liberals in 1957 to

[16] O. Kirchheimer, *Politik und Verfassung*, Frankfurt, 1964, p. 129.
[17] During a roll call which they initiated in May 1955 against the High Authority and the other parties *à propos* the consultations concerning investment policy in the ECSC.

stand up for the cartel and social policy of the High Authority as a 'government coalition'.[18] When, however, during the coal crisis, the High Authority dared to employ independently a minuscule portion of its supranational authority, in the area of coal pricing and cartel policy, the christian democrats and the liberals tried to block even this move.[19]

In other crises, as they arose, the socialists have continued to encourage the supranational executive, whereas the so-called 'government coalition' of the other European parties has tended to dissolve into national oppositions. In other words, when co-operation between national and supranational decision-makers yields to an autonomous intervention of the latter, the national considerations of the Council of Ministers tend to be faithfully and constantly reflected in the attitudes of the respective national delegations in the European Parliament. Only the socialists do not play this game but 'go into opposition'.

THE VOTE OF CENSURE AND THE QUESTION

In national governments, the control functions of parliaments as a whole have very often been shifted to the minority in op-position. Although the European Parliament does not 'govern', this process can also be noticed here. Acting in the European Parliament, the socialist opposition has assumed the function of 'controlling' the policy of the executive.[20]

For the first time there exists in inter-state relations a vote of censure, even if incompletely developed. The European Parliament can dismiss the Commission by a qualified majority, but its redesignation is the prerogative of the national governments. This instrument has however not yet been employed. If it were, then under present circumstances the best the European Community could possibly hope for is

[18] During the debates on the 5th Annual Report of the High Authority in June of that year.

[19] Only owing to the appeal by Pinay was the mild working of the High Authority accepted by the Common Assembly. See Kraft, 'Le groupe socialiste au Parlement Européen' (Thesis, University of Strasbourg, 1963), pp. 200 ff.

[20] A. de Block (socialist) 'We must resign ourselves that, lacking power, we shall determine the direction.' (European Parliamentary Proceedings, 21 June 1961, p. 80.) See also Strobel Report, doc. 110, op. cit.

that the national governments would reappoint the dismissed commissioners, who at least have long experience.

In the Common Assembly of the Coal and Steel Community, the vote of censure, which was originally a 'control' device for the two-thirds majority, became the instrument of protest for the one-third minority of socialists. Naturally the opposition did not intend to displace the executive; but by means of a declaration, which because of its contents was tantamount to a vote of censure, it expressed its disapproval of the supranational executive's actions, omissions or willingness to compromise with the national authorities.[21]

The socialist opposition in the European Parliament has abstained from making similar declarations against the Commissions of the EEC and Euratom. When the European Parliament incidentally recommended in a report that the Commission should resist the encroachment of the Council of Ministers[22] (particularly the reductions in its budget) by resigning their offices, the socialists rejected this procedure as inadequate.[23] Moreover if, as might happen, an economic crisis occurred in which the European Commission insisted upon maintaining its supranational competence, and a group of national oppositions were to employ the vote of censure to terminate the functioning of the supranational authorities, the socialists would form a minority capable of blocking the decision.

A much more effective method is the control of policy orientation by tabling written (or oral) 'questions' which, because of its continuity, enables the constructive opposition to exert influence. 'The art of questioning is part of the technique of opposition',[24] and in the European Parliament it is undoubtedly the most effective. As long as the initial phase of integration is not directly influenced by an articulate public opinion, democratic supervision is rendered possible by this procedure. This leads the administration, which must produce the answers, to become more thoughtful and cautious.

The drafters of the ECSC treaties intended that the Com-

21 See the votes on the 4th and 5th General Reports of the High Authority, and the declaration of the socialists against the High Authority in 1963.
22 See Janssen Report, doc. 113, 1962, *European Parliamentary Proceedings*.
23 See Kreyssig's speech, 23 November 1961, *European Parliamentary Proceedings*.
24 I. Jennings, *Parliament*, Cambridge, 1957, p. 103.

mon Assembly should exercise the right of question at plenary sessions.[25] Under the stipulation of strict separation of powers (characteristic of the initial stages of parliamentary evolution) the assembly as a whole formed the opposition to the new supranational executive.[26] This procedure was however recom-

TABLE 6

Written Questions from 1958 to 1965/66 (classified by institution)

	EEC		EURATOM		ECSC		
	Com- mission	Coun- cil	Com- mission	Coun- cil	High Author- ity	Coun- cil	Total
1958	12	5	6	5	12	1	41
1959–60	61	2	6	1	20	2	92
1960–1	80	5	13	2	37	3	140
1961–2	75	6	3	—	20	—	104
1962–3	146	8	5	4	25	1	189
1963–4	135	6	11	2	22	—	176
1964–5	132	8	7	3	18	3	171
1965–6	104	5	3	—	16	1	129
TOTAL	745	45	54	17	170	11	1042

Source: Secretariat of the European Parliament 1966.

mended only once during the lifetime of the pre-federative Common Assembly, and was not actually employed. In the European Parliament it was exercised once. This may be due to the fact that the supranational opposition insisted upon the right of question.

In 1958 the European Parliament extended its control (by question) over the Commission and the High Authority to the Councils (allowing two months for replies).[27] In 1962 the grow-

[25] See *Rapport sur les travaux 20 juin-10 août 1950*, quoted in P. J. G. Kapteyn, *L'Assemblée commune de la CECA*, Leyden, 1962, p. 191.

[26] This procedure was altered in a later draft of the treaty, allowing individual members to raise questions.

[27] The tabling of supplementary questions, intended to increase the reliability of answers by means of the element of surprise was, however, restricted to questions on the relationship between the European Parliament and the commission. The council asserted that its structure did not allow it to submit the answers of an individual minister as representative of the entire council without a prior vote.

ing burden of work of the European Parliament demanded more efficient procedures. With this in mind, parliamentary questions were speeded up, and interpellations (verbal questions with debate and voting) were introduced.[28] The verbal question, however, on which some sectors of the European Parliament set high hopes, has been used only rarely until the

TABLE 7 *

Written Questions from 1958 to 1965/66 (classified by political groups)

	Christian Democrats	Socialists	Liberals	UNR–UDT	Total
1958	10	14	1	4 †	29
1959–60	31	41	12	—	89
1960–1	40	73	43	—	156
1961–2	24	66	13	—	103
1962–3	56	117	19	—	192
1963–4	59	79	22	6 †	166
1964–5	47	98	20	1	166
1965–6	32	87	13	2	134
TOTAL	299	575	143	13	1030

Source: Secretariat of the European Parliament 1966.

* There is a difference between these figures and the yearly summarized figures in Tables 5 and 6. This can be traced to the fact that a large portion of the questions were put simultaneously to several institutions or came from members of several parliamentary parties.

† 1958 and 1963/64 without adherence to a political group.

end of 1966, and then in connection with the political structure and competences of the communities.[29]

A quantitative and qualitative evaluation of the written questions makes the intensity and trend of opposition policy more comprehensible. All the questions submitted to the Assembly during these years reveal that as the areas of competence of the three Communities widened, so the conscious-

[28] Earlier, representatives wishing to discuss a particular problem could only introduce a motion which had been previously debated and approved by a committee. The goal was to reduce the burden of the Committees and working groups, and to introduce parliamentary debates not based on a report.

[29] See, e.g., 27 November 1963 and 21 October 1964, 30 June 1966, European Parliamentary Proceedings.

ness of the European Parliament as a control agency has grown
stronger, particularly with regard to the Commissions, which
are partially responsible to the European Parliament. The 979
written questions which were submitted between 1958 and
1965–6 break down as follows: 1958, 29; 1959–60, 84; 1961–2,
101; 1962–3, 183; 1963–4, 161; 1964–5, 162; 1965–6, 129.

In Table 7, the lion's share of the socialists becomes evident,
since they initiated 55·8 per cent of all questions. One quarter
of the questions came from individual members of the Christian Democratic Parliamentary Party.

In 1965 there was a total of 18 joint written questions from
members of several parliamentary parties, in the following
combinations: christian   democrats/socialists;   christian
democrats/liberals; all parties; one oral question raised by the
socialists/liberals. These figures indicate that the parliamentary question is not in the European parties principally an
instrument which induces co-operation between the parties.

It is noteworthy that very few parliamentary questions are
initiated in the name of a parliamentary party compared with
those arising on the initiative of individual representatives.
Several written questions were introduced in the name of the
socialists. There were a total of eight socialist questions, one
from the liberals and not a single one from the christian
democrats.

Classification of the questions according to categories in
Table 4 shows that until 1965:

(1) Almost 50 per cent of the questions concern criticism of
    policy, that is to say individual measures of the agencies
    or their administration, and demand justification of a
    previous decision, or a prompt decision. Such questions
    are not aimed at the short term satisfaction of national
    or supranational interests by eclectic measures, but de-
    mand the long-term structural inprovement of com-
    mon policies as regards, for example, energy, or social
    and anti-trust policy. One can say that the socialists
    form the only group which continually pursues an up-
    grading of common interest through supranational
    measures. Their chief purpose is to keep under control
    the social and economic inequalities which could result
    from opportunistic compromises between Commission

and Council, and from the weak bargaining position of the non-producers.

(2) Almost 25 per cent of the questions deal with the relationship between the supranational executive and the member states. The opposition in this case has become the only regular control stage of the feed-back processes between the supranational executive and the national systems. It requires the supranational executive to maintain a more energetic attitude towards those practices of national enterprises which are designed to evade the decisions of the Communities. These practices are detected by the opposition, which demands to know what the executive intends to do about them, and whether or not governmental agencies are co-operative.

(3) About 15 per cent of the questions are requests for factual information, e.g. about the distributive processes in the economic systems of the individual countries (industrial capacity, import-export levels), on which the Commission has statistical data.

(4) About 10 per cent of the questions deal with the institutional structure of the Communities and the competence of the individual institutions. By means of questions of this kind, the representatives attempt particularly to supervise the co-operation between the Commission and the Council of EEC, in order to make the independent responsibility of both organs more evident.

To the extent to which the opposition supports the strengthening of the supranational competence of the Commission, it also becomes the advocate of democratic legitimation of what is now non-responsible bureaucratic power.[30]

The actual extent of the control exercised by means of the procedure of tabling written questions is difficult to assess. It can merely be gathered from the answers of the Executive and the Councils which are often evasive, imprecise, or which give no information at all. In these cases the opposition has not refrained from repeating the questions until it obtains a satisfactory answer. Because, in practice, the Commission is not institutionally dependent on the European Parliament, it has not

[30] See the linking of the Agrarian Fund with financial autonomy and budget control.

been possible for the Parliament, and in particular the opposition, to persuade the Commission to accept that the point of view of the Parliament should be ascertained by means of the 'question' *before* the Commission enters into negotiations with the Councils. On the other hand, consensus between Commission and Council, which results from bargaining, can be impeded if parliamentary majorities can determine the Commission's position.

Furthermore, the executives are composed of civil servants whose positions (characterized by the incompatibility of parliamentary mandate and executive function) do not allow them to develop parliamentary support for their own policy. This is underlined by the fact that they often exploit their right of invoking the 'professional secret' clause (article 214 of the EEC treaty) in order to avoid answering parliamentary questions. Therefore the question as to whether, in the shaping of their proposals, the Commission places more weight on the demands of the Assembly or on those of the member states, is falsely formulated.[31]

In spite of these restrictions, the parliamentary questions have a definite importance. They serve to inform the parliament and a broader public, and they are thus also a mechanism of control, in that the disclosure of irregularities can create awkwardness for an executive.

CONCLUSIONS

The behaviour of the opposition in the European Parliament is conditioned by their expectations with regard to the supranational allocation, regulation, and distribution processes which develop within the Communities. The transformations in the political structure and in the economic processes lead to a change in these attitudes. Accordingly, it has been noted that opponents of integration become supporters, that initial supporters become neutral or lose interest, while other initial supporters develop strong motives for continuing integration.[32]

[31] See written question No. 28, *Amtsblatt*, European Communities, 1961, pp. 10–11.

[32] In the German *Zollverein* unification was initially supported by the liberals against the opposition of the conservatives, concerned with sovereignty (partly with protectionism), though the political efforts of the latter brought about its completion.

It may be suggested that the following attitudes have developed since the establishment of the European Communities:

(a) The socialist 'precursor opposition'.
(b) The authoritarian right-wing anti-supranationalist opposition.
(c) The communist ideological, anti-capitalist, anti-supranational opposition.
(d) The opposition of free trade interests.

After a phase of five years of limited structural opposition to the 'clerical little Europe of the trusts', the diffuse ideological hostility of the socialists has been transformed, as a result of the success of integration, into long-term positive expectations, anchored after a time in socialist doctrine. Thereafter the socialist 'precursor opposition' turned against those national forces which were trying to hinder the construction of a supranational economic democracy.

It is unavoidable, in an 'institutionalized market' such as the EEC, that 'prior decisions' about production methods, sales, market organizations, etc., should be made between the producers and the allocating authorities. The representative institutions participate only in a consultative capacity. However, to paraphrase Dahl in a different context, the more the distribution of incomes and other opportunities is determined by a supranational authority, the more relevant become the ancient and inextinguishable controversies over the issue of equality versus differential reward.[33] The non-producers endeavour to make these controversies public, that is to replace co-operative bargaining, in which they are at a disadvantage, by competitive parliamentary voting. The opposition stresses the latent legislative power of the European Parliament. It demands voting on alternative principles, when the majority is inclined to insinuate itself into the diplomatic negotiations between the Council and the Commission.[34]

While the socialists evolved from an opposition hostile to the system to a 'precursor opposition', the christian democrats and the liberals, who initiated the process of European inte-

[33] See Dahl, *op. cit.*, p. 399.
[34] See the debates on the seat of the European Parliament in September 1964.

gration, have shown decreasing support. This seems to stem
from the fact that some of the christian democrat free traders,
and the liberals, had only short-term expectations from the
Communities. As these interests were met by a high level of
prosperity on the one hand, and on the other by a perception
of decreasing military danger, for which the system itself was
in part responsible, so these altered circumstances led to
diminished support for the supranational authorities.

Finally, the revolutionary left, in the course of its ideological
transformation and its reinterpretation of capitalistic integration, seems to be hinting that it has given up obstructionism
and is eager to participate in the organs of the Community.
'While the communist deputies, if represented in the Assembly, would certainly use that forum as they use their
national parliaments, their presence would nevertheless eliminate one feature of artificiality from the supranational
body.'[35] The more complex the economic and political com-
mitments become in the course of integration, the greater the
stress on the system caused by different kinds of opposition
forces. The stress may be alleviated, and the system may become more stable with the extension of the basis of representation in the European Parliament. If the 'conversion' of an
all-out opposition is brought about by the success of integration, then it follows that such oppositions should be brought
into the process. This appears to be particularly advisable
should the European Communities ever desire to participate in
an economic organization embracing both Eastern and Western Europe.

[35] See Haas, *op. cit.*, p. 409.

Contributors

Dennis Austin *is Professor of Government in the University of Manchester*

Rodney Barker *is Lecturer in Political Theory and Government at the University College of Swansea*

Bernard Crick *is Professor of Political Theory and Institutions in the University of Sheffield*

H. J. Hanham *is Professor of History in Harvard University*

Richard Hofstadter *was Professor of History in Columbia University, New York*

Gerhard Lehmbruch *is Professor in Political Science in the University of Heidelberg*

Kenneth R. Libbey *is Assistant Professor of Political Science in the University of Cincinnati*

Lauro Martines *is Professor of History in the University of California*

W. H. Morris-Jones *is Director of the Institute of Commonwealth Studies and Professor of Commonwealth Affairs in the University of London*

Michael Oakeshott *is Emeritus Professor of Political Science in the University of London*

Frank O'Gorman *is Lecturer in History at the University of Manchester*

Giovanni Sartori *is Professor of Political Science in the University of Florence*

Edward Shils *is Fellow of Peterhouse, Cambridge, and Professor at the University of Chicago*

J. E. Spence *is Senior Lecturer in the Department of Political Theory and Government at the University College of Swansea*

Silvano Tosi *is Professor of Political Science in the University of Florence*

A. Jeyaratnam Wilson *is Professor of Political Science in the University of Ceylon*

Gerda Zellentin *is a member of the Institute for Political Science and Research at the University of Cologne*

Index

Contributors' chapters are indicated by italic type.